Wine Country

An History of Napa Valley
The Early Years: 1838-1920

William F. Heintz

Capra Press
SANTA BARBARA

DEDICATION

The dictionary defines the word "dean" as the "senior member, in length of service, of any group, profession, etc." This book is dedicated to five men who have served the Napa Valley wine industry for 50 years or more: Roy Raymond (since 1933), Louis Martini (1933), Brother Timothy (1935), Robert Mondavi (1937) and Andre Tschelistcheff (1938).

Cover Painting by Grace Hodgson.
Text Illustrations by Cyndi Burt.
Typography by Bill Horton.

Library of Congress Cataloging-in-Publication Data

Heintz, William F.
    Wine Country : the history of Napa Valley : the early years.
1838-1920 / William Heintz : foreword by Brother Timothy.
        p.   cm.
    Includes bibliographical references.
    ISBN 0-88496-316-0 (cloth) : $29.95
    1. Wine and wine making—California—Napa River Valley—
History. 2. Viticulture—California—Napa River Valley—History.
3. Napa River Valley (Calif.)—History. I. Title.
TP557.H45   1990
338.4 '7663' 200979419—dc20

                                            90-36307
                                            CIP

Published by Capra Press
Post Office Box 2068
Santa Barbara, California 93120

FOREWORD

In "Wine Country" William Heintz has condensed the results of his many years of reserch into an authoritative and interpretative history of the exciting grape and wine industry in the Napa Valley.

This comprehensive history is the book for every vineyardist, wine worker, and wine lover to read and keep at hand as a ready reference. From it you will learn who made the first commercial wines of the Napa Valley, who was the first to introduce the Zinfandel grape, who were the notable men and women who established the vineyards and wineries and who were leaders in nurturing the high quality of Napa wines that brought worldwide respect for this area. Professional wine judgings in Europe and throughout America confirmed the excellence of our wines from the 1870s to the present day.

As "the best laid plans of mice and men gang aft agley,"* troubles appeared in our paradise. This book tell you about the root louse, *Phylloxera Vastatrix*, and about the genesis of the Prohibition movement, the two most serious calamities to strike our wine industry.

Believe it or not, Heintz tells us that the first motion pictures of a winery in operation were made in 1909. "Wine Country" is full of both landmark events and fascinating trivia. While reading, I became firmly convinced that the achievements and traditions of the past were the foundations on which current successes are based.

With a glass of wine at your side, you will be properly prepared to enjoy this informative book. I raise my glass of Napa Valley Cabernet Sauvignon to toast the future of all fine wines and the success of this book.

BROTHER TIMOTHY,
Cellarmaster, Christian Brothers

---

*Robert Burns, 1759-1796

INTRODUCTION

The wines of Napa Valley have dominated the domestic American wine market for so long that no one can recall when another region equalled its prestige. When the news media carry a story on wine, invariably they turn first to Napa Valley winemakers for views and opinions. How this came about is an intriguing piece of history, although it was not always the case.

California's wine industry was actually born in Los Angeles in the 1820s, founded by a French immigrant appropriately named Louis Vigne. He truly deserves to be called "Father of California winemaking." His annual production shortly before the Gold Rush of '49, sometimes exceeded 40,000 gallons. No one else even came close to equalling him.

In the decade following the Gold Rush came the dawning realization that truly fine, dry table wines could not be easily produced in the hot climate of southern California. Agoston Haraszthy discovered the Sonoma Valley and soon championed the north San Francisco Bay region as the place *par excellent* for producing wines equal to France and other parts of Europe. He set in motion what might be termed the modern era of wine in California.

Sonoma County surpassed Los Angeles in wine production about 1870, in part due to Haraszthy, and achieved considerable national notoriety. Unfortunately, a vine louse known as *Phylloxera Vastatrix* was already at work in the local vineyards, nearly destroying the wine industry within a decade.

This happened almost simultaneously in France. Thus it fell by happenstance that Napa Valley, in 1885, inherited the California wine crown from Sonoma, and almost from France as well. Fortunately for France, resistant root stock from eastern United States proved its salvation from the *Phylloxera* disease which had originated in America.

By 1889 French vintners were so relieved to find their vineyards returning to full production that American wines were invited to compete for the medals being offered at the World's Fair in Paris. The French had not granted this recognition before, especially to California wine, but now rumors about that region replacing France as the wine capital of the world could be laid to rest.

Nearly half the wine awards granted to American wine, brandy and champagne by French judges went to a place virtually unknown to most Americans, the Napa Valley. No American competitor was even close.

Napa wines were just beginning to gain recognition in San Francisco, but eastern wine consumers, who only allowed French wine to cross their lips, were startled by this recognition. Where was Napa Valley and who made the wine?

Reporters quickly hopped aboard transcontinental trains for California to get full details about Napa Valley for their readers. And for the next decade, this idyllic valley reaped a publicity bonanza. Its wines were compared favorably to the Bordeaux region.

Alas, the *Phylloxera* soon moved into Napa's vineyards too, destroying most of its vines. However, the discovery that the Rupestris St. George root stock was well suited to California's soil and climate, aided rapid replanting. Napa Valley's wine crown did not slip away after all and has never been usurped since those halycon days.

This is but a brief retelling of a segment examined in considerable detail in the book, including much more about *Phylloxera*. There are also surprises concerning the contribution of the Chinese immigrant who did so much more than pick grapes, sulphur the vines against mildew and dig wine tunnels. So many participated in the wine-making process including the first Italian, French and German immigrants.

Technical advances are chronicled including the first use of smoke as frost protection. Napa was the first region to try this age-old practice which originated in Europe. The rest of California soon followed suit.

Stories about individuals are told as well, from tragedy to triumph. Two prominent winemakers were murdered, John Osborne and John Weinberger. Both attempted to break up relationships between young daughters and hired hands. Josephine Tychson suffered tragedy too when her husband took his own life as they planned a winery. Undaunted, she went on to build the winery, probably the first woman in California to do so.

Much of Napa Valley's success can be traced to leadership from individuals of vision, especially concerning wine production, quality control and marketing.

Charles Krug, from the beginning, insisted that success could only come with high quality wine and urged his neighbors to grow European varietal grapes. He was right, as Paris and 1889 proved him to be. He has his contemporary counterparts in those who are legends in their own time, including Robert Mondavi, Brother Timothy, Andre Tchelistcheff, Warren Winiarski, Jack Davies, both Louis Martinis, Fred Abruzzini and many more.

None of these names were known to me four decades ago when I first came to California, nor any of the history in this book. My first taste of Napa Valley wine was in the old railroad car used as a tasting room for many years at the Krug winery. Considering my youth, I'm nearly certain it was a sweet Riesling.

Nearly two decades later as a corporate historian in San Francisco, I was unexpectedly asked to explore the background of the Simi Winery at Healdsburg. It planned to celebrate its centennial in 1976, having been founded in "1876" as bold numbers on its roof proclaimed. Much to my surprise the structure was discovered to date only from the year 1890, a fact well documented in local newspapers. Plans for a state landmark were promptly dropped, as well as any celebration. The disappointment was just too much.

Shortly thereafter, a San Francisco advertising agency asked for similar help on the Inglenook winery in Napa Valley. There was some confusion, since founder Gustave Niebaum, when still alive, advertising "Founded 1880" though winery owners, for most of this century, had used the date "1879." They too were making elaborate plans for a centennial celebration. (See Chapter 4.)

Since those first two projects in the early 1970s, more than a hundred have followed. Some have been brief, merely establishing founding dates and documentation to back this up for a wine label. Yet most of these projects have taken months to accomplish such as research for Beaulieu, Freemark Abbey, Villa Mt. Eden, Trefethen, Conradi, Far Niente, Stag's Leap Winery and Stag's Leap Wine Cellar, Pine Ridge, Chateau Chevalier, Talcoa, and Markham. These are just in Napa Valley.

I have also conducted research on appellations elsewhere in California including Temecula, Wild Horse Valley, Alexander Valley, Carneros, North Coast, Mt. Veeder and many others. Other research projects investigated when Chablis was first produced in California and whether it was sold with or without a "California" designation.

Almond Raleigh Morrow, first president of the Wine Institute, has been thoroughly researched as was the Mirassou family of San Jose and the Raymond-Beringers in the Napa Valley.

The greatest proportion of my time by far has been spent on Napa Valley subjects and this book is really the outgrowth of a suggestion by Robert Mondavi. After my long testimony covering the history of and use of the phrase "Napa Valley" in wine writing, advertising and public relations (at the Napa Valley appellation hearings), Mondavi urged this be expanded into a book.

No study in such depth has ever been undertaken on a single wine region in America. I believe the history presented here justifies this volume and the second which will follow in a year or two.

The challenge has often seemed overwhelming, but the offer from the publisher to present it in two volumes has made the task easier and more manageable. I hope too that the interpretative style used will assist the reader in placing the history in perspective and make it good reading as well.

WILLIAM F. HEINTZ

TABLE OF CONTENTS

I. Viticulture and the Gold Rush, 1838-1850

iticulture, a Latin word meaning the cultivation of the grape, was a subject virtually unknown to the first Americans to settle in California's Napa Valley. Grapes had nothing either to do with their arrival in the valley years before the great Gold Rush of 1849. These men from states such as Missouri, Illinois or Kentucky, had heard all about the rich farmlands of the valley and its healthful, mild climate. If a few had actually picked native American grapes back in Missouri, they knew they were to be eaten for food and not, God forbid, for the making of wine.

Even George Yount, the first white settler in the Napa Valley, apparently followed this belief. He planted a very small vineyard in 1838 (near what later became the town of Yountville), but the grapes were for eating and a source of sugar.

Yount, though a seasoned hunter and trapper and what might be described as a thorough mountain man by the time he reached California, was a product, too, of Missouri. He had moved there as a boy with his parents and listened like everyone else to the Bible-thumping itinerant preachers who often railed against the evils of alcohol. This has to be the explanation for his failure to produce even one drop of wine at his Napa Valley ranch until enticed by the demand for such beverages following the discovery of gold in California.

Few of Yount's neighbors in those early years in Napa Valley were trappers or hunters. These farmers came overland in wagon trains bringing their families because they had heard California's climate offered a far better alternative to mid-America's harsh winters and the summer "ague." That was a fever which befell many. Places like "Nappa Valley" were discussed for hours and debated long before names like "San Francisco" or the "Sierras" became widely known.

One man who listened intently to these stories was Enoch Cyrus. In the spring of 1846, he attended a meeting where he heard an actual eyewitness description of the lands which lay along the Pacific Coast and of a valley inhabited by a tranquil tribe of Indians known as the "Nappas." Cyrus was so taken by this account that within weeks he organized and led a wagon train of settlers bound for California. By late fall their destination had been reached.

Enoch Cyrus left no written account of these events, but he had a granddaughter who heard the story of the transcontinental journey many times in later years and recorded some of the details. Rachel Wright claims her grandfather had been told that every immigrant could purchase all the land he wanted in California, from the friendly Spanish-speaking Mexicans.[1.1] No mention was made that conversion to Catholicism was generally a prerequisite to land ownership. There were other portions of the glowing account of California which turned out to be untrue, but none of this dampened the enthusiasm of Cyrus and friends once they reached their destination. The landscape they saw was worth the journey across the American west.

By a rather remarkable coincidence, a traveler already in California, Edwin Bryant, met up with Cyrus and his party shortly before they reached the Napa Valley. He spent one night with them on the banks of Putah Creek, west of what later became the town of Sacramento. Bryant, moreover, recorded the event in a detailed diary he kept and three years later his notes appeared in book form as *What I Saw In California: Its Soil, Climate, Productions and Gold Mines*. It is one of the first books to be published about the land shortly to become the thirty-first member of the United States. (Besides being delightful reading, the book includes the first published account of travel in the Napa Valley.)

Bryant does not mention Enoch Cyrus by name in his book, but certain aspects of his description match the details provided much later by Rachel Wright. Bryant's notes of October 31, 1846 include this paragraph:

> Proceeding ten miles over a level plain, we overtook a company of emigrants bound for Nappa Valley, and encamped with them for the night on Puta[h] creek, a tributary of the Sacramento. Five of the seven or eight men belonging to the company enrolled their names as volunteers.

Bryant's "volunteers" were to be used in fighting the Mexicans if they offered further resistance to the Bear Flag revolt. Earlier that summer at Sonoma, a group of Americans had declared the region free from Mexico and raised a crude flag made of white cotton cloth with the drawing of a California brown bear. The militant, well-armed Americans easily overpowered the gentle Mexican residents of Sonoma, who actually outnumbered them about four to one.

Undoubtedly the emigrant party with which Bryant spent the night, kept him awake for several hours asking questions about the new land and the nearby Napa Valley in particular. Bryant had not, sorry to say, visited the spot as yet, but his notebooks did have the names of several men who had taken up residence on a permanent basis. Four days after this meeting, Bryant himself rode into the Napa Valley and wrote this description in early November:

> On the morning of the fourth, we found the trail described to us by Mr. Greenwood, and, crossing a ridge of mountains, descended into the valley of Nappa creek, which empties into the Bay of San Francisco just below the Straits of Carquinez. This is a most beautiful and fertile valley, and is already occupied by several American settlers.
>
> Among the first who established themselves here is Mr. Yount, who soon erected a flouring mill and saw-mill. These have been in operation several years. Before reaching Mr. Yount's settlement, we passed a saw-mill more recently erected, by Dr. Bale. There seems to be an abundance of pine and red-wood (a species of fir), in the *canadas*. No lumber can be superior for building purposes than that sawed from redwood. The trees are of immense size, straight, free from knots and twists, and the wood is soft, and easily cut with plane and saw.
>
> Arriving at the residence of Dr. Bale, in Nappa Valley, we were, hospitably entertained by him with a late breakfast of coffee, boiled eggs, steaks and tortillas, served up in American style. Leaving Nappa, after traveling down it some ten or twelve miles, we crossed another range of hills or mountains and reached Sonoma after dark.

The breakfast served by Dr. Bale, "boiled eggs, steaks and tortillas, served up in American style," is the earliest recorded menu of a meal served in the Napa Valley. Bryant, who later was elected an "alcalde" (mayor) in San Francisco, paid attention to such details because he was well-educated and well-traveled. His book is filled with copious notes on the vineyards he found as he meandered about the state plus observations on California wine and brandy. *He makes no reference to being offered such beverages by Bale or Yount.* Yount's vines were certainly producing well by that date and he seemingly should have had wine on hand.

Incidentally, the man Cyrus Enoch met back in Missouri earlier that year and who described the Napa Valley to him, more than likely was a member of Col. John C. Fremont's expedition to the Pacific Coast and California in 1843. Fremont directed a survey party that brought him across Carson Pass to Sutter's Fort, where they rested about a month before proceeding on south and thence eastward back to St. Louis.

During the Sutter's Fort respite, Fremont and a small group of his men made exploratory trips into the countryside, one of them reaching the Napa Valley. (Fremont personally seems to have left no record of this visit nor is the word "Nappa" used in his official report.

The Fremont survey party was just one of many direct sources for information about the Napa Valley in the 1840s. In Lafayette, Indiana, Overton Johnson and William H. Winter published in 1846 their notes and recollections of a journey made three years earlier to Oregon, southward to California and back to St. Louis.

Winter was the author of the detailed account on California in *Route Across the Rocky Mountains*. One of his observations refers to grapes:

> Nearly all the products of temperate climates except Indian corn, flourish here. Oats and clover grow spontaneously, in almost every part of the Province. The vine flourishes as well, perhaps in California, as in any portion of the world; and its fruit is the finest, and decidedly the most delicious, that we have ever tasted. There are many large vineyards [sic] in different parts of the country, from which several thousand barrels of wine are annually made.

Winter does not mention the location of any of the vineyards or whose wine he tasted. He most likely refers to Captain John Sutter at Sutter's Fort (now the city of Sacramento) for he had a most ambitious wine making establishment in that period and plenty of vines, both wild and domestic. Had Winter arrived a few years earlier, he might have witnessed wine making at one of the twenty-one Catholic missions in California. The Mexican government had ordered the missions be removed from church control, beginning in 1834, and most were in a sad state of decay by the time Winter arrived.

A biography of Winter published in 1873 does claim he visited the Napa Valley sometime in the year 1844, very likely in early fall:

> After returning to Sutter's Fort Mr. Winter came over to Napa Valley, and visited Mr. Yount's ranch, and then passed over to Sonoma. In the later place he fell in with Messrs. Fowler and Hargrave, and spent the Winter with them in that valley. In the following Spring, 1845, he and other parties from various portions of the State made Sutter's Fort a rendezvous, to form a party to go back across the Plains.*

Winter must have tasted the grapes of Yount that fall and, of course, those being raised by various individuals at Sonoma including the former Mexican commandante of the region, Marianno Vallejo. Grape cuttings could be had free from the vineyard at the Sonoma Mission, now under the control of Vallejo who was generous in handing them out.

With the discovery of gold in January 1848, at Coloma, due east of Sacramento, William Winter turned his attention again to California. Within months he was on his way westward and he settled at Mokelumne Hill, staking out his own claim on a nearby creek. He was either very lucky or persevering (a quality many gold seekers seemed to lack) because he was able to purchase 664 acres on Huichica Creek in southern Napa Valley in 1855. He added another 600 acres to his Carneros farm exactly one year later. He planted vines almost immediately and within two decades had the largest vineyard in all of Napa County.[1,2] He built a small stone winery on the banks of Carneros Creek, probably in the 1870s. The federal 1860 Agricultural Census credits Winter with making 20 gallons of wine, obviously just for home use.

Overton and Winter were so encouraging of migration to California that the suspicion is naturally aroused that they must have expected some financial gain, perhaps by acting as guides to the overland wagon trains. The book does provide this information on

---

*Historical and Descriptive Sketch Book of Napa, Sonoma, Lake and Mendocino, published in 1873, see pages 156-157.

the reception travelers might expect to receive upon reaching that part of the Pacific Coast ruled by Mexico:

> It is difficult to find a people, or even an individual, who has not some good trait of character; and even these Californians, with all their faults, are hospitable at their houses. If a stranger goes to one of their houses, he is made welcome to whatever it affords, and as comfortable as their limited means will allow; he must, however, furnish his own bed. It is always expected that a traveler in California will carry that article with him. [Winter meant bedding, not a bed per se. One explanation for this odd state of affairs is that fleas were a terrible problem. It may be that a friendly host did not want his bedding infested.]
>
> When he departs, nothing is demanded, and nothing will be received by them, as compensation; the almost universal and beautiful reply is, when payment is offered: 'No, God will pay.'
>
> There are now about five hundred foreigners residing in the country, and the principal portion are from the United States. Emigration from the United States is rapidly increasing, and it is probable that our citizens will possess themselves of the beautiful and healthy country, with its many vales of fertile land. They will soon outnumber the Spaniards, and gain the ascendancy over them. The consequence will be, to throw off their present form of government, establish a Republic of their own, and render this portion of our globe, what nature has seemed to design it should be, a prosperous and happy country.
>
> Grants of land are still obtained from the government, of from one to ten leagues. These grants cannot, however, be had at all times, or by all persons; only those who are in favor with the authorities, are likely to get lands.

The "Bear Flag revolt," which subsequently took place at Sonoma, had some strong supporters back in Indiana. The authors of this book, Winter in particular, openly encouraged taking California away from Mexico with force and making the land available to any and all who wanted it. What makes these ideas of considerable historic interest is that they are proof that the American action at Sonoma was hardly spontaneous. On the other hand, to Winter's credit, he had a very understandable desire for just a few hundred of those acres in the Napa Valley for the growing of grapes.

If Edwin Bryant and Enoch Cyrus and friends had met and camped overnight in the Napa Valley (instead of beside Putah Creek) in October 1846, their chance meeting would not have been quite so unusual. The valley was already in that year being crisscrossed by many travelers from eastern United States. Sonoma Valley pioneer Nicholas Carriger years later left a memoir with historian Hubert Howe Bancroft in which he tells of visiting the flour mill and farm of George Yount in the same year Bryant paid his visit. Major Stephen Cooper's autobiography published in 1883 as part of a county history in Missouri, has a flattering recollection about Yount in particular:

> We struck the Sacramento Valley on the 5th of October, 1846. That winter I stopped at Yount's ranch in Napa Valley— a man who, in my opinion, did more for the early immigrants of California than all the Sutters did. . . . On the 4th of July, 1847 George Yount and myself gave the first public 4th of July dinner ever given in California. We had a large turnout, and everything passed off pleasantly.[1.3]

Cooper's recollections are not quite correct since the first 4th of July celebration in California actually took place in 1836. That occasion came after Jacob P. Leese completed construction of the first building in what soon became the village of Yerba Buena, later renamed San Francisco. The Cooper-Yount dinner is still noteworthy in that it was probably the first social event held in the Napa Valley by Americans. *Cooper fails to mention if Yount served any Napa Valley wine at the dinner!* The "large turnout" does document further that the valley was already home to a number of new settlers.

One of the principal attractions of the Napa Valley and California in this period was the lack of sickness, particularly something referred to as the "ague." This was a common malarial fever in the mid-continent region of the United States, characterized by regular and recurring paroxysms. Escaping from this disease may have been the primary motivation for many of the families who undertook the long and difficult overland trip to California.

John Bidwell, who later settled at Chico, and became one of the state's most famous pre-Gold Rush residents, told a story of how he met a California traveler in the fall of 1840 with the name of Roubideaux. This happened in Platte County, Missouri. Roubideaux was quickly plied with questions about the land from whence he had just come, with this being number one, according to Bidwell:

> Generally the first question which a Missourian asked about a country was whether there was any fever or ague. I remember his answer distinctly. He said there was but one man in California that had ever had a chill there, and it was a matter of such wonderment to the people of Monterey that they went eighteen miles into the

country too see him shake. Nothing could have been more satisfactory on the score of health.[1.4]

Bidwell related this story in all honesty apparently, for Missourians did not take the matter of the ague lightly and assumed everyone else handled it in the same forthright manner. If Roubideaux had told his little story somewhat tongue-in-cheek Bidwell missed the humor entirely.

Among the first individual travelers encountered in the 1840s in the Napa Valley was George Yount.

Yount was from Missouri, too, of course, although a native of North Carolina, having been born there in 1794. It is doubtful he had more than the most rudimentary education and in his early teenage years was already working at various odd jobs. He enlisted in the army during the War of 1812 and though his formal army career seems to have been rather short, he claims to have participated in a number of Indian battles over the next several years. He quickly became a marksman with the rifle and some of his training in this regard probably came from his army experience.

When Yount was 32 years old, he married Eliza Wells and tried to settle down to family life. The fact that he did not marry until rather late in life, suggests he did not easily give up the bachelor's life which included the freedom to go off on a bison hunt with friends on a moments notice or take employment with a pack train of mules going to Santa Fe (New Mexico). He was an independent man and his marriage with Eliza must have been stormy from the start.

That Yount and his wife did not get along seems a safe conclusion based on the fact that he never returned home after taking on a job as a mule driver for a pack train to Santa Fe in 1826. The goods he transported could not be sold in Santa Fe and he found himself broke. Instead of returning home, he continued on westward, reaching San Francisco in 1833 and spent the winter at the Petaluma adobe of Marianno Vallejo. Vallejo was in charge of small garrison of Mexican soldiers stationed at Sonoma. He also controlled all lands belonging to Mexico which lay north of the San Francisco bay.

At Sonoma, Yount soon met Padre Jose L. Quijas, the priest in charge of the Sonoma and San Rafael missions. Since Yount was trained in a number of pursuits, from being a blacksmith to carpentry, Quijas quickly found several dozen tasks which required his urgent attention. Charles Brown told Hubert Howe Bancroft many years later that he and Yount made 1,000 shingles a day in these years for the Sonoma Mission and for Vallejo. Brown claims they were paid $25 a day.[1.5] Where or how the mission found the funds to pay the men seems rather strange since the Mexican government had the previous year ordered the mission be removed from the control of the Catholic church and its holdings sold. Yount and Brown may have received room and board, but little else.

One subject which Yount politely never spoke about in any of his memoirs of later years, is how his family survived while he traveled about the countryside. He and Eliza had three children before Yount left Missouri, a son Robert and two daughters, Frances and Elizabeth. Yount had no money to send back for their support.

It can be assumed that the land grant of 11,814 acres in Napa Valley given to George Yount in 1836 was in partial payment for the work he did for the Sonoma Mission and Vallejo. This is a safe conclusion since land grants by Mexican authorities in that period were given to outsiders only after they had converted to Catholicism and married into a Spanish (Mexican) family. Yount was baptized by Padre Quijas at the San Rafael Mission but never converted to the Catholic religion, and he did not marry the daughter of a Mexican ranch owner. He may have felt he could not take the latter step with a wife in Missouri, but in 1841 he found out from friends that his wife had divorced him.

Yount chose his "Caymus Rancho" lands carefully, picking out a location in the heart of the Napa Valley. He could have selected lands much closer to his new friends in Sonoma, particularly in the region shortly known as the Carneros. That he did not settle in the Carneros may be attributed to his background as an Indian fighter. Just north of what is now Yountville, Yount located a high hill which offered good protection on all sides should he be confronted by hostile Indians. He did not build his first "Kentucky fortress" on that hill but his attraction to this region of the valley seems to have some ulterior motive.

Most interviews with Yount claim he had a friendly rapport with the local Indians of Sonoma. He took several with him to aid in the construction of his first home. This was a Kentucky-style blockhouse, the first floor being smaller than the second or top floor. The first floor was one large room, eighteen feet square, the second floor was twenty-two feet square with portholes cut into the walls at convenient intervals to fire on unwelcome intruders.

The Wappo Indians that lived in the Napa Valley (of which the "Nappas" were but one small band) were far different from the Indians of the central plains or mountains of western United states. They did not have horses, which made them rather less of a threat to white settlers. There were as many as a thousand Indians in the valley in the 1840s, most living in small family units scattered widely from each other. They were supposedly rather passive, being content to hunt and live quietly. With no rifles and only a bow and arrows, it is difficult to conceive of anything approaching an Indian battle being waged in the Napa valley.

George Yount did, nevertheless, use his skills as a rifleman in putting down several Indian uprisings in the area and in defending himself against attack. He joined Marianno Vallejo two days after Christmas, 1840, in settling an Indian dispute at Soscol (several miles south of Napa City) and experienced at least one actual attack on his house. He told the story in 1859 to a writer from the *Hesperian* magazine of San Francisco:

At one time the Indians of Sonoma made a great feast and dance. The Indians of Mr. YOUNT's place took it into their heads to go to the feast; so a young Indian came forward and asked Mr. YOUNT if he might go; at the same time signifying that five or six more of the tribe would also like to attend. Mr. YOUNT readily gave his consent; but the young Indian became depressed in spirit, seemed moody and sad, and finally declared he would not go to the dance, and no persuasion of his companions could induce him to change his mind, so they departed without him.

The air was still and calm, and the night wore quietly away until just before daybreak, when suddenly arose upon the air the fearful warhoop! Louder and louder it sounded, as if the very fiends incarnate had been set loose; and Mr. YOUNT, grasping his rifle, sprang from his couch to find his house surrounded by a band of savages, who had come down from the mountains for the purpose of war and plunder. Thick flew the arrows, and the first one to fall was the young Indian who but the day before had refused to leave Mr. YOUNT. The Frenchman guarded the room below, while Mr. YOUNT fired from the port-holes above, killing many of the invaders, so they were glad to retreat, carrying their dead and wounded with them.

During the skirmish a little circumstance occurred, which serves to show the disposition of the brave settler. The friendly Indian women rushed to the door of Mr. YOUNT's cabin, for the purpose of obtaining protection from the flying arrows of the wild Indians;

but the Frenchman had the door strongly barricaded and refused
to open it.

At length their piteous screams reached the ears of Mr. YOUNT,
and in a voice like thunder he exclaimed: 'Open the door you old
rascal, and let those women and children in, or I will come down
and put you out among the Indians.' It is needless to say the door
was opened immediately, and the women and children given such
protection as the house afforded.*

Despite the overwhelming odds, Yount and his (good-guy) Indians
won, of course. Mrs. F. H. Day, author of the Hesperian article failed
to note in her journalistic zeal that the Napa Valley Indians may have
been attempting to dislodge these intruders onto their lands.

There are no reliable figures on the numbers of Indians living in
the valley during Yount's early years. Estimates vary from as low as
one thousand to as high as three thousand Indians. These "Wappos,"
as the white man later named them, roamed over a large area, from
the tidewaters of the San Francisco Bay to Knight's Valley (in
northern Sonoma County). For this reason they did not appear to be
very numerous, and travelers like Edwin Bryant do not mention
seeing Indians in the valley when he passed through in November
1846. Two decades later, most local Indians were dead, killed by
such diseases as smallpox or cholera, brought in by the white settlers.

Depending upon the size of George Yount's first vineyard,
Indians probably did the actual planting of those vines. These would
have been the workers Yount brought from Sonoma, as it is doubtful
the local tribes would have had any role in this historic event.

---

*The only known copy of the Hesperian for December 1859, from which this was
excerpted, was recently located at the library of the University of California, San
Diego. Pages one and two of the text are missing. Portions of the Hesperian
interview are to be found reprinted in the 1881 History of Napa and Lake Counties.

Yount's First Vineyard

George Yount may have looked upon the pursuit of agriculture with some horror, or at the very least with considerable apathy. He was not a farmer, never had been. He roamed the American West, hunting or following his curiosity and instincts at whim.

When he received his Caymus Rancho grant he was most concerned with building a structure that would serve as a home and protect him against the winter rains and when necessary, the local Indians.

This may explain why Yount seems to have only mentioned *his first planting of grapes* twice during his entire lifetime. It was a matter of no concern while he was alive. The excitement with viticulture in later years was another matter, entirely.

Both of Yount's very brief discussions of the subject came after questions were put to him by the Visiting Committee of the State Agricultural Society. The committee's task in the early 1850s was to encourage agriculture in California and did this by awarding prizes for the Best Farm, Most Improved Farm, etc.

The first visit of this select group of men came in the fall of 1855. At his home they observed his flour mill in operation, wheat having been grown by him "for eighteen years in succession" (or since 1837):

Mr. Yount's Ranch comprises three leagues of land, two of which are in the valley, and of which 800 acres are inclosed. It contains a fine assortment of fruit trees and a vineyard, with several thousand vines in bearing. *An old orchard and vineyard, planted long since, was attractive for its maturity and fine fruit.**

Yount did not mention the age of the vineyard or vineyards, there seemed to be a young vineyard and another of some years in age.

Yount did rectify the failure to mention the year his earliest vines were planted when the committee visited him again the following year. In the *Official Report of the California State Agricultural Society, For 1856*, the traveling farmers record that Yount told them he had been a "twenty year resident of the valley" (or 1836) and they added:

> Mr. Yount's Farm comprises about 13,000 acres of land—8,000 acres of which lies in the valley, all first class land; 800 acres of it enclosed, containing good variety of fruit trees; an old Orchard and Vineyard planted eighteen years ago, was attractive for the great growth and healthy appearance of the trees and vines.

One or two committee members may have made a quick mental calculation and came up with the year 1838 for his very first vineyard.

About this same time a local minister named Rev. Orange Clark began jotting down the recollections of Yount, especially as they referred to his hunting exploits in California. Yount did not mince words and later his second wife went through the manuscript and removed many pages which had unflattering remarks.**

If the grape was not of overwhelming interest to Yount, or of even enough significance in later years to recall it in conversations with friends, his first neighbors would have treated the subject no differently. This included Englishman Dr. Edward T. Bale (who married a Mexican woman and converted to Catholicism, thereby gaining a large Mexican land grant some miles north of Yount), Nicolas Higuera, Salvadore Vallejo and Cayetamo Juarez.

---

*First published in the California Farmer, October 19, 1855.

**This manuscript was published many years later by the California Historical Society, San Francisco as *The Chronicles of George C. Yount. California Pioneer of 1826.* The date is likely in error as Yount did not come to Sonoma until 1833 and it is believed he never returned to his Missouri home after once reaching the Pacific Coast. References in the manuscript by the editor to viticulture often appear ambiguous, there being little certainty when Yount is being quoted or when historical background is being added.

The traditional approach to farming and ranching in California before the influx of Americans, was casual, unhurried and required no great expenditure of energy. Why should it? There was no business in farming. Each rancho was largely self-sufficient. A few hides might be traded with passing ships (if the rancho was near enough to the sea coast). The large herds of cattle roamed for miles before a few horsemen might venture out to round them up and head the leaders back toward the rancho headquarters.

When the California sun heated the long summer days and the coastal breezes stopped, all activity ceased.

William Winter in his book claimed the "principal business of all classes, is attending to animals; there are some, however, who cultivate small patches of ground" but his remarks further indicate these were the exception, not the rule. Higuera incidentally, was granted in 1836 his rancho (which later would include all the land for the city of Napa); Salvadore Vallejo, brother of Gen. M. G. Vallejo was granted "Napa Rancho" in 1838 and the "Tulocay Rancho" was given in 1841 to Juarez.

The individual most likely to plant or cultivate grapes after Yount was Dr. Edward Bale. He was as colorful and communicative as Yount and built himself a mill, too, which for years afterward served as a landmark when traveling in the valley. It was called simply "'Bale Mill.'"*

Bale was granted the "Carne Humana Rancho" in 1841 and moved there two years later. Very much opposite of Yount in some respects, Bale's quick temper made it difficult for many to get along with him, most especially his relatives. One story was told that he challenged his wife's uncle, Salvadore Vallejo, to a duel, because Bale suspected some sort of romantic involvement between uncle and niece.

This would have been only a minor scandal in that early period. Eligible lovers were not easy to find. The younger and stronger Vallejo easily defeated Bale in the clash of swords and he may even have used his sword to flay the backside of Bale. Disgraced by such degrading treatment, Bale then attempted to shoot Vallejo. Since this

---

*Believed to be one of the oldest structures in Napa County, the mill is California State Landmark #359 and a state park.

was all among "family," Bale survived without any incarceration but the fracas did his health no good. He died at the age of forty-one in 1849.

Bale seems about as unlikely an individual to cultivate the vine as Yount and probably did so only out of necessity. He had no interest in the soil, only in what it might produce for eating and certainly left the real labor to local Indians. On the other hand, the grape might have come as the *second order of business*, after the construction of home and barn. It was too far and too dangerous to travel to Sonoma frequently for supplies, if some could be bartered. Since grapes grew easily and abundantly and provided a quick source of sugar, they would have had a high priority. (Grapes left to mature on the vine until very late in the season, will attain a high level of sugar and this was used to sweeten foods during cooking.)

Bale, incidentally, deserves some small place in the annals of Napa Valley's history for his entertaining the writer-traveler Edwin Bryant, as we reported earlier.

Many Americans from Missouri and other points eastward and several Europeans, began moving into the Napa Valley in the early and mid-1840s. E. Barnett stayed briefly with Yount before bravely going to Pope Valley (where Yount had fought one of his Indian skirmishes). William Pope actually obtained ownership of the valley named in his honor, in 1841, and moved with his family to the locale before Barnett arrived.

William Fowler and sons Henry and William reached the Napa Valley in 1844, followed by William Hargrave and Harrison Pierce. The following year, Col. J. B. Chiles returned for his second visit and purchased land in what later was named "Chiles Valley." After that the list of new settlers grew so rapidly that it would take a small book to list them all: Clyman, (Enoch) Cyrus, Nash, Coombs, York, David and William Hudson, Elliot, the Grigsbys (who helped raise the Bear Flag of revolt at Sonoma), Baldridge, Kilburn, Hopper, Pierce, Boggs, Tucker, Keseberg, Ritchie, Jesse, Nash and Harbin.

This unusual early settlement is acknowledged in a special story in the San Francisco *Alta California* newspaper of August 30, 1866:

Pioneers.

No one part of the State can boast of so many pioneers among its inhabitants as Napa. In the Upper Valley, most all of the settlers are of long standing, *and belong to that little army of hardy ad-*

venturers that penetrated these Western shores long before the discovery of gold. It is an interesting sight to see, here and there, over the valley, the log cabins that sheltered the pioneers of a State still young, but mighty in her sudden growth. (Italics added.)

Some of these pioneers had short memories about their accomplishments. This was especially true of who planted the first vineyards.

John York, who settled in 1845 near what later became Calistoga (with brothers-in-law David and William Hudson), claimed in later years to have planted the first vineyard in Napa County *of any commercial consequences.* On several occasions the St. Helena *Star* published this claim and no one wrote in to contest it or the editor failed to publish the letter.[1.6]

Actually York's assertion contributes to the assumption that Yount did not produce wine until after the Gold Rush and barely raised enough grapes in the early years for his own use. York may be quite correct that he was the first to sell grapes, that would have made his vineyard definable as "commercial."

Not far behind York in turning over the valley's soil for the propagation of the grape were F. E. Kellogg and William Nash. Both men purchased parcels of land, near Bale's Mill and set out orchards and very small vineyards between the years 1845 and 1847.

Kellogg and Nash were among some "seventy or eighty" Americans living in the Napa Valley by late 1847. This rather informal census is from a story about the Napa and Sonoma valleys published in the *California Star*, San Francisco, in two installments in January 1848. Titled "A Trip Across the Bay," the material clearly was gathered during the preceding fall harvest as these excerpts indicate:

> We arrived at Farmer Y[ount] in the evening, late and pushed on to Dr. B[ale]. George Yount arrived in the valley in the summer of 1832 and shortly after settled here.
>
> The valley of which we speak, presents over its surface, scarce a rise of ground deserving the name of hill. . . . The soil is of richest quality, and yields, as we shall in a little time show, immensely and with comparative slight labor. Delicious water may be found within ten or twelve feet of the surface in any part of the valley. . . . of white residents, the valley contains seventy or eighty souls.
>
> . . . The next day, however, we were led through the cultivated lands of the aged pioneer, and first farmer of the valley, Mr. Yount. Within his vineyard, the young vines bending with the luscious fruit, perfectly ripe, in great purple clusters, over which the dew of the passed night seemed delightful to linger.

(There is no reference to wine being made or offered to the journalist.) These vines almost certainly were located on what is now Yount Mill Road and about two miles north and east of Yountville. At this location, marked by a California State landmark, Yount constructed his blockhouse, about 1836. Yount had at least three vineyard sites during his lifetime. One is now under the waters of Rector Dam. Another was located at the north end of what is now State Lane, in Yountville, and this was his last home. His original vineyard was planted between his blockhouse and Napa River, and located directly across the river from his mill.

The only evidence for the location of *the first vineyard in Napa Valley* is an eyewitness account given on April 19, 1861 by Henry Fowler in a legal suit brought against Yount by the United States government (Land Case #32). The dispute was over the northern boundary of Yount's Caymus rancho. Fowler and his father spent the summer of 1845 with Yount and he testified in detail as to the Yount farm at that time including the vineyard.)

This is the first description of the Napa Valley to be published in a California or San Francisco newspaper. By coincidence, the publication came in the same month that gold was discovered at Sutter's Mill, or what later became the town of Coloma. The reference to "white settlers" in the valley, probably included all non-Indian inhabitants, that is the Spanish or Mexican families like the Vallejos, Higueras, Juarez; Englishmen like Bale and then the many Americans from Missouri or other nearby states.

Of the small communities which sprung up near the great bay of San Francisco before the Gold Rush (usually close to an old Catholic mission such as at San Jose, San Rafael or Sonoma), *Napa Valley was now second only to San Francisco in population*. It did not have much of a town. Napa City was nothing more than an embarcadero for small ships and the residents were widely scattered. Still, there were more of the so-called "white settlers" per square mile in the Napa Valley than in any other part of the bay region except the village of Yerba Buena (San Francisco).

It is difficult to comprehend what the Napa Valley must have been like just prior to the discovery of gold in California. Many of the Indians had already died out or were pushed back into the hills and they posed no serious threat to the newer settlers. Besides, there was then plenty of space for both the Indian and white farmers to coexist quite peacefully. That seems to have been the tradition established after Yount's few disputes which were settled by force, namely with the rifle.

The valley was overrun by wild animals, particularly bears, and they were a greater threat to farmers than the Indians. *The Chronicles of George Yount* describe in detail Yount's bear hunts, which had become legendary by the time he died. Animals such as the elk, existed in herds numbering in the hundreds and the watery lower portions of the valley near the bay, were their favorite habitat. Deer were everywhere and were easy to kill when the summer drought drove them to raid the newly seeded fields of wheat or other crops. Ducks by the thousands often wintered in the lagoons or marshes, which then existed far up into the valley. Food was certainly no problem for the seventy or eighty white settlers in the valley by 1847, at least the procuring of fresh meat.

The near wilderness aspects of the Napa Valley changed dramatically within months after the discovery of gold. At first just a few sailors arriving at San Francisco jumped ship and headed for the Sierras to search for gold. Then hundreds of sailors abandoned the high masted sailing vessels which had brought them to California in search of whale oil, hides, tallow and other products. Anyone with an extra horse for sale, quickly had callers at the front door. Sometimes the horse was stolen while negotiations were in progress by someone else not so polite. Increasing numbers of these gold seekers wandered through the Napa Valley, a little off course, but following different routes to Sacramento and the Sierra foothills to the east.

By 1850, Napa County's population had tripled from just two years previously. The official census figures gave the county 405 residents, 159 of them living in the now thriving town of "Nappa City" as the first four pages of the census are labeled. George Yount, at 56, was about the oldest resident of the county. His real estate was valued at $150,000, which made him easily the richest man in the valley. Sharing his home then was Jesse Yount, 46, and John Yount. There were six individuals from England, Wales and Ireland already living in the valley, and one from Switzerland. By far the majority of the residents listed "Missouri" as their last address, but the Bale family (he was from England, originally) called themselves "Californians" as did anyone with a Spanish surname. Yount, who had been in California longer than Bale, insisted on being listed as coming from "North Carolina," his nativity state.

The United States Census for 1850 included a special Agricultural Census which lists Napa County as having 52 farmers. Yount's agricultural pursuits are the most detailed, of course, of any farmer. He had 100 acres planted to various crops, 200 head of horses, 20 milk cows, 4,000 cattle, 100 pigs and held in storage: 20 tons of hay, 100 bushels of barley, 50 bushels of Irish potatoes and 30 bushels of peas. *There was no category on the census form for "Grapevines," but there is a column labeled "Wine, gallon of:" with nothing listed under Yount's name!*

Yount's bounty quickly became inadequate as the months passed and thousands of men stayed on permanently in the valley. The California Legislature ordered a special census in 1852, because of the swelling population and this time Napa County had a population of 2,116, five times the figure of two years earlier. The disproportionate balance of males to females can be readily seen from the fact that only 252 women are listed in Napa's population. California's total population was hard to estimate, thousands of men literally racing off to a new gold strike once word spread, but it was about 100,000 men, women and children, from every state east of the Mississippi River and most countries of Europe, Mexico and Central and South America and China.

Napa Valley residents seemed fond of celebrating the 4th of July in grand style in this early Gold Rush period. As mentioned previously, Major Stephen Cooper and Yount hosted a dinner in '47, which they erroneously thought was the first such holiday feast in California. On the 4th of July 1850, a much bigger celebration was held in "Nappa City." Fortunately, an Englishman with pen and notebook in hand, attended the day long festivities and left a rather detailed description, including the wild explosion of a cannon which nearly killed two men. The account by Frank Marryat, was published in 1854 as part of the book *Mountains and Molehills:*

> On approaching Napa . . . we entered a very beautiful valley about three miles in breadth, studded with oak trees, and bounded on either side by mountains that rose abruptly from the plain, and whose summits were crested with heavy masses of the redwood tree and white pine.
>
> As yet there was no sign of cultivation or enclosure, nor did we see a dwelling-house until the village of Napa appeared in sight; but the whole of this rich and fertile valley was shortly to be made productive, and it was to supply the wants of the many settlers, who

were now on the eve of improving this wild tract, that the little bunch of houses called 'Napa City' had sprung into existence.

We had to cross a small stream in a ferry-boat to enter Napa, and we found the little place in a lively state. Music was playing, the stars and stripes were waving from each house, whilst the street was thronged with people.

The outside settlers had come in to celebrate their fourth of July, it was now the fifth, and they were in the thick of it, and there was to be a 'ball' in the evening.

At twelve o'clock they prepared to fire a salute from three old honey-combed cannons that had probably been fished up out of the river; whether or not, a serious accident immediately occurred–the first gun fired exploded like a shell, blowing off the arm of one man and destroying the sight of another, besides peppering the spectators more or less seriously.

This damped temporarily the pleasure of the afternoon, but the public dinner, which took place under an enormous booth, seemed to restore cheerfulness.

The settlers were nearly all "Western people," small farmers from Missouri, and other Western states, who emigrated with a wife and half-a-dozen children to California in search of good land; on this they squat until the land-claims are decided, and with their thrifty habits made money, not only more surely and comfortably, but faster than the miners, whose wants they supply.

The soil here is admirably adapted for the growth of wheat, barley, potatoes; and although the price of labor is so great that these immagratory agriculturists, having little or no capital, can only till a patch of land at first, yet so rare a luxury is a vegetable, that large profits attend their earliest efforts, and the settler of these valleys, if prudent, is a rising man from the moment his spade first raises the virgin sod.

During the day a Mexican tight-rope dancer performed to the crowd: I considered him rather a bungler at his work, but my opinion was not shared by the spectators, one of whom, an old farmer, 'kinder, reckoned it was supernatural,' in which he was supported by an old backwoodsman, who said 'It warn't nothing else.'

I left these good folks in the height of enjoyment, and should not perhaps have said so much about them, but that having all very lately come from the United States across the plains, they had brought with them, and as yet retained, the manners and wants of a rural population. These people form the most valuable portion of the emigration for they come as permanent settlers, and they continue permanent improvers. Under their hands forests are cleared, and valleys enclosed, grain is raised and mills are erected, the country no longer relies on foreign ventures for its chief wants, and monopolizing flour companies cease to fatten at the expense of a hard-working population.

'I did not wait for the ball,' as I wished to reach Sonoma that night, the luggage having gone on. At our first arrival at the Creek, the ferryman, who was an American, had refused all toll on the strength of the 'Anniversary.' We could not but admire such a striking instance of real charity, as it enabled many of the surrounding farmers to cross over with their numerous families, which at the rate of one dollar for each person they could not have afforded to do. But there was nothing said about going back for nothing, and our Yankee friend having succeeded in filling the village gratis, now had the satisfaction of emptying it at a dollar-a-head.

With so many new residents arriving in the year of 1849, it quickly became imperative that a better system of laws be formulated for the county and individuals hired to carry out both the meaning and spirit of the law. If a sheriff was needed and deputies, someone had to hire them and this required some type of county council. On February 8, 1850 the county of Napa was formally created. This was seven months before the United States Congress approved a bill admitting California as a state. Napa County was one of the original twenty-seven counties forming the new state (there are now fifty-eight counties).

The more than two thousand people who called Napa County home by 1852, created an enormous demand for food, much more than could be met by Yount and the few farmers who were well established before gold was discovered. The immediate need, almost an emergency, was for someone who could supply seeds, young trees and grapevines. As a consequence, one of the first nurseries in California was founded at Soscol, five miles south of "Nappa City" in 1852.*

The man who stepped in to fill this need was Simpson Thompson, from Bucks County, Pennsylvania. Thompson was nearly fifty years old when he left Pennsylvania to come to California, and his original plans were to help set up a gas plant in the young city of San Francisco and light the streets. He even brought with him some of the fixtures and equipment needed for the project.

---

*It should be noted that originally "Soscol" was spelled "Suscol"—who or when the change was made cannot be determined.

NATHAN COOMBS

J. B. CHILES

GEORGE C. YOUNT

SIMPSON THOMPSON

Life in San Francisco was too wild and chaotic for such civilized ideas, and Thompson quickly gave them up. Within weeks he found himself in Napa Valley and obtained from Marianno Vallejo at Sonoma, the land he wanted south of Napa City. He had probably journeyed to Napa City by boat and on a warm summer morning passed the exact spot he then and there decided would be his new home. There was even an exceptionally large oak tree on the property, which served as a guidepost for returning to the site.*

Thompson first had to construct ditches and dikes to control the Napa River and drain the precise location he wanted for his orchard. His first young trees came from Rochester, New York and from a nursery in New Jersey. It is claimed that he picked ripe peaches within sixteen months of planting his first seedling and given richness of the soil and with a mild winter, he may have actually done so. Thompson is even credited with producing apples within two and a half years from seed.

Thompson had similar success with grapevines for a Visiting Committee of the California State Agricultural Society in the summer of 1856 found a vineyard of 8,000 vines, "comprising thirty varieties of native and foreign grapes.[1.7] Two years later the Society's touring committee counted 15,000 grapevines of forty-five varieties.[1.8]

Simpson Thompson was soon joined in his nursery by two sons, James and Thomas. Whether by agreement among the three of them or from some individual observation on the part of the father, the nursery quickly established a precedent in California by not irrigating its trees, shrubs and vines! Irrigation was assumed to be an absolute necessity, by the eastern Americans who could not quite fathom how any plant survived in California all summer without water (there is usually no rainfall between June 1 and September 15).

The state's first agricultural newspaper, the *California Farmer* of October 30, 1857 described the Thompson Nursery and added:

> Among the Nurseries that stand prominent for reliability and fairness in dealing, we are most happy to name Thompson's Suscol [sic] Nurseries. . . . It should be remembered that trees in these Nurseries are raised *without irrigation* and in great perfection.

---

*Menefee in his *Historical and Descriptive Sketch Book*, claims William Thompson, brother of Simpson, was the first owner of the Soscol ranch. Whatever the truth of this statement, Simpson was the man who founded the nursery.

Sixteen years later in a biography of Simpson in the *Historical and Descriptive Sketch Book* of Napas history, C. A. Menefee wrote:

> This gentleman is well known all over the Pacific Coast as the proprietor of the celebrated Soscol Orchards, and is entitled to the honor of having introduced the system of fruit culture in California without irrigation.

(This latter honor has been widely accredited to Agoston Haraszthy of Sonoma; though being a leading proponent of the concept of nonirrigation of grapes and one who wrote and talked frequently on the subject, he more than likely adopted the idea from the Thompsons. Haraszthy, who did not arrive at Sonoma until 1857, most certainly would have visited the Soscol nursery and purchased from it any grape varieties he did not have.)

Simpson also deserves some special honors for winning the first prize ever given for a Napa Valley wine though, unfortunately, this was not a grape wine. The State Agricultural Society in 1859 awarded a "Special First Premium" of $15 to Thompson for his "white currant wine, one year old" and also a "First Premium" for the "greatest number of good native varieties [of grapes] and best grown specimens, three bunches each."*

The award was in part for the "greatest number of good native varieties . . ." and this may be interpreted as either the native "Californicus" grape or, more than likely, the long-established "Mission" and "Los Angeles" grape. There has always been some question of how well the native Californicus grape did in the Napa Valley. Menefee claimed in his 1873 book:

> Wild grape vines abound along every stream, and used to afford the grizzly a considerable portion of his provisions during the fall (p. 35).

There appears to be no record of such grapes being harvested by the first Americans in the Napa Valley, though John Sutter gathered the grape which grew abundantly along the Sacramento River and even made wine from them as early as the 1840s.

Another individual to do almost as much for viticulture in the Napa Valley in the early 1850s was John Osborne. In 1856 his farm

---

*George Yount exhibited a "third-dozen" bottles of Native wine at the State Fair of 1858 but won no award, either for the exhibit or the contents.

won the First Place Premium given by the State Agricultural Society for Best Farm in California. With the Gold Rush already declining in importance as an economic factor and agriculture moving up rapidly as the major income producer for the state, Osborne's award drew considerable attention to the Napa Valley. (Osborne's murder less than ten years later by a disgruntled farm employee caused almost as much publicity.)

Osborne may have been the first person to use the fine Napa Valley sandstone for the construction of farm buildings. By 1856 he had a stone "granary" capable of holding eleven thousand bushels of wheat and a stone building to house the fresh milk, butter and cheese he made. It was more than likely these stone structures that won for Osborne his First Premium for Farms in California.

Osborne's vineyard then was second only to the Thompson's, with six thousand vines, of which three thousand were foreign varieties. There was no standard spacing of vines in that early period, though six hundred eighty to the acre (planted eight feet apart each way) may be taken as an average (this would mean Osborne had about ten acres in grapes). Among all of his foreign vines Osborne had growing a grape he called the "Zinfandel," and it may be that Agoston Haraszthy in nearby Sonoma obtained his first cuttings from him (rather than as the famous story of this grape has it, from his native Hungary).

The Zinfandel was grown in New England hothouses for many years before its introduction to California, although the spelling of the grape varies considerably (it was usually spelled "Zinfandal"). John Osborne was a native of New England, from Massachusetts.

He and other New Englanders, especially Frederick W. Macondray of San Mateo, were ardent experimenters with grape varieties and exchanged viticultural information and cuttings. The Zinfandel was available in the San Francisco Bay Area for some years before Agoston Haraszthy settled at Sonoma in 1857.

At least one individual claims to have firsthand knowledge of how Haraszthy acquired the Zinfandel from Osborne's Napa Valley farm. This was William M. Boggs who was Haraszthy's closest neighbor in Sonoma for several years. Boggs wrote a letter in June 1885 to the *St. Helena Star* with this recollection:

> About the year 1859 we organized the Sonoma Horticultural and Viticultural Gardens, of which Col. Haraszthy was President, and the writer one of the two Directors, as these gardens were owned by joint stock by members of the association.

Col. Haraszthy, in company with Judge Tott, and several of his friends who were visiting him, paid a visit to J. W. Osborne, the former owner of the Oak Knoll ranch, Napa County, now the estate of the late R. B. Woodward, and there Mr. Osborne showed these gentlemen his grafted vines and the success of his experiment in grafting foreign cuttings on Mission vines. The crop of cuttings was large and thrifty.

Col. Haraszthy reported the fact to the Board of Directors and recommended the purchase of the entire lot of trimmings from these grafted vines, which Mr. Osborne's gardener had kept carefully labelled, although a severe late spring frost had badly damaged the growth of that years cuttings. Many thousand were planted from them the same season in the nurseries of the Horticultural garden under my supervision. Among them were the Zinfandel.

(Boggs letter might have been given more credence in the later Zinfandel controversy if it weren't for the fact that so many grape varieties were misidentified in those early years. The propagation of pure strains of various vines is a science and the Zinfandel grown today may only be a close cousin of the Zinfandel or Zinfandal grown in New England hothouses.)

The high state of agriculture advancement in the Napa Valley may explain in part the reason for the forming in March 1854 of the first county agricultural society in California. A constitution for the Napa County Agricultural Society was adopted at a meeting on March 23 in Napa City with John W. Hamilton elected President, and the other officers and directors including John Grigsby, W. Kilburn, Nathan Coombs, William S. Jacks, Riley Gregg, E. Kellogg, J. Evans Brown and B. R. Pierpont.

One of the resolutions adopted at the meeting had serious portents for the future viticultural societies in the valley:

On motion it was agreed that every member exert his influence to extend the circulation of the farmer's own journals published by Messrs. Warren & Son, San Francisco, and called the "California Farmer."

The corresponding secretary was then directed to transmit to the agriculture newspaper, all news of the society. Needless to say, the complete words of the motion, plus a story on the formation of the new group, were carried in the Farmer (April 13 1854). Thereafter, the California Farmer published every piece of agricultural news it was sent on the Valley, and editor Warren made frequent visits to see for himself what was transpiring. *This may have done more to establish the Napa Valley as a premier farming region in California than John Osborne's First Prize or Thompson's pioneer nursery.*

A year after the agricultural society had been formed, the County Assessor's Report for 1855 was carried in full in (where else?) the *California Farmer*. Napa farmers now had a grand total of 57,500 vines or about 85 acres.* More than 15,000 acres of farmland were now estimated to be under cultivation, two-thirds of that sown to wheat. There were 16,002 apple trees, 66,692 pears, over 4,000 head of horses and nearly 10,000 head of cattle, to enumerate only a part of the listed items in the Assessors Report. To say Napa Valley and county were expanding rapidly was to put it mildly. It was booming.

An eyewitness to all of this who had pen in hand and recorded it for later generations, was John Russell Bartlett, a member of the U.S. and Mexican Boundary Commission. Bartlett's travels in the early 1850s covered much more than the boundary in dispute. He galloped up and down California, viewing everything including the Geysers north of Mt. St. Helena. On March 10, 1852 he rode into the Napa Valley for the first time:

> Here we entered Napa Valley. The hills on both sides as well as the valley were covered with a luxurious growth of wild oats, and immense herds of cattle were roaming about feasting on them. Wild flowers of varied hues were thickly scattered around, and everything showed that the heavy and continued rains had given new life to vegetation. Our course was now a northerly one, directly up the valley. ... The valley soon became perfectly level, without a hill or depression. In many places ploughmen were at work turning up the soil, which was of the richest description. Barley appeared to be the principal grain sowed, this being in more general use for horses than oats, and found to give a better yield. In one place I noticed a hill, the whole of which had been sowed with barley, presenting a field of more than a hundred acres.

---

*Figures published in the *Transactions* of the California Agricultural Society for 1858 give Napa County Only 22,700 vines in 1856, at considerable variance with the Assessors Report. Neither is probably accurate, no one paying that much attention to precise records though considering the interest in vines in the valley, 33 acres of grapes would be rather low.

Bartlett spent several days as a guest of Osborne, noting in his diary:

> Mr. Osborne's place was the most beautiful and picturesque I had seen in the valley. In fact, it was the only house where there was any attempt at taste and comfort; for the country was too new to expect much in the way of comfort.

His observation, "A road has just been laid out through the [valley's] centre," documents the fact that by 1852 a road ran the entire length of the valley.

Bartlett's diary was eventually published as *Personal Narrative of Explorations and Incidents* in California and the various other states he traveled. Bartlett also stopped at the Yount farm, noting he "has cultivated very little of it, but has used it like the other great landholders of the country, for a cattle range." There are several pages of footnotes, retelling the best hunting stories of George Yount and his first explorations of the Napa Valley by boat, which seem to be at odds with the historical record. *The descriptions of the Indian villages (with drawings) at the Kellogg farm in Knights Valley, offer some of the best early records available on Napa Valley Indians.* (Knights Valley is not in Napa County, but the Indians living there were from Napa tribes as this was a portion of the Wappo extended hunting area.)

The first town to be laid out in the Napa Valley (and county) was Napa City. (The word "City" was frequently used in the early years to make sure newcomers did not confuse the town with the county.) Natham Coombs was its founder, having secured the townsite from Nicholas Higuera* in return for constructing a farm house on his rancho. Coombs surveyed the townsite in 1847 and drew up a formal map which was largely ignored during most of the Gold Rush period. The first building in Napa City, Harrison Pearce's saloon on Main Street, was abandoned within days of completion when the discovery of gold was announced. The only men who supposedly remained in the town during that fateful summer of 1848 were George Cornwell and J. P. Thompson who had just opened a small store.

---

*Obtaining an accurate spelling for many Napa pioneers is nearly impossible. Higueras first name was spelled either "Nicolas" or "Nicholas." His last name can be spelled with a double "r".

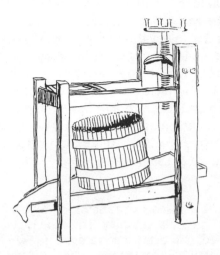

The First Napa Valley Wine

Since George Yount planted the Napa Valley's first vineyards, it seems only natural that he would have been the first to make wine and do it on a commercial basis. Yount should have built the first winery in the valley, but there is no evidence that he did so. Few visitors who left a record of his generous hospitality ever mention being served wine! There is an explanation perhaps, in Napa being so "dry" in those early years and it has to do with the many residents from Missouri.

As mentioned previously, the majority of Napa's settlers before the Gold Rush, and many who came immediately afterwards, were from Missouri. Enoch Cyrus and his family were from Missouri. A former governor of the state, L. W. Boggs, was an early resident, though like nearly everyone else in Missouri, had been born elsewhere. English writer Frank Marryat visiting Napa in 1850 observed "the settlers were nearly all 'Western people,' small farmers from Missouri, and other Western states . . ."

Most Americans who moved to Missouri in the 1820s and 1830s brought with them their strong, conservative religious background. They were the prelude to the Baptist Fundamentalists who nearly established their beliefs as the state religion in some southern and mid-western areas. The use and most certainly any abuse of liquors, was portrayed as a sin worse than breaking any of the conventional Ten Commandments of the Bible.

It does not quite follow that Yount would have adhered to this strict code since he was so independent that he readily forsook his Missouri homeland to follow the trail westward to California. But in the drinking of alcoholic beverages, Yount may have been a believer in the Baptist codes. There is no record of Yount drinking to excess or ever consuming too much even at the dinner table. This seems strange for a rough and tough Indian fighter and fur trapper.

The earliest documentation confirming wine making by Yount is a brief item carried in the *Alta California* newspaper of San Francisco, dated February 2, 1854:

NAPA WINE

We are indebted to Mr. Geo. C. Yount for some wine from his ranch in the upper portion of Napa Valley. The wine is evidently new. It is clear, bright red, and bears a good deal of resemblance to the Bordeaux wines, but is better than most of the claret offered in the San Francisco market, and probably, with more age, and, perhaps, a little better management, would equal the best French red wines.

Yount then walked down the street the same day to the offices of the *California Farmer* and provided the editor there, too, with several bottles of wine. In its issue of March 16, this brief item appeared:

CALIFORNIA WINE

We have received, by the polite attention of George Yount, Esq. of Napa City, two bottles of wine made from his vineyard, from the Los Angeles grape. The wine has a good flavor, like the 'Bordeaux claret'; has a fine body and free from the objectionable taste usually found in domestic wines. Mr. Yount manufactures about one thousand gallons.

If Yount made a thousand gallons in 1853, had he stopped during the years 1855 and 1856 when the Visiting Committee of the Agricultural Society came by? Almost certainly they would have mentioned any wine operation, especially the latter year when there was some attention paid to the subject. Yount would not have made the wine himself, his abilities were diverse but overseeing fermenting grapes? He hired someone to oversee this task but to Yount's credit, he did the selling of it, or seeking out news coverage of this achievement in San Francisco newspapers.

The two San Francisco news stories on Yount's wine strongly suggest this venture was a new one for him, i.e., "The wine is

evidently new," "with more age, and, perhaps, a little better management, would equal the best French red wines." Had Yount produced
wine previously, it seems almost certain that he would have visited
the news journals in a like manner and this recorded for posterity.

The Rev. Orange Clark, the Episcopal minister who jotted down
Yount's reminiscences during the 1850s, left a reference to wine
making at Yount's rancho in the year 1855. Clark's manuscript
carries these words with reference to the subject of Napa Valley wine:

> His lands are cultivated with remarkable success—from Four to
> Eight Hundred acres of Wheat annually is the product of his farm—
> Two Hundred Hogs, Seven Hundred Sheep, Five Hundred Horses
> & Two Thousand head of Horned Cattle, until the intrusions of
> squatters, have been the number of his Flocks & herds—One year
> ago, he marked & turned off into his pastures, Seven Hundred
> Calves, the productive annual increase of his herd of Cows, his
> vineyard yields him annually Two Hundred Gallons of wine, & his
> Orchards & gardens are studded with fruit trees of every kind—His
> fig trees yield him two crops annually—all these are the proofs of
> his industry and enterprise . . .[1.9]

Yount had no structure set aside for the making of wine, no winery,
and therein lies some of the problems with acknowledging his efforts
in this regard. When the Visiting Committee of the California Agricultural Society came on their inspection tour in 1855 and again in 1856,
they must have been permitted to look inside all of his farm buildings.
Either they saw no barrels of wine (or leather bags) or what they saw
did not impress them at all (wine stacked perhaps, in an outbuilding
also used for cattle?).

(Nearly a dozen farms with vineyards are described in the
Report of the Agricultural Society for 1855, among them A. Delmas of
San Jose: "The fine wine exhibited to the committee gave evidence of
superior skill in manufacture." Committee members C. I. Hutchinson,
B. Cahoon, R. Robinson and A. H. Meyers sampled the Delmas wine
to make this discrete observation.)

When the editor of the *California Farmer* paid Yount a visit in
September 1856, he could write for the October 3 issue that he had
been "refreshed with new wine from the new-pressed grapes." There
is no mention by the editor of seeing a winery in operation or how
much wine was being produced.

The same issue of the *Farmer* carries an excellent description of the town of Napa which is worthy of repeating in its entirety:

THE VALLEY OF NAPA

The Napa Springs.

Some two weeks since our duties called us into the Valley of Napa, and we were surprised at the improvements of the city in one year. The very handsome block of brick buildings erected by James & Co., are an ornament to the city, and a source of profit to the owners. Other new buildings are going up to join them; the splendid new Court House, of which we have before spoken, is a great credit to the county. The new Church will soon be finished, and will add to the character and credit of Napa—this is the first and only Church in the county, we believe.

We visited the warehouses, and we believe there is now stored in Napa city more than two thousand tons of wheat, owned by men that are able to keep it—the Farmers.

Napa is progressing sure; the brick for the Court House was made in Napa, the stone quarried, and the lumber found there. The grain growers are prospering, and everything wears a cheerful aspect. Hotels are full, and the stores are doing a good business.

We made our home at the Napa Hotel, kept by the well known firm of Gilmore & Taylor. This is as good a house as the size and convenience it offers can be, and the proprietors do all they can to please their numerous patrons. Napa, however, needs a larger and better hotel, for the accommodation of so large a place; and as the travel to the Springs is rapidly increasing, we would hope some public spirited citizen will see such a Hotel erected very soon. We were very much indebted for kindness and courtesy to Messrs. G. and T., and we hope they will soon have a new and fine building, when they can do all they desire to please their increasing patronage.

There has been one evil corrected there since our last visit, which is worthy of note. A toll bridge, at the entrance of the city, which was a heavy tax upon the citizens, has been purchased by the county, and the burden and evil remedied. Toll bridges and toll gates on plank roads, we consider a nuisance that should be abated at once; it is a poor policy that dictates or permits it. Napa has set a good example, which we hope will be imitated by every other county in the State.

Napa Valley's First Winery

To George Yount goes the distinction of being Napa Valley's first wine maker. He produced at least one thousand gallons of wine in 1853 according to the *California Farmer*, although Rev. Orange Clark put his production at only "Two hundred gallons" annually in the early to mid-50s. After that initial burst of wine public relations in San Francisco, Yount seems to almost drop out of sight for a half dozen years. Two hundred gallons is not what might be called "commercial wine making."

There is another individual who vies with Yount for the title of Napa Valley's first vintner—an immigrant Englishman named John Patchett.

Patchett did not begin wine making until three or four years after Yount, but he shipped wine regularly from 1857 onward and won a great deal more press notice for the valley's wine than the man from Yountville. Moreover, *Patchett built Napa Valley's first bona fide winery*, a structure measuring 50 x 33 feet of native stone! The year was 1859, two years before Charles Krug was able to fashion a small winery at St. Helena out of an excavation dug into a hillside. Patchett's winery was, unfortunately, struck by a rare lightning bolt during a rainstorm in January 1878, and was severely damaged.*

John Patchett is easily the most obscure figure in the long and fascinating history of wine production in the Napa Valley. His name

---

*This may explain why the ruins cannot be located in what is now downtown Napa even serving with some mortification as a garage or other outbuilding.

is rarely to be found in any accounts of the valley's viticulture or wine past. (He is not even a part of the oral history tradition of the county, which has greater breadth than current contemporary writing on wine.) The most simple explanation for this peculiar obscurity is that he died with no heirs, no children to remind later generations of their fathers contribution.

John Patchett was born in Lincolnshire, England in 1797. In 1817 he immigrated to the United States, settling in Pennsylvania. Two decades later he began moving westward, never remaining long in any one place. He was a brew master by trade and had difficulties finding employment in the western outreaches of the country, which then had not crossed the great barrier of the Missouri River. He took up farming but this seemed only a temporary occupation.

By the time of the great California Gold Rush, Patchett was an old man, at least for that time, of some fifty plus years. After the tenth or twelfth story about the richness of California had wetted his appetite, he left his Iowa farm and headed westward.

In the fall of 1850 he was mining for gold near Placerville and like the majority of other miners, soon followed the crowd to a new site whenever someone had "struck it rich." He was well acquainted with the Gold Rush towns of the Sierra-Nevada mountains within a matter of months.

Patchett had more patience than many of the other younger miners, and eventually had enough gold to invest in his own California farm. In 1852 he journeyed to the Napa Valley to see what all the agricultural excitement was about and purchased his first vineyard. From James W. Brackett, he bought in May for $3,000, a one hundred acre parcel near the junction of Napa Creek and Napa River (this is now right in the heart of the city of Napa). Patchett added eighty more acres to the south of this parcel, two years later.

C. A. Menefee in his *Historical and Descriptive Sketch Book* claims:

> The first one to plant a vineyard of any consequence one for any other purpose than for grapes for table use was J. M. Patchett. As early as 1850, a small vineyard had been planted on the property which he afterwards purchased. The year of his purchase he planted a greater number of vines and also an orchard. In 1859 he was so well convinced that wine making could be made remunerative that he erected his cellar, now standing . (p. 203).

Menefee was the first but not the only Napa Valley pioneer to record Patchett's early achievements. William A. Trubody who arrived in the valley in 1847 left a memoir many years later which stated:

> Yount had a small vineyard an acre or two. The first to have large vineyards were Paget [sic], Krug and Dr. Crane. [I.10]

Frank Leach who arrived in Napa City as a youth in the 1850s wrote years later:

> The first vineyard for wine making purposes was planted in the latter part of the 50s by John Patchett on a piece of land about a mile northwesterly from the court house in the town of Napa. Here the first wine on any scale was made. [I.11]

This was not the first place he made wine, however, that was in an adobe built by or for Nicholas Higuera, closer to the junction of Napa Creek and Napa River.* The source for Patchett's historic wine making in the Higuera adobe is none other than Charles Krug himself, considered the father of the wine industry in Napa Valley. On December 19, 1890 the *St. Helena Star* published a long account written by Krug on the history of Napa Valley viticulture. He recalled:

> In October 1858 I made the first lot of wine ever made in Napa county, at the place of John Patchett, Napa city. As a cellar used an old pioneer adobe house built on the banks of Napa creek and close to the lot where at present stands the Napa college (Calistoga Avenue at Seminary Street).

Krug quickly clarified his recollection by stating his was the first lot of wine made other than by the old Spanish process, of foot stomping the grapes in a leather bag.

Menefee's *Sketch Book* adds additional details of this first crush:

> In 1859, having become convinced that the business of raising grapes and wine making could be made remunerative, he [Patchett] erected a stone cellar 33 x 50 feet. He had made about 600 gallons

---

*The Patchett vineyards and orchard may have been located in part on the site now occupied by Fuller Park in downtown Napa. This is directly west of the courthouse. Old-timers like Mrs. Frank Noyes of Napa, who was born in the town in 1900, can recall playing in the "Patchett Grove," now occupied by Fuller Park.

Patchett's winery, the 50 by 33 foot stone structure, may have been in the park or possibly a few blocks further west, just across Jefferson Street, a main north-south artery in the center of Napa City.

of wine the year previous, selling it at $2 per gallon. The stone for his cellar was quarried out of the hills back of the residence of Cayetano Juarez. The cellar is still standing and is as good as ever (1873).

Menefee also credits Patchett with the first shipment of wine from Napa County and that this took place in 1857. Patchett sent six casks and six hundred bottles of wine, probably to San Francisco.[I.12]

In keeping with the example set in 1854 first by Yount and then by the Napa County Agricultural Society, Patchett, too, sought publicity for his success with wine making. The ever attentive editor of the *California Farmer* described Patchett's efforts in the issue of March 18, 1859:

> We have always believed that California would *make her mark* as a wine growing country; for years we have urged attention to this all-important subject, and most heartily rejoice to see our citizens turning their attention to it. We were pleased to receive a call from one of our subscribers at Napa, John Patchett, Esq. and to learn that he had been very successful that past year in growing the vine and making wine. He kindly informs us that he has now about twenty-six acres of vines, and they are doing well. They are principally the Mission Grape, although he has some ten varieties of foreign grapes, all doing well.
>
> The wine brought to us by Mr. Patchett was a fine White Wine, of very superior character in flavor, much resembling the Hock Wine. Most earnestly do we commend the enterprise to every man having land. . . .

One year later, the editor of the *Farmer* paid the Patchett ranch a visit and found a vineyard of 11,000 vines in full bearing and 12,000 young vines, or about 55 acres. (There was no vineyard of comparable size in the county.) Patchett's winery is described as having one wine vat capable of holding 1,600 gallons (probably a fermenting tank), and his white wine was "light, clear and brilliant, and very superior, indeed his red wine excellent; we saw superior brandy, also."[I.13] Patchett, though trained as a beer brew master, had the good sense to hire experienced wine makers. Who assisted him in 1857 is not known. Krug made or helped make his '58 vintage and Henry A. Pellet worked for him in '59 and '60.

By the mid-1860s John Patchett was no longer in good health, he was nearing his seventieth birthday and suffering from "cancers." There is no record of his winery operating after about '65, although this may be due to the fact that bound volumes of Napa newspapers for the period were later destroyed by fire. The only total production figure for his winery on an annual basis is that supplied by the United States Agricultural Census for 1860, which credits him as making 4,000 gallons. It is certain that wine production had long since ceased when the thunderstorm moved over Napa in January 1878, and a bolt of lightning caused the "roof to cave in" and severe cracks in the walls.[I.14]

John Patchett fortunately did not live to see his winery treated so harshly by this whim of Mother Nature. He died August 13, 1876 having "been a sufferer from cancers for a long time." The obituary notice in the *Napa Reporter* adds that his death came in the family residence but does not give an address or location. (This is crucial, of course, to locating the most likely site for the Patchett Winery.)

Fortunately, Martha Patchett's death (his widow) elicited a lengthy obituary in the same newspaper on August 30, 1904. She passed away "at the family home on West Second street, near Jefferson. ... She was 82 years and 14 days of age at the time of her demise, and was born in Manchester, England. She came to California and Napa in 1861, forty-three years ago, and has been a resident of this city ever since. Mr. Patchett came to California about 1850, and purchased in 1852 the place in Napa where both he and his wife lived and passed away."

In 1873, Patchett created the "Patchett Addition" to the city of Napa and began selling off most of the land he owned surrounding his family home. (The Patchett Addition is now bounded on the north by First Street, on the east by Jefferson, on the south by Laurel and on the west approximately follows Seymour Street. It is most likely that Napa Valley's first winery, and one made of stone at that, would have been located in this area. There seems to be no structure in anyone's backyard roughly approximately 50 by 33 feet, a building which could now serve as a garage, for example. Hopefully the site, because of its historic importance, may be located precisely at some future date.)

There is still the question of how much credit Patchett deserves for helping establish or found the Napa Valley wine industry. He appears to be the *first really commercial winemaker*, Yount's efforts seemingly being for personal use except for the year 1853 when he did make a thousand gallons. There is no evidence Yount repeated this production until much later in the decade.

Some sort of private feud seems to have existed between Patchett and Charles Krug. Neither man gave any credit later to the other for those pioneering years of wine making.

For example, Krug's memoir in the *Star* of December 1890 includes this often quoted observation:

> In October 1858 I made the first lot of wine ever made in Napa county, at the place of John Patchett, Napa city. . . .

Patchett never mentioned this fact once in any publicity he sought for his wine endeavors, including a lengthy biography in the 1873 *Historical and Descriptive Sketch Book of Napa* . . . Krug, on his part overlooks the fact that Patchett and/or his wine maker, produced wine as early as 1857 (if not the year previously) and shipped, according to the *Sketch Book* six casks and six hundred bottles of wine.

Krug, of course, did much more than Patchett to promote wine and viticulture in the valley, attending every meeting or convention held in the state dealing with wine. He served as a Commissioner in the 1880s for the Board of State Viticultural Commissioners and even wrote in great detail about his viticulture experiences for publication. When anyone forgot that contribution after his death in 1892, the family was there to restore that honor.

John Patchett, on the other hand, died in Napa before wine making had caught on so widely in California, half a decade before the great viticultural boom of the 1880s. He had no children to mourn him, to renew his wine legacy when it needed renewing in the anniversary publication of a local newspaper. (A stepson survived Patchett, but never accepted any filial responsibilities in this regard. Patchett deserves at the least, to be honored as a co-founder of the valley's wine industry and the builder of the first winery.)

Viticulture as a California Occupation

When John Patchett first began purchasing land for the planting of grapes, viticulture was a subject being held out to potential California farmers as a new and tantalizing farming endeavor. Only a handful of the thousands of young men attracted to the state by the Gold Rush had ever worked in a vineyard and most of these were Europeans. The cultivation of the grape, and even more so the making of wine, was a mysterious occupation so very timely for California. Each individual had stepped onto California soil knowing full well this was a land of uncertainty, risks had to be taken. Risks were taken just to reach this wild outpost of civilization. Viticulture fit in perfectly in this new approach to living.

Half a dozen years into the 1850s, newspapers in Northern California began what amounted to a campaign to stimulate the growth of agriculture. The source of this movement is not difficult to discern. The 1856 vigilante movement in San Francisco offered a fearful demonstration of what can happen when strong young men are idle for long periods of time. Crime and violence reached a point in the city where the death of an individual, by mysterious circumstances, hardly warranted a brief item in the newspapers. Something had to be done to change all of that.

The Monterey, Ca. *Sentinel* in April 1856 offered this suggestion for those who sought a new direction in life:

> From the first settlement of the country to our time, nothing has given continental Europeans, who have visited California, more admiration and surprise than the extraordinary facility with which different species of the grape have succeeded in our mellow and

fertile soil. . . . Germans, Frenchmen, Spaniards, Italians and traveled Englishmen and Americans, with concurrent testimony, invariably affirm that there is no country of the Mediterranean or of interior Europe which can excel or even equal California and its adaptability of soil and climate for the cultivation of this fruit, and the manufacture of every quality and fineness of wine and brandy.

The Monterey reporter took note of the fact that the valleys of the Sierras had already demonstrated how well the grape grew there and that since 1848, in around San Francisco, "there are many fine vineyards, planted mostly for the vending of the fresh grape, which promise this year to lower the price materially." It was also claimed that not one instance had occurred of the failure of the grape to produce in Sonoma, Napa, San Jose or Contra Costa counties.

If the making of money was the motivation for turning to agriculture, rather than say, the love of the soil, much wealth could be made here too, claimed the *Petaluma Weekly Journal* in April 1856:

In France, in 1694, a vineyard was sold for one million francs.... The average value of vineyards in France, per arpent (100 rods and 22 feet of our measure), is $210—but the very best vineyards are worth from $2,000 to $3,000 per arpent.

The *California Farmer* began beating the drum vigorously for viticulture before other publications and success in this field is in large part due to its editor, James Warren. In July 1857, Warren devoted two and a half columns to "The Commerce of the Vine, Olive and Mediterranean Fruits." He pointed out how easy it was to grow such products in California, which compared favorably to their natural home in Italy or Greece. Warren, like the editor of the Petaluma newspaper, appealed to more than just the desire to till the soil. He reprinted government figures showing the importation of wine, brandy, champagne and dried raisins into eastern United States offered a yearly market worth $7,235,000. He asked why the farmers of California could not share in this agricultural wealth?

Warren's figures, incidentally, show that 8,000 gallons of Burgundy wine was imported into Boston, New York and other East Coast ports between June 1855 and June 1856. Americans also drank 44,000 gallons of Madeira wine in that same period, 398,000 gallons of Sherry, 265,000 gallons of Port, 1,500,000 gallons of Claret, 1,800,000 gallons of Brandy and 197,000 dozen bottles of champagne. The California firm of Kohler & Frohling had exported a few hundred gallons of wine to New York by this date and there may have been the same amount sent from Los Angeles, but otherwise the market belonged to European producers.

There were more grape growers in Santa Clara County in the early 1850s than any other location except for Los Angeles. Although most of these were French immigrants, L. A. Gould was singled out for special attention in an early wine story on the county:

> We are constantly reminded of the excellent quality of the wines of California. We tasted some of the wines made by L. A. Gould of Santa Clara, some two weeks since, that would vie with the best hock wines of Germany. Mr. G. has been very successful in making wine, although in small quantities. He has a vineyard of the Isabella and Catawba, that promise wonderful things.[I.15]

The various newspapers and other publications even began arguing with each other as to whom should or could take the most credit for the growth of agricultural interest in California, and wine making in particular. The following excerpt appeared in the *Farmer* of November 27, 1857:

> The *Alta California*, in its issue of Sunday, the 22nd, complains of the *Scientific American* for giving credit to the *California Farmer*, for an article on the 'Wines of our States.' The *Alta* says: 'The *Scientific American* contains a long article on the *Wines of California*, including several extracts from an article published in the *Alta* several months ago, on *the general advantages of our State for Wine-growing over all other countries.*'
> The italics are ours, for here seems to be the material point: the *Alta* would claim all the credit of having pointed out to the *Scientific American*, and all journals in other States, the advantages of Wine-growing in California. . . . the form of language in which it was printed may have been taken from the *Alta*, and was undoubtedly so taken; but the same material facts, and columns more, have been published for years in the *California Farmer*, and have been often quoted.

Warren, the editor, probably was correct in what he said of the *Alta* or any other journal for that matter. Agriculture, after all, and grape growing, were primary subjects of interest to his publication and his readers.

German-born Charles Krug and a Hungarian named Agoston Haraszthy, were among the first to seriously heed the advice of Warren, et al. Both men had lived for some years in eastern United

States, but Haraszthy had caught California fever first. He liked to be referred to as "Count Haraszthy" and was an entrepreneur quite suited to the times in San Francisco.

He would invest in almost any venture. He had planted vines in San Diego, then moved his grapes to San Francisco and upon learning that could be a fatal mistake, uprooted the well-traveled grapes and hauled them south to San Mateo County. He also held a job with the U. S. Mint in San Francisco.

How or when Krug and Haraszthy met is not known. Both were working in the Mint in 1856, both had vineyards near Crystal Springs, San Mateo County. Their backgrounds in viticulture and most of all in political intrigues in their home countries, gives the impression they came from somewhat the same mold. Krug, at the age of 22, had immigrated to the U. S. and briefly lectured at the Free Thinkers School of August Glasser in Philadelphia. When political discontent swept Germany in the late 1840s, he returned to join what he thought was to be a revolution. Like Haraszthy in Hungary, it turned out he was on the wrong side and ended up in jail. Imprisonment was brief, fortunately, and he quickly fled back to the United States.

In California in 1852, Krug accepted the task of editing the German language newspaper *Staats Zeitung*. He planted his San Mateo vineyard, then accepted a post with the Mint which is where he and Haraszthy must have plotted the Sonoma Valley viticultural boom of the late 1850s.

San Francisco's leading daily newspaper then was the *Alta California*, followed by the *Bulletin*. The *Alta* had carried brief items on vine planting at Sonoma, but the first major story describing a wine boom in the Sonoma Valley occurred December 6, 1858:

> Sonoma Valley is going into the vine business extensively. The vine was introduced there by the Missionary priests about thirty years ago, and it has thrived admirably. The wine of Sonoma is different from that of the southern portion of the State, being lighter and more like the French wines. The red wine of Col. Haraszthy has taken some of the highest premiums at our late fairs. The fitness of the soil and climate of Sonoma for the production of excellent grapes and wine has incited the people there to plant vines extensively, and they are now in the beginning of the wine fever.

This story listed thirteen grape growers who were planting new vineyards, among them Charles Krug who had 15,000 new vines. Nearly two hundred thousand vines had been planted that year alone, that was more vines than had existed in the entire valley previously. Haraszthy, and perhaps Krug, deserve some of the credit for this "wine fever" as the *Alta* called it. The infection had begun even earlier, however, for County Assessors figures show a 656% increase in vine planting in the years 1856 and 1857. Haraszthy did not settle in Sonoma Valley until the latter year.

The vine excitement spread to nearby Napa Valley as well, but on a smaller scale. John Patchett, of course, was already active and as early as 1854 had begun expanding his vineyards. John Osborne began doing the same even before Haraszthy and Krug moved to Sonoma. The Thompsons at Soscol, anticipating a grape boom perhaps, had thirty varieties of grape cuttings for sale in '56. George Yount also seems to have begun expanding his vineyard about the same time.

The first St. Helena resident, or resident-to-be, to catch the wine fever, was Dr. George Crane, who found himself soon caught up in the excitement:

> My first visit to Napa was in May, 1858, thirty two years ago, when I was surprised by the muddy roads contrasting so broadly with Santa Clara valley, where the plows had been mainly idle for years for want of rain. My attention was then drawn to the fact that while the prevailing Summer winds in San Jose, where I lived, were from the North, they were on the same days and hours there blowing toward the North.
>
> This apparent anomaly I found was explained by the Sierra Nevada mountains. They arrest the atmospheric current which comes landward through the Coast range at the Golden Gate, when in obedience to hydrostatic law it divides and like water, takes the course of least resistance. This brings a portion of that air, fresh from the ocean, ladened with its evaporation, up through this valley.
>
> Here, pent in a comparative narrow defile by the collateral mountains and obstructed in its progress by grand old St. Helena with a summit towering 4,000 feet plus above the sea, its moisture is condensed into rain drops by the lower temperature of the mountain tops and precipitated into the valley. This explains why Napa grain growers were jubilant while the same class of men in Santa Clara and other more rainless valleys were paying three per cent a month for money to meet unavoidable expenses.[I.16]

Crane's weather observations are not quite correct, although he understood in part why the cooling, refreshing fogs of summer sweep into the Napa Valley (a thermal low in the San Joaquin Valley draws the cooler marine air through the Golden Gate). The winter following Crane's first visit to the valley, he purchased 335 acres of land at St. Helena and shortly began planting his first vineyard. Within a few years more, he turned to the making of wine, sharing with Krug the honors of being the first to be a "St. Helena vintner."

An amusing aspect of this entire pre-Civil War vine planting saga north of San Francisco is the motivation behind Charles Krug's decision to leave Sonoma and settle in the Napa Valley. In 1858, he borrowed an apple press from the Haraszthy's and at John Patchett's in Napa City, crushed his grapes and assisted in the making of wine. The following year, Krug made wine for the Bale family south of St. Helena and in 1860, was the winemaker for George Yount. In August of this latter year, Krug inserted the following advertisement in the *California Farmer:*

NOTICE.

Vineyard for Sale. The Undersigned offers for sale his Beautifully located VINEYARD MONTEBELLO, consisting of 16,000 to 17,000 VINES (some of them foreign). One-fourth of the Vines will bear next year. A Young ORCHARD of 125 choice FRUIT TREES, together with Two small Dwelling-Houses and a Stable. The place, 35-1/2 acres, with several living springs upon it. The soil is eminently adapted for Vines, and adjoins the well-known Vineyards of Col. Haraszthy, Gen. Williams, and Mr. Dresel.

Having in view to commence a more extensive plantation, this place will be sold cheap, the owner not being able to carry on both. Terms easy. Apply by letter, or personally, to CHS. KRUG, Sonoma.

Krug's little farm was right in the heart of what soon became the vine capital of California. One of his neighbors was none other than the man quickly gaining the most fame for viticulture in the state, Agoston Haraszthy. (Maybe there wasn't enough room in Sonoma Valley for both of them?) Another neighbor was Army General C.H.S. Williams, and many nearby vineyardists were fellow Germans. Why give this all up and move to the Napa Valley?

The explanation seems to be that he had fallen in love with Caroline Bale, the daughter of the late Dr. Bale. Krug had made wine

for the family in 1859. As heir to a portion of the Carne Humana
Rancho land grant, Caroline was due to be given a good portion of
that land on her marriage. It may have been that Charles Krug was
as interested in his wife's dowry as the ability of the soil of the Napa
Valley to produce fine wine grapes. Caroline and Charles were
married December 26, 1860, the day after Christmas.

Krug never left any hint in many subsequent letters on viticulture
history, as to his real motivation for leaving Sonoma. Thirty-two years
later he did describe in detail, for the *St. Helena Star* the status of
grape growing and wine making in the valley as he first witnessed it
in the late 1850s:

> When I first visited Napa county I found less than a dozen small
> vineyards of so-called Mission vines, about six or ten years old, all
> planted for the purpose of enjoying the sweet, juicy fruit and partly
> to sell the grapes at splendid, paying prices. The old pioneer, Capt.
> George Yount, near the present Yountville, had several acres of
> vines. On Dr. Bale's rancho was about one acre of vines in a
> flourishing condition.
>
> David Hudson and John York, near St. Helena, were proud
> owners of about half an acre of vineyard each. C. C. Griffith, now
> of Vineland, had furnished both gentlemen the cuttings for planting
> from the above mentioned *Buena Vista* vineyard, 1849.
>
> There were a few acres of vineyard near Dr. Bales flour mill, at
> present the property of W. W. Lyman, about an acre at George
> Tucker's place, the vines having been planted by Colonel Ritchie,
> a few vines planted by Mr. Owsley on Lincoln's farm, and about one
> acre of vines near Calistoga at the place then belonging to Henry
> Fowler. Most of these vines, as a matter of course all Mission, are
> not any more in existence.

Krug's memory seemed to be failing him in 1890 for he overlooked or
ignored the three largest vineyards which were thriving in the valley
when he arrived: John Patchett's near Napa City, the Thompson
Nursery and vineyard at Soscol and John Osborne's farm at Oak
Knoll.

Krug's rather lengthy letter to the *Star* fails to reflect the extremely active and promotion conscious young farmers who wanted
to put Napa Valley "on the map" by the late 1850s, particularly the
Napa County Agricultural Association. In September 1856, a special
meeting was called at Napa City to consider the possibility of hosting
the annual fair sponsored by the State Agricultural Society. The
committee named to investigate the matter included: John Osborne,

Natham Coombs, F. Kellogg, George Yount, Wells Kilburn, William Nash, J. Hamilton, Edward McGrarry and J. Day.

The efforts of these men did not succeed, largely because Napa City was just too small a village to host a statewide fair. The primary energy behind this movement is traceable, in part, to that hard-working editor of the *California Farmer*, James Warren. It was at this meeting that Warren succeeded in obtaining passage of a resolution urging all able-bodied mechanics, farmers and working men to subscribe to the *Farmer*.

There was a mini-boom in vine planting in Napa as in Sonoma before the American Civil War began. Records kept by the State Agricultural Society, and published in its yearly journal *Transactions*, indicate a doubling in size of vineyards in Napa County from 1856 to 1857. The actual number of vines in the first year was 22,000, one year later, 55,000. The following year Napa County had 90,000 vines. (With a vineyard spacing of 8 by 8 or 680 vines to the acre, by 1858, the county had 132 acres in grapes).

Viticulture was so new an undertaking in this period that every farmer eagerly sought the advice of others who seemed to have more experience. In the spring of 1859, the "Sonoma and Napa Horticultural Society" was formed with the first two speakers, John Osborne and Agoston Haraszthy. "The plan is to establish a Garden, similar to those of Europe, for introducing new products from every clime, and practically testing their adaptability to our climate." The Gardens were to be established at Sonoma and it was here that Haraszthy brought his first cuttings of the Zinfandel grape, purchased from Osborne in Napa Valley.[1.17]

In the same year, Horace Greely came to California to see for himself why he might want to urge the young men of America to settle in the great American West. Already a famous journalist and newspaper editor, Greely's comments on the potential of California for growing grapes only served to fire the boom already in progress:

> Of Grapes, it is hardly yet time to speak so sanguinely as many do; for years will be required to render certain their exemption from the diseases and the devastators known to other lands of the vine. But it is certain that some kinds of Grapes have been grown around the old Jesuit Missions for generations, with little care and much success; and it does not appear that the more delicate varieties recently introduced are less thrifty or more subject to attack than their Spanish predecessors, and Vineyards are being multiplied and expanded in almost every farming neighborhood; single vines

and patches of choice varieties are shooting up in almost every garden throughout the Mining region, and there can be little doubt that California is already better supplied with the grape than any other State of the Union. That she is destined soon to become largely and profitably engaged in the manufacture and exportation of Wine, is a current belief here, which I am at once unable and disinclined to controvert.[I.18]

In spite of the cautious tone to Greely's comments, this could be considered a strong endorsement of grape farming in the state. Just the acknowledgement by so famous a writer and traveler as Greely, meant that countless readers in eastern United States were suddenly aware of the vines' existence here. Since Greely's comments were carried in the *California Farmer*, in full, they were widely read in the Napa Valley.

The Third Annual Fair of the California Horticultural Society was held in San Francisco in September. The First Prize for "Best Display of Fruit" went to John Osborne of Napa Valley, and Simpson Thompson won Third Place honors. D. Gibbs and Thompson won First and Second Place as well for "Largest and Best Variety" of apples and peaches. Gibbs, Thompson and Osborne won awards in many of the other categories as well, although in grapes Napa Valley did not do so well. Antoine Delmas of San Jose took First Place honors with the only local award going to Thompson, a Second Place for Native and Atlantic varieties.

Of more interest to farmers everywhere and those in attendance at the Society's Fair, was an afternoon session devoted to grape culture, particularly varieties suited to climatic regions of the state. Antoine Delmas of San Jose presented a long list of dozens of varieties he thought best for the region south of San Francisco and perhaps for much of Northern California. The conclusion, however, of the session was that such a list was premature:

> Let the new beginner but note this difference [of climates] and in his planting, if for profit, choose only those varieties having these marks of adaptation to his locality, and he will ensure success. Our Society is too young and has yet too little experience to make perfectly reliable fruit lists for every locality, but much information has been elicited and recorded, and we think, albeit many a man's old favorite has been stricken off, will be found to be reliable.[I.19]

The State Agricultural Society had appointed a "Special Committee" on the Culture of the Grape-Vine many months earlier and its report was issued late the same year. John Osborne of Napa Valley, one of seven vice-presidents of the Society, may have had some influence in bringing about this special study.

One of the findings of the Society was that irrigation was not necessary for vines except in the hot Sacramento and San Joaquin valleys. Eastern American farmers could not fathom growing any fruit or grapes in the state during the long, dry and often hot summer, without some watering. Numerous pioneers stated the trees and vines would send roots down to the water table, not far below the soils surface. In the coastal valleys or the foothills of the Sierra-Nevada range, irrigation simply was not necessary.

The Committee bemoaned the fact that so much French wine and brandy was imported when it all could be produced here:

> It would be an interesting fact to publish, if one possessed it, the amount of gold drawn from our soil never more to be returned, by the French wine and liquor merchants. We may venture the assertion, that since eighteen hundred and forty-nine, the people of California have paid, and the gold has gone into the public and private coffers of France enough to build the Atlantic and Pacific Railroad. . . .[1.20]

This report also carried such recommendations as the immediate necessity of collecting and classifying the many varieties of wild grapes in California and of the state government providing assistance in the propagation of the vine throughout the state.

Vine culture was not an all-consuming passion for Napa Valley farmers, obviously. The cereal grains and cattle were the mainstays of every farm with the racing of horses possibly requiring more hours of both idle and serious time than any other subject. A "Jockey Club" was formed at Napa City in 1858 whose members did nothing but argue the merits of "horseflesh" and exchange gold dust in private bets. A favorite Sunday occupation on many farms, was the coming together of neighbors and racing of their best horses down a dusty stretch of valley roadway.

It was also very common to lay out a very generous table of food after the races were over and beverages to slacken the thirst. Some farmers or most especially their wives, frowned on the drinking of spirits on the Lord's Day, or any day for that matter. With each new acre of vines planted, there was bound to be some grapes which could not find a ready market in the town; or the farmer did not have the finances to ship them to San Francisco. These grapes were crushed and fermented into wine.

Much of this local wine could not have been of very high quality and probably tasted as if it were made by an Illinois or Vermont farmer. There were not many residents to admire them like Charles Krug, who had grown up in Europe amidst vineyards and wineries. This early wine making was strictly an amateur undertaking. Grapes fermented easily, however, if the sugar is high enough in late fall. By the end of the 1850s, Napa Valley wines must have been available for many of the participants in the Sunday afternoon horse races.

Since wild game such as bear, deer and elk, or wild duck were staples, too, of the big Sunday dinners, a good hearty red wine would have been a perfect complement to the strong flavors inherent in such meat (a result of the animals feeding on marsh grasses or hillside vegetation).

Fish abounded in the Napa River in that period, the water table being so much higher year-round. Salmon could be caught by the dozens, far upstream, and must have also been a perfect complement served fried or baked, with the early homemade Napa Valley Rieslings.

II. The Birth of the Napa Valley Wine Industry, the 1860s

There is no editorial explanation in San Francisco's *Hesperian* magazine of April 1860 as to why the publication carried a long story called "Notes On Napa Valley." No general circulation magazine in California had done anything similar on the small farming region because it did not have a major tourist attraction. There was nothing to compare to neighboring Sonoma County's mountainous and ominous valley of geysers and fumeroles (the Geysers).

No gold strikes occurred in Napa County such as those which made the Sierra foothill counties household words. There is just an outside possibility that some readers had inquired as to the location of the valley after Mrs. F. H. Day's vivid account of the life of George Yount. That story had been published one year earlier.

More than likely the magazine carried "Notes On Napa Valley" because freelance journalist John Hittell simply decided one cold January day to do a travel piece on Napa. *Hesperian's* editor, coincidentally Day, may have been the first to see the piece and purchased it on the spot. The combination of circumstances if true, was fortuitous for publicizing Napa Valley and judging from the opening lines of Hittell's story, he seemed to think most of his readers had never heard of the region:

> North of San Pablo Bay and opening upon it, are three valleys side by side parallel with each other and with the coast, their general direction being N.N.W. and S.S.E. Each is drained by a creek bearing its own name, and bounded by a steep range of Mountains on both sides; and each is rich in wealth different from that of the others. Petaluma has the dairies, Sonoma has the wine, and Napa has wheat. The latter, of which I propose now more particularly to speak, makes a better appearance than either of the other two.

Hittell's observation that "Petaluma has the dairies, Sonoma has the wine, and Napa has wheat" probably reflected what was then generally known about agriculture in these three valleys north of San Francisco. Agoston Haraszthy's speeches and published writings about Sonoma had brought that valley some measure of publicity regarding wine making, but he had no counterpart in Napa.

The growing of wheat and cultivation of apple orchards were the farmer's main concerns, claimed the San Francisco journalist, with the valley, "in proportion to its size, the richest and most productive grain district in the State." Salvadore Vallejo had one field alone which measured 2,200 acres in size! Hittell provided the names of two dozen farmers who were also major growers of fruit, the county having more than 150,000 fruit trees, about two-thirds being apples. Vallejo's grain fields were being tilled by an Italian named "Basciano." He is possibly the first Italian immigrant to settle in the valley.

"Notes On Napa Valley" provides much history on George Yount, of course, and documents the fact that Napa Valley was the destination of many pre-Gold Rush settlers:

> About 1842 the Fowlers, father and son, and Mr. Kilburn, settled in Napa, and in 1844 Mr. Bartlett Vines [son-in-law of George Yount]. *In the fall of 1846 a number of Americans arrived in California from Missouri* by way of the plains.* Of these, James Harbin, Arch Jesse, the Stilts brothers, and the Long brothers, the last now residing in Solano County, took their families to Mr. Lorent's house, and themselves went off to join Fremont in fighting for the country. In 1847 Nathan Coombs and Captain John Grigsby, who had been in California some time, settled in Napa Valley.

---

*One of these certainly was led by Enoch Cyrus and the group Edwin Bryant camped with on Putah Creek.

Despite the lavish compliments heaped on the valley by Hittell, vineyardists like Patchett, Krug and in particular John Osborne, must have despaired of his failure to mention grapes or wine making. Hittell merely observes: "These 'orchards' include some vines, and more vineyards have been planted since my visit to the valley." Not one word about Napa Valley wine!

There is an explanation, perhaps, for this oversight. The writer never clearly stated the time of year of his visit, but his mention of seeing "fifty-five roses" in bloom at Yount's farm "on the 27th of January last" is an indication of when his visit transpired. In January the farmers were busy seeding wheat or inspecting its young growth while the small scattered vineyards in their dormant state, were barely visible among the many fields of wheat.

The San Francisco writer probably made the trip to Napa City in just over four and a half hours on the small steamer "Paul Pry." That is, if the tide was not out, necessitating a stop at Soscol and changing to horse and wagon. An account of one trip made in August 1860 by a newspaper editor listed some of the places and views to be seen:

> The steamer stops at Vallejo and Suscol, giving a view of Mare Island, the Navy-Yard, Vallejo, and all the inland views on the creek up to Napa, which are really beautiful, showing the wide expanse to the hillsides, with grain-fields and orchards, and proving the great fertility and productiveness of this section. The very circuitous winding of the creek affords interest to the passenger, and takes away much of the monotony of such trips.[II.1]

Eight days after the first transcontinental telegraph was completed, connecting California to the East Coast, a party of U.S. government surveyors arrived in Napa Valley, camping at Soscol. They were here to survey the valley and county and record various aspects of its flora and fauna plus whatever else excited their imagination.

The man in charge of the survey party was 32-year-old William H. Brewer, a graduate in agricultural science at Yale. Brewer kept a diary of his daily activities and his nearly two weeks spent in the valley. His lengthy notes on everything he saw in California were published many years later as *Up and Down California* in 1860-1864.[II.2]

Brewer records drinking Napa Valley apple cider and although he does not mention it specifically, probably sampled valley wine, as well. They were made by a farmer living near Yountville:

I lounged down to the Tavern to read the news. While there, a rough but intelligent-looking man entered into conversation and invited me to his house a few rods distant for a 'glass of good cider.' I went, got the cider, the best I have tasted in this state, and went into his house. I found him an intelligent man, quite a botanist, and even found that he had some rare and expensive illustrated botanical works, such as *Silva Americana*. . . . He does not own the ranch, is merely a hired man, having charge! There is an orchard of ten or twelve thousand trees and a vineyard—he makes wine and cider and sells fruit.

On the following day he visited the farmer-vintner again, identified only as a "Mr. Beardsley" and indulged himself in drinking more cider but does not mention the wine! Brewer at least documents that wine was available to passing travelers in the fall of 1861. Since his notes were intended to be included in the survey party's official records, he may have prudently not mentioned any consumption of wine!

Brewer's description of the valley is remarkable, to say the least. The burning of "tule" along the marshes of the Napa River, which went on for several nights, offered he and his associates long hours of fascinating viewing:

The swamps bordering all the rivers, bay, or lakes, are covered with a tall rush, ten or twelve feet high, called *tule* (tu-lee), which dries up where it joins arable land. On the plain below camp, fire was in the tules and in the stubble grounds at several places every night, and in the night air the sight was most grand—great sheets of flame, extending over acres, now a broad lurid sheet, then a line of fire, reflected from the pillar of smoke which rose from each spot—a pillar of fire it seemed—was magnificent.

There was wild game in abundance in the marshes for the surveyors, especially geese and the flavor was exceedingly fine, according to Brewer. Goose was the major portion of their diet on many days.

After a long visit at George Yount's ranch (no mention of wine), Brewer and an associate climbed the hills east of Napa Valley where he recorded what he saw lying below him:

The view from the top is finer than any we have had since crossing the bay, more extensive and more grand. San Pablo Bay gleams in the distance; the lovely Napa Valley lies beneath us, with its pretty farms, its majestic trees, its vineyards and orchards and farmhouses. Its villages, of which three or four were in sight, the most picturesque of which is St. Helena, are nestled among the trees at the head of the valley, a bold broken country around us.

Although Brewer only mentions the vineyards of Napa Valley twice, and briefly, and its wine but once, he was a plant scientist and these vineyards may have made a greater impact on him than can be surmised from the diary kept as part of his official duties. Individuals with his kind of expertise on California agriculture and vineyards were rare on the East Coast.

After Brewer returned East in 1864, he taught at Yale for many years. He may have been consulted, or wrote, the *Atlantic Monthly* article called "California As A Vineland," in May 1864. The detailed account of viticulture and wine making on the Pacific Coast does not mention Napa Valley by name, but the story is a milestone in East Coast wine journalism. Its opening remarks had to be especially eye-opening to Easterners:

> It has been reserved for California, from the plenitude of her capacities, to give us a truly great boon in her light and delicate wines.
>
> Our Pacific sister, from whose generous hand has flowed an uninterrupted stream of golden gifts, has announced the fact that henceforth we are to be a wine-growing people. From the sparkling juices of her luscious grapes, rich with the breath of an unrivalled climate, is to come in future the drink of our people. . . . We are to make wine as common an article of consumption in America as upon the Rhine.

There were in California more than ten and a half million vines, the writer claimed, mostly young and not yet bearing, and three-quarters of a million gallons of wine made annually. This production compared to one and a half million gallons made in all of the other states (eastern) combined.

These claims made in the *Atlantic Monthly* were not always well received. California soon had a reputation for boasting that everything grew bigger and better along the shores of the Pacific, and it is conceivable that this worked very much against the wines of the state.

Eastern Americans, during much of the nineteenth century, developed a wine snobbery against so-called "Native Wines" that made it difficult, almost impossible, to sell Napa Valley or California wine in many of the first-class hotels and restaurants. Wine from eastern states such as New York or Ohio fared even less well, it should be quickly noted; it was the French label that was preferred on the wine bottle.

Fortunately, few Napa Valley farmers who turned to raising grapes or making wine in the decade of the 1860s, had to deal with the eastern market. Only two California wine merchants were shipping wine eastward, although this would change dramatically at the end of the decade with the completion of the first transcontinental railroad.

Napa County and Valley now had a population of 4,872 individuals, according to the U.S. Census of 1860. This compares with 405 residents a decade earlier. Six hundred and forty of the men living in the county gave their occupation as "Farmers" in the special Agricultural Census.

Only nine of those farmers also told the census takers they were vintners. The nine pioneer wine makers of Napa Valley were: Lolita Bruck, 400 gallons; Reason P. Tucker, 200 gallons; Samuel Tully, 65 gallons; A. Chamilla, 80 gallons; and Thomas Knight, 1,000 gallons (all of St. Helena); William H. Winters, 20 gallons (Carneros); John Patchett, 4,000 gallons (by far the largest vintner in the valley); and G. C. Genno (the illegible handwriting makes the spelling here uncertain), 1,500 gallons, both of Napa City. At "Sebastopol," shortly changed to "Yountville," Joseph B. Chiles is credited with 280 gallons but there is no listing for George Yount. A story in the *California Farmer* later that summer stated he would make 2,000 gallons of wine, apparently the same amount as the previous year.[II.3]

The Agricultural Census credits Napa County with producing 8,745 gallons of wine, but the above figures for individual production only add up to 7,525. Yount's 2,000 gallons would push the final total to 9,525 and if John Osborne were making wine or Simpson Thompson, and it is very likely they did, the county would have a total of over 10,000 gallons.* The official Census figure for all wine produced in California is 246,518 but could be off, too, by thousands of gallons.

---

*Ernest P. Peninou and Sidney S. Greenleaf have made a comprehensive study of wine production in California in 1860, based on the Agricultural Census and other sources. They conclude that the census missed wine producers Yount, Thompson, Thomas Allen, George Crane and Florentine Kellogg, but they offer no other production figure. See *A Directory of California Wine Growers and Wine Makers in 1860* (Berkeley, Ca., 1967).

As journalist John Hittell stated, wheat was the principal interest of farmers in Napa County, and the Census strongly confirms his observation. Only one other county in California produced more wheat than Napa, and that was San Joaquin County with 685,000 bushels. Napa farmlands yielded 591,375 bushels of wheat with its next closest competitor being Santa Clara County. Cattle raising, the principal occupation of the preGold Rush settlers, was of minor importance to the economy by 1860 with only 22,000 range cattle and 5,947 dairy cows.

It is easy to see why wheat and not cattle should have such a strong position in the local economy when the size of the average Napa farm is considered. Of the six hundred and forty farmers in the county, nearly four hundred cultivated farms of five hundred acres or less. Two dozen farmers held farms between 500 to 1000 acres in size, and a dozen men owned lands totaling more than one thousand acres. Individually owned cattle herds required thousands of acres of grazing land, not a few hundred. Napa County clearly was not owned by a few cattle barons, as quickly became the case in many California counties.

This diversified ownership of the arable lands of the county by 1860 is one of Napa's early strengths, for it attracted men with interests in all areas of agriculture, from grape growing to wheat, from apples to the lowly potato. These farmers could shift their crops readily depending upon rainfall, or as market prices dictated.

It is difficult to ascertain clearly who fathered Napa Valley's grape growing industry, no one individual seems to deserve most of the credit. George Yount certainly paid little attention to his vineyards until most of his neighbors began cultivating the vine. There is no record of anyone coming to him for viticultural assistance in the 1850s. He was, of course, an old man by Gold Rush standards. John Osborne was an avid vineyardist but his life was soon to end in a tragic murder. Dr. George B. Crane of St. Helena may have created the most initial enthusiasm for grape growing in the valley, although his early experiences were enough to discourage all but the most avid growers.

An unknown writer in the 1881 published *History of Napa and Lake Counties, California* credits Crane with beginning the viticulture boom locally:

> ... so he came into Napa Valley and purchased the place he now owns near the town of St. Helena. Here he planted the pioneer

vineyard of the great St. Helena district for wine purposes. What a grand pride must swell the heart of the hardy old pioneer in wine vineyards when he now looks forth upon the broad acres of the lovely valley all covered with thrifty, bearing vines, saying to himself in the meanwhile, 'I set that movement on foot which has accomplished all this!' And did he not? He broke the path, and what followed was in his footsteps (p. 203).

The author may have had clippings from the San Francisco *Alta California* to support his comments on Crane. In a March 11, 1866 issue, a brief story datelined "St. Helena" reads:

In this vicinity, there is quite a furor about grapevine planting. The soil for several miles around, both valley and hills, being well adapted to its growth, almost every landowner is putting in more or less the present season. Dr. Crane—just across the Sulphur Creek from this village—besides owning what is considered the number one place for such purposes, is a sort of leader in the enterprise, having a vineyard of considerable size, planted five years ago [1861] and, of course, now in full bearing. He had made some very good wine, both red and white, from a variety of grapes.

The *St. Helena Star* of August 25, 1876 honored Crane's viticultural work, too, but limited his sphere of influence slightly:

Fourteen years ago [1862], Dr. Crane inaugurated the wine business in St. Helena by making two pipes—about 300 gallons. Today, three quarters of a million gallons a year are made.

Even Charles Krug in his declining years, credited Crane with being one of the valley's real viticultural pioneers:*

When I moved in the Fall of 1860 from Sonoma to St. Helena, at that time a little village of not much more than a dozen houses, Dr. G. B. Crane showed me his 8,000 vines, then one year old—the first vineyard planted in Napa county for the purpose of wine making. This gentleman, about 1864 or 1865, was the first to use redwood tanks in which the crushed grapes fermented for claret. Up to that

---

*Krug's comment "the first vineyard planted in Napa county for the purpose of wine making" is confusing; or the mark of a man whose memory was failing. He may have meant a vineyard planted with only wine grapes, rather than one mixed with table and wine varieties. John Patchett's vineyard was certainly planted for wine making purposes. Yount probably had an equal balance of table and wine grapes.

time small tubs and pipes with one head taken out had served us as vessels for fermentation. [II.4]

Crane many years later gave an account of his early experiences with the vine in which he admitted initially to knowing next to nothing about his subject. He purchased five to six thousand cuttings, "all I could find for sale within 100 miles," and stuck them two feet into the ground! Neither a plow or spade had turned over any of the soil beforehand. He did not state how many cuttings survived.

Dr. Crane had been told by Marianno Vallejo that his wine cellar should not be any larger than roughly 16 by 24 feet. Crane neglected to tell Vallejo he had seven *acres* of vines under cultivation and his first good crop when crushed must have nearly inundated the small cellar. Apparently at Vallejo's suggestion too, Crane purchased only a very small crusher and press, about the size, as he put it, of "a Yankee cheese press."

> I made what proved to be the costliest blunder of all in shipping East before I had learned that there swindling was the rule and honesty the exception. Had I knocked in the heads of all my pipes at home, and spilled the wine, as it turned out I should have been $20,000 better off in 1870; but I have prepared the way to success for later shippers of California wine and I have survived my own misfortunes. [II.5]

Crane, although a major figure in the history of valley viticulture, is nearly as obscure an historical figure as John Patchett. (Both men have rarely been mentioned by historians. Even those periodic special editions put out by Napa Valley newspapers which salute the local wine industry and include summaries of viticulture history, usually fail to mention Crane or Patchett.)

George Belden Crane was born in 1806 in Dutchess County, New York, and upon completion of high school and passing other minor requirements, took up the profession of teaching. At the age of twenty, he enrolled in the State University of New York, majoring in medicine. For nearly twenty years, he served as a country doctor before the lure of adventure and the California Gold Rush caused him to head west. In 1853 he settled at San Jose, taking over the post of director of the City and County Hospital.

There is nothing in the known background of Crane that would indicate he had an interest in the cultivation of grapevines or the making of wine. On a trip to Napa City in May 1858, Crane happened to pass the vineyards of Patchett and stopped to take a closer look. He was so impressed with the vineyard, then just leafing out, that he began a systematic reading of all available literature as to whether this business might earn him as much money as the practice of medicine.

The only hesitation on the part of Crane came from the fact that he would eventually produce a beverage that led to the intoxication of some individuals who abused it. Many of his friends were in the temperance movement (which had very strong adherents in Santa Clara County), and he was faced with a delicate problem of justifying to them this new direction in his personal life. That Crane created many enemies among his former friends is one conclusion easily derived from a long biography published in the 1881 *History of Napa and Lake Counties, California*. Several pages are devoted to the subject of temperance with long refutations of various charges about wine as an intoxicating drink.

Crane was present at a religious meeting led by a preacher who asked in his prayers that "God would blight the vineyard business now being commenced in the valley." Crane quickly rose to his feet and in a voice clearly heard by everyone present told the preacher, "That prayer won't go six feet high." Crane took pride in noting afterwards that in his lifetime, no "blight" had ever visited local vineyards.

Crane's lack of business experience, especially attempting to sell wine wholesale on the East Coast, almost soured his interest in wine making as a career.

In the late 1860s, he shipped several thousand gallons of red and white to New York City and journeyed there himself to supervise its sale. He apparently could not find a dealer who would even purchase one barrel of his wine, the market being taken completely by imported, mainly French wines. The problem was one he had not anticipated: Eastern American wines from native grapes (rough, foxy, were commonly used adjectives) were of a far different taste than French wine. It was assumed by Eastern dealers that California wines would taste the same. The few newspaper stories already published on the high quality of California wine, had not been able to open the doors of New York wine merchants.

Crane's bitter disappointment with the Eastern wine trade came some years after his success with growing the vine in St. Helena, of course, and his influence on others led to the miniboom in plantings, especially in the immediate vicinity. By time the Napa County Fair was held in 1864, many proud new vineyardists came forward to exhibit grapes; men like W. S. Jacks, H. N. Amesbury, S. Wing, R. S. Thompson, J. S. Trubody and Henry Boggs.

The wine exhibit at the '64 fair was rather disappointing, but not unexpectedly so, given the youth of the business, and included six bottles made by Wing, nine bottles from Krug, nine from R. H. Sterling and a half dozen from T. Vann. With the "father" of it all, George Crane, Napa Valley could easily count about two dozen men all patiently planting, pruning and eagerly picking the clusters of grapes in the fall.

About twelve months earlier, German-born Jacob Schram climbed the rugged hillsides between St. Helena and Calistoga and began burning off the chaparral and trees for a small vineyard site. Whether he planted grapes in 1863 is not quite certain but economics historian Titus Fey Cronise acknowledges that year for Schram's first plantings. Cronise wrote a book in 1868 called *The Natural Wealth of California*, and found in Schram the perfect example of the immigrant who seemed to work by day (at barbering) and planted vines by the moonlight:

> The career of the proprietor of one of the Calistoga vineyards, affords such an excellent illustration of what a 'poor man' with no other capital than intelligence and industry, may accomplish in California, that we give some particulars about Schram, and his vineyards as an example worthy of imitation.
>
> Schram is German by birth, and a barber by profession. When he arrived in the states less than seven years ago, he had neither money nor friends, and could scarcely speak our language; but he had tact and courage. Believing that the hillsides around this valley would produce a superior quality of grapes, he procured a tract of land for a trifle—being covered with timber and underbrush, it was not considered to be worth anything.
>
> By dint of hard labor, he cleared a few acres and planted them with vines, acting as a barber at the springs* on Saturday and Sundays . . . He now has, at the end of five years, 15,000 vines growing, about one-half of which bear fruit, from which he has made sufficient wine to pay for considerable improvements (p. 181).

---

*White Sulphur Springs resort in St. Helena.

There is no evidence as to precisely what year Schram had his first crush. If his vines were planted in late 1863, the first possible crop could not have come before 1865 or '66. He had a crush in '66 because the following year the *Alta California* described his wine and cellar in an April 28, 1867 story:

> His cellar, cut into the rock, has scarcely room for three to stand in, and he has only one barrel of wine, all the rest being in kegs.

The newspaper adds that his vineyards were now composed of 14,000 vines.

Schram appears to be one of the individuals responsible for Gottlieb Groezinger first tasting Napa Valley wines and then carrying them in his small wine shop in San Francisco. Or Charles Krug may deserve the credit here, for all three were German. Groezinger liked what he found in the valley and shortly began buying bulk Napa wines and blending them to his taste. He also purchased Napa grapes and had them crushed at his store, controlling completely the wine making process so as to improve its quality.

The quality of California wine disturbed Groezinger. He was far less concerned with how the grapes grew or the cultivation of the soil. His primary job was to sell wine at the retail end of the trade, and he knew what his customers said about the taste of the product. He was also very successful as a wine merchant, one publication crediting him with doing "the best 'Home Trade' in wine, of any house in this city." "Home Trade" meant California or "Native Wine" as the distinction more commonly was made.

It did not take Groezinger long to arrive at the conclusion that he had to buy vineyard land in the Napa Valley and build his own winery. There was an enormous future market for Native wines. He found the vineyard land he wanted at Yountville. He felt he had the advantage on every other wine maker in the valley for he came into the business from the opposite direction of his neighbors, that is, a wine dealer first. He became the first Napa Valley vintner to place the emphasis in the young industry on how good the wine tasted, rather than simply producing a palatable wine. (His brick winery, enlarged many times after construction began in 1870, still stands in the center of Yountville.)

Within a few years after the realization that Europe's finest grapes could be grown many places in California, the arguments began as to whether the state's wine makers could match the highest quality wine, as well. It was one thing to grow grapes, any competent farmer could do that, especially given the rich, youthful soils of California and its temperate climate. Whether the chemistry of the grapes could match France or Germany was questionable.

Californians were filled with enthusiasm but short on experience, observed its wine critics. The fact that most of the wine makers were sons of old European wine making families was always blithely overlooked.

The debate over California wine quality heated up dramatically when the largest wine firm in the state, Kohler & Frohling, began regular shipments to New York for the first time. The *California Farmer* carried a story on its front pages on November 16, 1860, which sums up why the criticism intensified:

> It is, perhaps, for the interest of persons engaged here in importing and dealing in foreign Wines, to throw discredit upon our California production, and thus prevent it from supplanting the foreign. And this may account for the articles which have lately appeared in several papers, endeavoring to cry down our Native Wines, and to make it appear that our whole production is of inferior quality.

A story with this orientation had recently been published in New York's *Mercantile Gazette* after news was carried in the daily newspapers of shipments of wine to New York. The story was reprinted in San Francisco by the *Daily Bulletin*. The strongest criticism leveled at California was that on the East Coast the wine was sold for only seventy-five cents a gallon; it could not possibly be any good at that price. The firm of Kohler & Frohling, one of two shippers to the East, replied, with a brief history of wine retailing:

> The article commences by saying that the cultivation of the vine is destined to become important in the State, etc., which is all true; but the writer adds: 'It is a lamentable fact, that our wines have not at all improved in reputation within the last three or four years.' A few facts will show that this statement is wide of the truth. We commenced the business of producing and selling native wines about six years since [1854], and then we had but a few hundred gallons. Scarcely anyone knew that native wines were anywhere to be had. None of the saloons kept the wines, for there were really none for sale.
>
> Now we produce more than 100,000 gallons per annum, and find a market for the whole quantity. Our city trade is more than a hundred times greater than it was four years ago, and so is our

country trade. . . . Almost every saloon in this city keeps the native wines on sale, and the demand is rapidly increasing.

Kohler & Frohling had begun shipping wine to Boston in 1858 and in 1860 established its own agency in New York. The other California wine firm shipping to the East Coast was Sansevain Bros. of Los Angeles. The K&F wines sent were all vintages of the years 1857 and 1858, and included California brandy.

Editorial comments on California wine quality were sometimes so subtle that the casual observer would miss them. An *Atlantic Monthly* article on California wine concludes:

> It only remains for the vintners to keep their wines pure, and always up to the highest standard, and to take such measures as shall insure their delivery in a like condition to the consumers, to build up a business which shall eclipse that of any of the great houses of Europe.

It wouldn't do, in other words, to produce a fine wine in San Francisco and have it arrive on the dining table in Boston or New York tasting even less than a European *vin ordinaire!*

Two months after the *Atlantic Monthly* story of May 1864, the editor of the *California Farmer* again picked up the "quality" theme when he wrote:

> California Wine LIKE every other 'good thing' in this world, it will be more or less spoiled. California Wine can be made to bear a good name and only a good name, if the true friends of our State will exert themselves to this end; but in this State and abroad there is to be found so much vile stuff, bearing the name of 'California Wine,' that we are not surprised it holds as yet a second place, when it should be first.[II.6]

The publication noted that Gottlieb Groezinger seemed to be doing the best trade in local wines, largely because his wine, in their opinion, rivalled "much that is sold for Rhine wine it has all the 'bouquet' of the best Hock, imported." It is difficult to determine if this was just a journalistic plug for an advertising client in the publication; yet the theme had been constant with the editor for many years and the story seems to be legitimate. The same high compliments were given to John Patchett's wine, but no one else in the Napa Valley was accorded such treatment.

Although wine quality may have been of some concern to Charles Krug when he settled in the Napa Valley, he seems to have made no special attempt to improve on what he found. A San Francisco reporter thought his wines "rather strong," a not-too flattering comment although admitting at the same time that he might have "tasted a little too much."

There is a much more substantial reason for suspecting that Krug did not have wine quality on his mind during his early years in the Napa Valley. His first winery, "cellar" is a better word here, in the dictionary definition, was about as primitive a structure as could be found anywhere in California. It must have resembled the early grass and pole dwellings built by the Franciscan priests when they established the missions a half century earlier. The Napa *Reporter* for January 4, 1873 carries the best eye-witness account of the first Krug wine "cellar":

The pioneer wine cellar of the valley now stands near the new one on the premises, and is quite a curiosity.[*] Mr. K. intends keeping it to mark the difference between then and now. It is 14 x 20 feet, sunk 2½ feet into the ground and raised some 5½ feet above, covered first with straw, then with earth, and over all with lumber and shakes that had served their time on the pioneer saw mill of the valley, after it had exhausted the stocks of redwood in the vicinity, and had become useless property.

Gordon Backus, reminiscing twenty years after he arrived in St. Helena, wrote ". . . when I arrived in St. Helena in 1870, Krug had a cellar (a hole in the ground), Mr. Pellet one above ground."[II.8] This was a little harsh, perhaps, and even inaccurate for Krug had enlarged his cellar several times by then.

It did not, of course, require much of a building for the making of only one hundred gallons of wine, Krug's first crush. Seven years later, as recorded by Titus Fey Cronise, Krug had 41,000 vines and he could have been producing as much as fifty thousand gallons of wine. For this he would have required much more room than the 14 x 20 foot

---

*Why the reporter should use the phrase "pioneer wine cellar of the valley" is curious. Patchett's stone wine cellar, though closed was still standing and built before Krug's. It was only a few blocks away from the Napa Reporter office. Krug may have used the phrase in the interview with the reporter since his boasts about pioneer wine making continued thereafter.

structure, half buried in the ground. According to the same Napa *Reporter* story just quoted, of January 1873:

> The rapid growth of the vineyard and large increase of wine necessitated building additional cellar room from year to year . . .

With Krug's unbounded energy, Crane's high example of a man with education and intelligence going into the vineyard business, and the early success of Patchett at wine making, Napa Valley farmers turned to the challenge with considerable spirit. *Two hundred and fifty thousand vines were planted in the first three years of the 1860s.* This amount and more were spaded into the soil before the decade was half over with the County Assessor reporting 700,210 vines and a production of 50,000 gallons of wine for the year 1866.

"Probably at no past period in the annals of Napa City and county has property changed hands and been held at such high figures as at the present time," claimed the *Napa Daily Reporter* in early December of that year. The newspaper added that San Francisco was now filled to overflowing with money, much of it coming from the bonanza of silver being dug out of the Comstock Lode in the hills of western Nevada. The timely stories in newspapers and magazines on the emerging wine industry of the state, with flattering words especially for the wines of Sonoma and Napa valleys, turned the attention of investors to wine making.

The spread of vineyards in the valley was apparently so rapid that some "old-timers" began objecting to all the changes taking place. One or two had complained in the public press that vines were destroying the pastoral beauty of the valley. A resident of St. Helena promptly responded in an April 1867 issue of the *Alta California*:

> The charge that we are converting grain producing land into vineyards, though untrue, suggests the consideration of a most important politico-economic question. By far the largest portion of the cultivated lands of this State cannot be made to yield a remunerative return to the farmer, and very large portions are comparatively or entirely valueless for pasture.
>
> Shall this extensive territory remain forevermore a sterile waste— a disgrace to our country? or, shall we profit by the proof already obtained of its capabilities when used as nature evidently designed, and make it, by viniculture, a source of individual and public wealth, exceeding in value all other agricultural productions combined?

Why a Napa Valley resident should object to vines being planted in place of wheat is not entirely clear since vineyards enhance the natural beauty rather than detract from it. The objection probably had nothing to do with which plant is more esthetically pleasing to the eye, wheat or vines.

The objection may have been to the end product of the vine, Napa Valley wines. Many southern or midwestern farmers had braved the long trek across the western deserts to find this Garden of Eden and had prayed, no doubt, that the serpents of temptation, in the form of alcoholic spirits, had been left behind.

Wheat was an important staple to the economy of Napa and once harvested, it could be handled much more easily than grapes, and even wine. Napa City had four large grain warehouses: that of Capt. Phillips, the Napa Warehouse, Lawler & Co. and Capt. Mighell. Smaller storage facilities were scattered across the valley. The Napa warehouses alone could handle 6,000 tons or put in the terms of the day, two hundred thousand sacks. Wheat was not transported in bulk, it was all sacked and carried about by teamsters.

Wheat was the inspiration for the settling of Napa County's Berryessa Valley in the mid-1860s. A town site, to be called Monticello, was surveyed "two miles from the upper and last crossing of the Putah creek," apparently everyone understanding instantly that geographic location. The work on a wagon road to the valley was begun in 1867, and would wind a total of 24 miles over hillsides and through Wooden and Capell valleys directly to the warehouses and flour mills of Napa City.

"There will be over 100,000 sacks of grain produced in Berryessa Valley alone, this season," observed the Napa *County Reporter* that same spring and the financial returns to the city could not be ignored.

Most of the wheat produced in the county was quickly loaded at high tide into the small steamers which plied the river or on barges, and then sent scurrying back downstream to ocean traversing ships. There was a good market for California wheat in England and in other portions of Europe. Some of the wheat was ground into flour at the "Vernon Flour Mill" or the "Napa City Mills." A "Mr. Ault" ran the latter mill, his reputation based on several prizes won at state fairs and his flour could be had at $11 per barrel. He also ground corn into meal and this retailed at $9 per barrel.

The weather in Napa Valley and California often seemed at cross-purposes with the agricultural boom then in progress. The

G. B. CRANE

H. A. PELLET

CHARLES KRUG

JOHN LEWELLING

JACOB SCHRAM

valley went through a severe drought in the early portion of the 1860s, then witnessed severe flooding a few years later and, heaped upon the cares and woes of the young farmers, a bad frost. It was almost enough, or perhaps it was enough, to send many men back to the Sierra foothills to dig for gold.

The drought came in the winter of 1862-63, following a previous winter which saw localized flooding in the valley. By summer, moisture was so critically short that range cattle had to be sold because there was neither grass on the hills to feed them nor enough alfalfa cut and stored.

There were a few large cattle herds in the county, remnants of the early Mexican period of settlement. Many farmers pointed to the healthy young vineyards, however, as a sign that their newly found interest had the approval of higher powers. (Vines put down deep and vigorous roots, especially when moisture is short.)

The following two winters were again moderately wet, which prompted the Napa *Daily Reporter* of November 23, 1866 to offer the opinion that the coming months would be dry:

> Old settlers in the mines generally predict that this will be a dry winter, and the prediction is based upon their experience for many years in this climate. We have now had two winters in succession in which larger quantities of rain and snow have fallen. . . . Experience has proven that every third season, or fourth, in California, is a dry one.

The newspaper also reported that when the winters tend toward an unduly large amount of rainfall, severe storms show something of their capabilities by Mid-November, and the fall had been very dry so far.

The "old-timers" proved to be wrong, indeed very far off course in their weather forecasting. The heavy rains came just before Christmas, beginning December 19. By the 21st, water was coursing down Main Street in Napa as if the Napa River had decided to change channels. Captain Phillips' grain warehouse, just mentioned, had water up to the second story. Bridges disappeared and a major portion of the railroad embankment west of town gave way. No lives were lost and few losses of farm animals were reported, but the high water was placed at or near the same height as in the floods of '61-62.

Frost was severe in the valley in the spring of the same year, and was widespread over all of California. William Nash and Frank Kellogg, between St. Helena and Calistoga, suffered the greatest losses. The oldest vines, some sixteen years old, suffering less injury than the younger vineyards, a condition no one could explain. "The frost appears to act according to some law not well understood. In some neighborhoods, it attacked some vineyards and missed others, without any apparent reason. Generally, those on high ground escaped with little injury," reported a local vineyardist.

There were many distractions to the weather in the valley, one being the arrival in St. Helena in the fall of 1862 of the first commercial photographer. Most residents had never seen an "ambrotype" likeness of friends or relatives and the novelty was an amazement to everyone. W. A. Maxwell was the itinerant "photographer" who advised potential clients he would be in town "but a short time." He could preserve the likeness of someone like Charles Krug or Dr. Crane on a glass plate for far less money than a portrait artist charged.

There was also the murder of John W. Osborne and the hanging of his murderer in Napa City to take attention off the weather. No one of Osborne's reputation had been murdered in Napa County. Unknown men passing through Napa had been found occasionally shot or knifed to death and like the frequent and similar fate of many young men in San Francisco or the gold mines in the 1850s, most residents paid scant attention. But the shooting of Osborne in April 1863 was much different; he had done so much to assist in the agricultural development of the valley and bring publicity to Napa.

Osborne had employed a young man named Charles Britton and when the two began to have some personal difficulties, Britton was discharged. Britton was paid for his last days of labor with a draft or check on a San Francisco bank and sent on his way. When Britton sought to cash the draft, the bank advised him that his former employer had insufficient funds. Britton assumed he had been paid knowingly by Osborne with a draft that was of no value, and this added insult to injury.

Britton acquired a revolver, took the steamer to Napa and made his way to the Osborne ranch just a few miles north of Napa City. Osborne and Britton argued briefly, according to other workers at the ranch, and Britton pulled out the gun and shot Osborne with a volley of three shots. Britton did not attempt to flee and was promptly arrested.

The hanging of Britton was the first in Napa County carried out under sentence of law, although the story in the Napa *County Reporter* of August 8, 1863 required but one paragraph of space:

Execution of Britton—This individual was hung by the neck, and suffered the 'extreme penalty of the law' about 4 o'clock yesterday afternoon, for the murder of J. W. Osborne, of Oak Knoll. He was hung in the jail yard, in presence of some fifteen or twenty of our citizens. The culprit was attended by his spiritual advisers, but no impression could be made upon him by their kind and Christian admonitions. He met his fate with the most stoical indifference—requesting the Sheriff to bury him as 'a gentleman, for he had always lived like one.'

A little over a year later another death of a pioneer viticulturist saddened valley residents. George C. Yount died October 5, 1865, in his 71st year of life. By the standards of the day, Yount was an old man, indeed. Yount did not live long enough to see the name of the village he had established, changed from "Sebastopol" to "Yountville." That took place formally on May 14, 1867. He had been honored in so many ways already that naming the village after him might have seemed incidental.

Mrs. F. H. Day's interview with Yount in the *Hesperian* some years previously, had elevated Yount to the stature of "grand old man of Napa Valley." With four thousand new residents during the decade of the 1850s, many had known little about him previous to the Day interview. There had been a brief flurry of excitement in the Yount home in 1858 over the establishment of a college in Yountville (Sebastopol), and some of the financial backers had urged it be Galled "Yount College." That idea lasted but a few months and then was quietly forgotten.

Yount's death was not marked by any special services or attention in the local press. The words spoken by the minister who buried him are not preserved, and it seems neither he nor anyone else in the valley lauded Yount's pioneering viticultural work.

There is an explanation, in part, for this oversight. Grapes and wine were rapidly growing in importance in the valley's economy, but the proportion of two or three dozen vineyardists out of a total of 640 farmers (counted in the last census) meant that most local residents were barely aware of the new trend in agriculture. It is likely more people in San Francisco were paying attention to the possibilities of

planting (investing) in Napa Valley vineyards, because of the growing publicity on the subject, than the local residents.

During the early 1860s reports of gold and silver discoveries
kept circulating in the valley, one more reason for most local citizens
to ignore the grapevine.

In the winter of 1860, a vein of silver was supposedly discovered
in the King's Canyon north of Calistoga. Miners by the hundreds
flocked to the site, staking off claims on land that gave no hint
whatsoever of any precious metal.

A miner who did witness silver being dug from Napa County
mines later in the nineteenth century, said of the first mining
excitement:

> Many small holes were dug and sham assayers and silver sharps
> reaped a small harvest. At that time our American citizens had not
> learned anything of the nature, appearance of localities of the
> precious white metal and they had everything tested from blue
> mud up to the volcanic rocks, with varied and most generally
> unsatisfactory results.[II.10]

A metal of much greater quantity in the hills of Napa County was
discovered in February 1860, in the Geysers region of Sonoma and
Napa counties. If the search for silver was confounding most of the
men out digging for it, as reported in the above quote, none knew
anything about cinnabar mining and the means of extracting quicksilver. Therefore the red cinnabar was to lie undisturbed, for many
years to come.

One hindrance to the development of a wine industry in the
upper portion of the Napa Valley, was the lack of good roads to Napa
City and/or some other means of transporting wine to her waterfront
docks. Even San Franciscans were aware of the sad plight of the
valley's thoroughfares, as the San Francisco *Alta California* reported
in the spring of 1866:

> Napa county certainly needs one good public thoroughfare, for a
> large portion of the year her roads are impassable.

Napa's roads were often submerged under water or mud for
great areas of the valley were swamps which had never been drained
and prepared for habitation by farmers. Traveling by horse and buggy
to St. Helena meant constantly taking detours around the "wet
spots."

The first road up the length of the valley was laid out in 1852. John Russell Bartlett recorded this fact in his section on the Napa Valley in his *Personal Narrative of Exploration and Incidents*. The phrase "laid out" meant exactly that as the road was not completed until the summer of 1860.[II.11] This presumably meant that a roadbed was prepared which was higher than the surrounding land, that it was reasonably well drained and was covered with some type of coarse gravel making it useable in winter. (This route has virtually remained unchanged in the last one hundred and thirty years and is now designated Highway 29 or the "St. Helena Highway.")

Transporting pipes or puncheons of wine by horse and wagon on a nicely gravelled and drained road from St. Helena to Napa City for water shipment to San Francisco was still not the best way of moving large quantities of wine. It must have been with a great sigh or relief that up valley wine makers heard the news of the proposed Napa Valley railroad.

The first mention of a railroad through the valley actually dates to December 1863 when a company was organized in San Francisco to pursue such plans. San Franciscans were always coming up with new ideas to spend the money of the gold miner or those who had been enriched through various schemes, so most Napa residents did not take any of the plans too seriously.

In March of the following year, a bill was introduced in the State Legislature by Chancellor Hartson providing for the issuance of county bonds of $225,000 to aid in building a Napa Valley railroad. This time the idea was much more sensible since it provided for funding by a county tax on property. The builder would receive $10,000 per mile for the first five miles (starting at Soscol, in heavy marshes) and $5,000 per mile for the remaining thirty-five to Calistoga.

The tax funds provided by the county only raised a portion of the total cost of the railroad. In keeping with the generous nature of the citizens, much of the right-of-way for the roadbed was donated by the farmers and a public subscription raised another $60,000 within a few weeks time.

The contributors' names would shortly become a Who's Who of the wine industry, perhaps because most of them stood to benefit so much: E. J. Weeks, $5,000; 5. Brannan, C. Mayne, A. A. Cohen, R. B. Woodward, W. R. Garrison, H. Barroilhet, C. F. Lott, 5. Alstrom (all contributing $3,000 each); C. Hartson, N. Coombs, J. Graves, T. Knight, G. C. Yount ($2,000 each); J. H. Goodman, A. Y. Easterby, J.

Lawley, Smith Brown, 5. C. Hasting, G. W. Crowey, George Fellows, J. S. Trubody, H. Fowler ($1,000 contributors); E. Stanley, J. F. Lambdin, C. H. Holmes and W. Hargrave ($500 each). Samuel Brannan, the man who first made public the discovery of gold in California in January 1848, gave an additional $5,000.*

The ground was broken for the railroad November 21, 1864, the builders either anticipating or praying hard for a dry winter. (There had been a drought the previous winter season; this one turned out to be moderately wet.)

Within the record time of fifty-two days, the five miles of railroad from Soscol to Napa City was completed! The total cost came to $32,000, the actual construction being handled by Patterson, Gray & Co. Apparently, the railroad company could pocket the difference between the total allotted for construction ($50,000) and its actual cost.

The construction moved ahead so rapidly that the organizers of the railroad company did not have time to purchase the train engine and cars needed for the railroad. As a consequence it was not until July 11 that the first train formally passed over the track, which entered Napa by way of Main Street and stopped at the end of the line at Third Street.

A bit of nefarious scheming then began to finance the remaining twenty-five miles of the road to Calistoga.

Napa Assemblyman Chancellor Hartson, who sponsored the original railroad bill in the State Legislature and also got himself named president of the company which ran the railroad, introduced a new bill at Sacramento calling for a payment of $15,000 per mile for completion of the line. A petition from local citizens protesting the Hartson bill, in part because they believed the line could not operate at a profit, failed to influence the Legislature and the Hartson bill passed.

---

*In a special article on "Railroading" for the *Star* of Dec. 19, 1890, "G[ordon] Backus," who professed to know most of the details of the building of the railroad, added this observation: "Had there been no railroad through Napa valley where would be the fine wine cellars of Beringer Bros., Weinberger, Krug, Laurent, Lyman, Sciaroni, Lewelling, Wheelers, and last, but not least, the magnificent cellar of W. B. Bourn...and others, all in Napa valley and looking to railroads to give them rapid transit to the markets of the nation, yes to the markets of the world, for the finest wines produced on earth...

Further delays came when opposing ideas were put forth as to the route of the rail line. Nearly everyone favored a route on the west side of the valley and parallel to the existing valley road.

There were two logical reasons for this routing: the first was that the county road followed an elevation somewhat higher than any possible rail bed would be on the eastern side of the valley. Secondly, most of the farms were located at or nearer to the original county road and thus could be serviced more easily by a west side route. In the spring of 1867, survey work was completed parallel to the county road and grading of the roadbed began. This time the construction seemed to go much slower, and the railroad was not completed to Calistoga until October 1868.

With the railroad came another change to the valley, this time in the ethnic makeup of the population. Chinese laborers were not unknown in the county since several ranches used Chinese cooks and some businesses in Napa City engaged Chinese as general laborers. The railroad employed dozens of Chinese in the preparation of the dirt and gravel roadbed, and their noisy singing and chatter could be heard at some distance.

As a matter of fact, the Chinese became the center of much curiosity and general delight in Napa Valley. The Chinese brought a welcome change in the boredom of the long, hot summer days and many farmers drove for miles to see them work and listen to their peculiar language, which certainly was different from anything else to be heard in California. Incidentally, the Chinese seemed not to have been hired in the construction of the railroad from Soscol to Napa City in 1864, as there is no record of their employment.

The success of using Chinese workers in 1865 in the construction of the first transcontinental railroad led to thousands of Chinese being recruited in China just for that purpose. Two years later there were plenty of Chinese available for Napa Valley railroad building, as well. *Napa Valley's railroad was completed only seven months before the Golden Spike ceremony at Promontory Point, Utah*, which joined the two sections of the transcontinental railroad.

Previous to the arrival of the railroad in the upper end of the Napa Valley, there had not been enough buildings in the village of Calistoga to warrant using the term "village." Napa City, St. Helena and Yountville were the first three towns to be established in the valley.

John York purchased land in 1845 near what later came to be Calistoga and planted a small vineyard. With the Bear Flag revolt the following summer and the consequent unrest throughout the countryside, he abandoned his farm and vines. Capt. John Ritchie held the title to the future town site in 1859 when wealthy San Franciscan Sam Brannan arrived and nearly smothered him in gold pieces. This marked the beginning of the town.

Sam Brannan was an enigma to the people of the Napa Valley. In spite of all that he did to strengthen the local economy, including spending vast sums of money, he was not well liked. In the late 1860s, Brannan literally created a national reputation for Napa Valley through his development of the hot springs as a health spa.

It was not wine or wheat or cattle which attracted so much attention to the valley in the years after the American Civil War, but Brannan's flamboyant way of going about creating the Saratoga of the West, including the name for the town: "Cali" from California, and "toga" from Saratoga, to form "Calistoga."

Brannan was best known for being a major figure in the founding of the city of San Francisco. He arrived in the then village (named Yerba Buena) in 1846, with a ship loaded with fellow Mormons, nearly half of whom were women and children. He brought along a printing press on which to print San Francisco's first newspaper, the *California Star*.

Brannan happened to be at Sutter's Fort one day in May 1848 when John Sutter could not keep the discovery of gold to himself. Brannan took the secret back to San Francisco and the world where he told everyone and began preparing for the Gold Rush which would surely follow. He invested in property, built merchandise stores, and every dollar invested came back the proverbial hundred fold.

By 1859 Brannan became convinced that the wealthy in San Francisco needed a playground, and he would provide it in the Napa Valley. After acquiring the springs from Ritchie, he built cabins and bathhouses. He waited for the guests to arrive. There was a slight miscalculation: few people came to bathe in the warm waters or enjoy the warm summer evenings, something he knew instinctively should appeal to the residents of the city, tired of the cold summer fog.

The immediate problem appeared to be transportation—there was not even a good all-weather road to his health spa. To attract large numbers of visitors, the only solution was a railroad. For this reason, Brannan quickly became a close friend of Napa's representative in Sacramento, Chancellor Hartson.

Six months before construction began on the second stage of the railroad, from Napa City to Calistoga, the first store was built in the soon-to-be village of Calistoga. Henry Gettleson and M. Friedberg put up the wooden building of 26 by 36 feet at the invitation of Brannan. (Friedberg, incidentally, was Jewish and perhaps so also was Gettleson. Robert Louis Stevenson would later write about him in his book *The Silverado Squatters*, using the name 'Kelmar.') Other commercial structures soon followed and by the time the railroad arrived in the fall of the following year, the town was ready for San Francisco's elite.

It is difficult to ascertain when Brannan's promotion efforts really began to take effect with the press of the state and especially in San Francisco.

An example of this achievement is an article in the San Francisco *Alta* of May 7, 1866. The story takes up an entire column on the front page and is titled "Trip to Napa Valley and Calistoga." Signed simply "Pioneer" (he may have written it himself), the article first describes the trip by steamer to Napa City on the "Paul Pry," the coach ride up the valley and then the narrative turns to exactly the reader Brannan most wanted to influence:

CALISTOGA

I found a number already of the beauty and fashion, and 'chivalry' of San Francisco, and other portions of the State, promenading through the delightful grounds, which are embellished with a profusion of aromatic shrubbery and the fairest flowers. Feeling somewhat tired, I seated myself beneath the whispering foliage of a locust, and looked out upon the magnificent amphitheater of hills, while a living fragrance filled the air. Deeper fell the shadows upon the scene, and there I sat wrapped in profound reverie until the night winds warned me to retire. But, oh!

'Night and darkness, we are wondrous strong

As is a dark eye in woman.'

The account by "Pioneer" is lavish in heaping praise on Brannan for what he had accomplished at Calistoga and the large sums of money being spent on exotic trees and plants, dams for fresh water and bathing, a brand new flour mill, trout ponds and the hotel and cottages which could accommodate 200 guests.

There were three separate vineyards within walking distance of the grounds, the closest of only 10,000 vines but the second contained 280,000 vines and the third, 40,000. Brannan obviously intended to provide his guests with all the wine and brandy they might wish to drink.

Several months later another story in the *Alta* summed up rather more succinctly for the general public the goals Brannan had in mind in the upper end of the Napa Valley:

> Napa is remarkably fortunate in her possession of so many places of interest. Her mineral springs, with the exception of the Geysers, are without rivals. Their situation in most picturesque districts adds much to the fame they are yearly acquiring. Calistoga in its natural attractions, is bound to be our Saratoga. The qualities of the water, surrounding country, and many other advantages, conspire to that end.[II.12]

An attempt to murder Sam Brannan in April 1868 at his Calistoga sawmill offers a good example of his remarkable ability to antagonize people, especially individuals employed by him or associated with him in business ventures. Brannan and a man named McDowell had a disagreement about some aspect of the mill's operation, and both decided to walk to the mill from the Calistoga store. McDowell hesitated momentarily, leaving Brannan and a friend named Swift, to walk ahead.

When both men approached to within fifty feet of the mill, a man inside named Snyder ordered Brannan to halt. Brannan told Snyder he was to get out of the building posthaste. Shots were fired, felling Brannan and Swift within minutes.

That Brannan survived this attempt on his life is truly remarkable. According to one account of the dispute, his body took eight shots—whether these were separate bullets or shot or pellet from a shotgun is not clear. One bullet entered the neck, passed near the trachea and esophagus and injured the "Adam's apple." He also was hit in the right arm and near the hip, the projectile passing near the spine. Although Brannan recovered, he must have suffered from the injuries for years afterward.

The Napa Register, believing that Brannan was about to die, carried this editorial comment:

> Mr. Brannan has done more, perhaps, than any one or two other men for Napa County—has expended his means freely and exten-

sively in developing the resources of the valley, and should his
death follow from his wounds, his place would not be filled. It is
only now, when death seems about to rob us of him, that his good
qualities are recognized and appreciated according to their real
merits.[II.13]

The success of Brannan's publicity efforts during these years is not
difficult to measure. Hubert Howe Bancroft in San Francisco, had
begun compiling a series of scrapbooks of press clippings on all
subjects for each county in the state. He had plans to eventually write
a history of California, and this was to be just one of many resources
for the writing of the book.

Of all the subjects covered in the Bancroft clippings on Napa
Valley and County, by far the greater percentage dealt with the health
resort of Calistoga. If the material is any yardstick of public interest
in or knowledge of the valley by the late 1860s, dipping in hot mineral
baths was the main attraction in the Napa Valley.*

Incidentally, by the summer of '69, visitors to the health resort
disembarked from the San Francisco steamers directly at Vallejo, and
there climbed into trains waiting to take them to Calistoga. The total
time from the pier in San Francisco to the train station in Calistoga
was only six hours. The trip could begin at 7 a.m. or 4 p.m., seven days
a week.

"No one who has resided in San Francisco for any length of time
can fail to find here any day at least one familiar face," wrote one
reporter, this may have been enough to sell out the available space
for the remainder of the summer at a time when vacations were not
taken to get away from one's friends as much as to leave behind work
and the cold winds which blew all summer long in the city by the bay.

When Brannan began spending his vast wealth on developing
the Saratoga of the West, he unhesitatingly ordered land cleared for
vineyards, as well. His first vineyard was planted in 1861, the same
year during which Charles Krug founded his vineyard. By the middle
of the decade, Brannan had, according to one source, 330,000 vines,
which made him the largest grower in the Napa Valley.[II.14]

The land devoted to vines by Brannan may not have been quite
so extensive as the above numbers suggest. Economics historian
Titus Fey Cronise visited the valley too, during this period and

*The Scrapbooks are available to the public at the Bancroft Library, University
of California, Berkeley.

recorded a much more conservative account of Brannan's involvement in viticulture. Cronise provided the following list of growers in his 1868 published book *The Natural Wealth of California*:

Name	No. of Vines	Name	No. of Vines
Samuel Brannan	100,000	Hardman	20,000
Sigrist Bros	60,000	J. T. Dewoody	20,000
Charles Krug	41,000	J. Van	20,000
J. York	35,000	P. Kellogg	15,000
Capt. Phil. Christensen	35,000	E. Kellogg	15,000
Dr. Crane	32,000	P. Pettet	15,000
General Keyes	30,000	Oak Knoll	15,000
Lewelling	30,000	R. Kilburn	12,000
D. Hudson	24,000	C. Westfall	12,000
Dr. Rule	20,000	Wm. Hudson	12,000
F. Kellogg	20,000	D. Fulton	10,000
Mr. McCord	20,000	Mrs. Mills	10,000
C. Cowa	20,000	M. Vann	10,000
Henry Boggs	20,000	Geo. C. Young (estate)	10,000

Missing from this breakdown were the names of grape growers in the Soscol and/or Carneros area of the valley, especially William Winter. Cronise gives the Soscol district a total of 10,000 vines, plus another 250,000 vines in the county growing in vineyards smaller than that of the Yount, Vann ranch, etc. *The economics writer reported a total of 1,000,000 vines for all of Napa County.**

Cronise's description of the valley opens by acknowledging indirectly the influence of Brannan's Calistoga publicity:

---

*Attempting to arrive at a general figure for grapes planted per acre in this period is no easy task. *Southern Vineyard*, Los Angeles, Ca. of Oct. 2, 1858 claims: "The average yield of vines may be placed at ten pounds per vine, and a thousand vines per acre." The *Atlantic Monthly* of May 1864 states: "In Los Angeles County most of the vineyards have 1,000 vines to the acre. In Sonoma the number varies from 680 to 1,000." The *Sacramento Daily Union* of Feb. 18, 1865 states: "In Los Angeles County the distance is six feet each way, or one thousand vines to the acre. In Sonoma, the distance in the vineyards set out before 1865 is eight feet or six hundred eighty vines to the acre." Seven hundred vines to the acre for Napa Valley seems a good average based on these and other sources consulted.

On the road through Napa valley, towards Calistoga springs, an attractive picture is presented of a California farming district— substantial private dwellings, well fenced fields, broad patches of vineyards and fruit orchards, alternate with grain fields, extending as far as the eye can reach. On either side of this fine valley are mountains covered with pine and fir, with here and there a clump of cedar; the lower ranges full of thickets of nut-hazel, buckeye, California bay, *oreodaphne Californica*, the most odoriferous plant that grows on this coast; the California lilac, a species of ceanothus; several varieties of oak, the ash, and a dense undergrowth of grasses, clover, wild oats and flowers which afford food and cover for an immense number of quail, hare and rabbits.

About 500,000 bushels of wheat were harvested in this valley in 1867. The average yield of all the land sown to this grain, being thirty bushels to the acre, without the use of any fertilizer or artificial irrigation. Fruits of all kinds, and the vine in all its varieties are also very productive. The lower hills are covered for miles with vineyards, and the area of this cultivation is rapidly extending.

To illustrate the perfection the foreign varieties of grape attain on these hill-sides, Mr. H. N. Amsbury, in 1867, raised bunches of the White Nice measuring thirty-two inches in circumference, and weighing upwards of eight pounds each. In another vineyard, bunches of the Flame Tokay were gathered, weighing five pounds each. The vines on these hillsides are never irrigated—they produce a wine essentially different from that made from grapes grown on the low lands, or where watered.

Cronise adds the observation that "there appears to be considerable difference in the quality of the wine made from grapes grown in different localities." This may be the first published recognition that the valley offered some variation in the quality of wine which could be produced, based not on the individual wine maker or his equipment, but on the chemistry of the soil and/or climate.

The long quotation just given from Cronise's work should not be construed to mean that the emphasis in his section on Napa was on wine making. Grapes and wine take up only a small portion compared with the pages he devotes to the health spas or resorts of Napa County. Calistoga receives the most attention with statistics on the temperature of the mineral waters at various levels below the surface of the earth.

Many San Franciscans and other Bay Area residents with poor quality drinking water were discovering that "Napa Soda Springs" soda water offered an excellent alternative, especially if chilled and served on warm days. Consuming mineral or soda waters for health reasons was very popular, so Cronise provided a breakdown of the mineral content of Napa Soda Springs water which included, according to one "Dr. Lanzweert," bicarbonate of soda, magnesia, lime, sodium, iron, sulphate of soda, silicious acid and alumina (aluminum oxide).

DIRECTORY

OF THE

GRAPE GROWERS, WINE MAKERS AND DISTILLERS

OF

CALIFORNIA,

AND OF THE

PRINCIPAL GRAPE GROWERS AND WINE MAKERS OF THE EASTERN STATES.

PUBLISHED BY THE

BOARD OF STATE VITICULTURAL COMMISSIONERS OF CALIFORNIA.

SACRAMENTO:
STATE OFFICE, : : : : : A. J. JOHNSTON, SUPT. STATE PRINTING.
1891.

(Pacific Coast Business Directory For 1867)

There is one curious omission in *The Natural History of California*: Nowhere in the text on Napa is there a mention of how much wine was produced that year. Although a visitor to the valley might get the impression that all of the vines were too young to produce, winemaking was expanding very rapidly. In the latter years of the decade, more than fifty thousand gallons of wine were being fermented each fall, five times the production estimated to have taken place when the decade opened. (See chart opposite from the *Pacific Coast Business Directory For 1867*. The figures are probably from County Assessor's records provided each year to the State Board of Equalization.)

In the United States Special Agricultural Census of 1860, Los Angeles was the leading wine producing county with 162,980 gallons of wine. Second in the tabulations and far behind is Mariposa with 10,700; Santa Barbara at 10,550 gallons; Napa, 8,745; San Bernardino, 8,520; Alameda County, 8,040; and El Dorado with 6,464 in seventh place among the top counties. Sonoma County is shown as producing only 1,990 gallons, this figure is in error and should be about 100,000 gallons. The county had 344,000 vines by 1858.[II.15]

Napa County had fallen to seventh place in the chart just presented, but with its five-fold increase in wine, and all of the young vineyards just coming into bearing stage, the future looked very bright, indeed. Nearly fifty thousand gallons of wine fermenting in its wine tanks in 1867 meant to other Californians that the valley was on its way to becoming a major wine region of the state. There was more than hot mineral water baths to be taken or soda waters to be tasted when visiting the valley.

There were a number of other notable growers and wine makers established in the valley in this period. Swiss-born Henry A. Pellet deserves to be ranked among the pioneers of the county since he began making wine for John Patchett in 1860.

Pellet was born in 1828 in Switzerland and took up the trade of watch repair when he was eighteen years old. Somewhat like Krug and Haraszthy, and perhaps many other immigrants whose background is little known, Pellet quickly found himself involved in politics and revolution. His fight was with the King of Bavaria and the battles his home county in Switzerland waged to break free of Bavarian rule. Pellet left Switzerland in 1848 and returned to watch repairing, this time in St. Louis, Missouri.

In the spring of 1850, the California Gold Rush was too much for Pellet to resist, and he joined a wagon train for the Pacific Coast.

Pellet panned for gold in the Sierras, made enough money to invest in other business ventures, most of which failed, and returned to gold mining a half dozen times. Finally, in 1858 he purchased land near Napa City and devoted his energies to farming. Leasing Patchett's vineyard two years later, Pellet began making wine for himself and Patchett.

Pellet must have preferred the viticultural potential of St. Helena, as was demonstrated by Crane's success with the grape, for he moved there in 1863 and purchased forty-five acres. He quickly joined Crane in making wine or, to be more accurate, probably became wine maker for Crane who knew little about the process. Three years later, St. Helena banker-to-be D. B. Carver invested with Pellet in a winery, the "Pellet & Carver Winery," quickly gaining fame for the quality of its product.

John J. Sigrist and his brother Theodore, set out a vineyard northwest of Napa City about 1860, near the entrance to what is now called Brown's Valley. In his book Cronise credited the Sigrist brothers with having the second largest vineyard in the county. By the end of the decade they had a winery capable of handling one hundred thousand gallons of wine.

The Sigrist brothers may have found an ally in Gottlieb Groezinger's attempts to improve the quality of wine he sold in his San Francisco store by fermenting each grape variety separately and keeping the wine the same way. Many vintners crushed only two kinds of grapes in these early years: white grapes for white wine and red grapes for red wine.

This attempt at upgrading California wine quality is borne out by this brief story in the *Napa County Reporter*:

> We direct the attention of vineyardists and wine-makers to the advertisement of Mr. Sigrist, one of our most extensive wine manufacturers, who is importing Rhine wine casks, primarily for his own use and secondarily for the benefit of other wine growers who desire to produce the best quality of wine of which their vineyards are capable.
>
> Mr. Sigrist is laboring earnestly and efficiently to elevate and maintain the character of our California vintage, and to that end will, as he informs us, take pleasure in giving instructions and assistance in the proper manipulation of the grape, to young vintners, and small grape growers, or any one who may desire the benefit of his extensive practical experiences.[II.16]

Julius Fulscher built the above winery in Calistoga in the late 1870's but Louis Kortum acquired the cellar in 1880 and made rather famous wines thereafter. As late as 1884, Kortum was still the only winemaker in the town despite all that Samuel Brannan had attempted two decades earlier to attract the socially elite of San Francisco to his resort and spa.

This was the first winery built in Napa Valley's famous Carneros district although the ruins are now well-hidden in the dense undergrowth along Huichica creek. William Winter built the winery circa 1872. George Husmann later brought considerable notoriety to the old "Talcoa Winery'" with his winemaking skills and describes the cellar in detail in his 1883 book American Grape Growing and Wine Making.

Winemaking at the Charles Krug winery. Frequently misidentified in wine books, this photograph of the winery dates after 1894 when the California Wine Association was formed and leased the building. Its name is in the lower right hand corner. Krug had died two years earlier. The structure was built by Krug in 1874.

Gustave Niebaum's Inglenook winery was begun in June, 1883 but only the left wing was completed. Two years later, the right wing was added and finally the central tower. Hamden W. McIntyre was the architect, designing many of northern California's grand stone or wood wine cellars.

Josephine Tychson was undoubtedly famous in the Napa Valley for being the first woman to construct a winery entirely on her own but she was gossiped about more often for how fast she rode or drove her horses. Her home, shown here was directly across the main county road to Calistoga from the Tychson winery completed in the summer of 1886.

Until about 1890, the Chinese laborer carried out nearly all of the viticulture work in California, including picking grapes. There are only two shown in this photograph (identified by their peculiar inverted woven hats) and the other dozen workers are likely Italian immigrants. The latter group replaced most of the Chinese when the height of the grape vine trunk was raised from eighteen inches off the ground to waist high. Caucasians usually refused to tend vines close to the ground.

In the years immediately proceeding Prohibition when hundreds of Italian or Swiss-Italian immigrants swarmed into Napa Valley, most built homes with wine cellars in the basement. Luigi Domeniconi built his home on Silverado Trail in 1902. The stone wine-cellar basement was entered on the left in the above photograph. (Today this is the site of the Pine Ridge winery and the original basement cellar is still intact.)

Winery appearances prior to Prohibition had little to do with the quality of the wine produced inside. This is obvious in this photograph of the Stanly winery (which burned in 1936). Stanly wines were among the most highly prized and priced in Napa Valley in the 1880s and '90s. The building, however, would not have won an architectural award and certainly could not have withstood a severe earthquake.

Highly unusual for its square design (66 x 66 feet) the Larkmead winery was completed in 1906 for Battista Salmina and his nephew Felix Salmina. The entire bottom floor is five feet thick of solid concrete and interior redwood timbers are so huge a small railroad engine could easily be well-supported. Designer-builder Wilbur Harrison made the structure to withstand any size earthquake. (Hanns Kornell Champagne cellars now occupy the building.)

Wine Cellar, "Far Niente", Oakville near St. Helena, Cal.

Taken from the newly popular picture postcards, this photograph of the Far Niente winery dates to shortly before the death of the winery's founder, John Benson, in 1910. Benson, a wealthy San Franciscan, traveled frequently to Italy from whence he borrowed part of the phrase "dolce far niente" for the name of his winery completed in 1886.

Henry W. Crabb was living in southern Alameda County in 1868 when his former neighbor, John Lewelling, stopped by to tell him about the Garden of Eden he had discovered at St. Helena, Napa County. Both men had grown up in eastern states which had native grapes (South Carolina and Indiana for Lewelling; Ohio for Crabb) and a developing wine industry. When gold was discovered in California, they came west but quickly returned to the soil and farming for their livelihood. When Lewelling saw how well the grape thrived in California, he caught viticulture fever. He spread the fever to many of his neighbors, including Crabb.

Lewelling had purchased land in lower Napa Valley as early as 1864 but sold it and moved to St. Helena four years later, the year Crabb arrived in the valley. Both began clearing and draining their farmlands preparatory to planting grapes.

Crabb was not quite so enthusiastic about St. Helena and settled for 240 acres west of a spot which would eventually become the town of Oakville. (Both men would shortly become major figures in the valley's wine industry, Crabb even naming Crabb's Black Burgundy, a grape variety after himself. He shortly replaced Haraszthy as the leading experimenter with grape varieties in his Oakville nursery.)

When the *Illustrations of Napa County, California* was published in 1878, the section on viticulture includes this observation:

> The greater part of the wine making of Napa Valley is conducted by persons of foreign birth, and generally by those who have had experience in the business elsewhere. They are from Switzerland, Germany, France and Italy (p. 6).

Among the Swiss immigrants who settled in the valley (Pellet has already been mentioned) was Frank Salmina who purchased land on the east side of the valley just north of Napa City (where few people were settled as yet). From Germany, via Indianapolis, came John C. Weinberger in 1869. He selected land near what later became Tychson Hill, a very modest rise of ground two miles north of St. Helena. (This put him close to Krug and Schram and this is where the Beringer brothers would eventually settle.)

From Italy in 1866 came the grape grower and wine maker, Giacomo Migliavacca. Like most nineteenth century Italian immigrants, Migliavacca did not have the funds necessary to go into viticulture immediately so he opened a small grocery store on Main Street in Napa City.

Migliavacca's first advertisement in the Napa *Daily Reporter* of November 15 proclaims his selling "Family Groceries and Provisions" and "Fresh Fish received by every boat." He must have brought the fresh fish in the front door, for the back of his store was quickly converted to the making of wine from local grapes. Migliavacca's wine reputation grew rapidly which does suggest he did not mix his selling of fish and wine. (In due course he would build Napa's second largest winery, a huge brick structure along the river.)

Civil War general Erasmus D. Keyes spent a few years in the valley after his retirement and founded what later became known as the Edge Hill Vineyard and winery. The site he chose was at the mouth of Sulphur Spring Canyon, southwest of St. Helena, not far from John Lewelling.* Keyes barely had time to bring his vineyard of 12,000 vines into production before he sold it to another Civil War military leader, Gen. R. W. Heath. Heath began winemaking on the property in 1872.

Newspaper editor C. A. Menefee helped put all of these events of the decade in perspective when he wrote, just three years into the 1870s, about the coming of the railroad to Napa Valley:

> Looking at the facts thus far presented, it would seem that the County has made a very bad bargain. But in fact, the County has been evidently a greater gainer. An impetus has been given to every branch of business, and both County and City have awakened as if from a long slumber. The value of land in the upper half of the county has been enhanced from 100 to 300 per cent, and this advance alone would repay the subsidy four-fold.
>
> The railroad, by giving us the means of rapid communication with San Francisco, and all parts of the State, and the East, has called attention to our town and valley, and caused a heavy immigration of the best class of citizens. If the railroad were to be removed, a million dollars would not cover the loss. It is not here intended to defend or apologize for the management, or heavy rates of fare and freight charged on this road, but merely to state the general proposition, that nothing yet has done so much to call forth the latent resources of the County, and increase her wealth and population, as the railroad.**

---

*Now the private home of St. Helena wine maker Louis Martini and his wife Elizabeth.

**Historical and Descriptive Sketch Book . . . page 56-57.

The first railroad built in California was a twenty-four mile line in 1854, between Sacramento and Folsom. The second, and what might also be termed a passenger line similar to the Sacramento railroad, was completed between San Francisco and San Jose in 1863. This makes the Soscol to Napa City line, completed in 1864, only the third passenger railroad in the state.

By 1868, when the Napa Valley railroad was completed all the way to Calistoga, Napa County was the first to have a railroad span its entire length. No other county could make that boast. (Neighboring Sonoma County, for example, saw its first railroad construction start in 1869 and end upon completion to Cloverdale in 1872.)

Transporting wine easily and relatively inexpensively played a crucial role in the development of the wine industry in the Napa Valley. In the latter half of the 1860s, wine production climbed dramatically.

Of a more crucial role, however, were the men of vision who helped found the valley's young wine industry in the 1860s. John Patchett's pioneering efforts rated much serious attention, as did those of George Crane. And though Sam Brannan's wine and viticulture role seems to have lasted but a decade or so, he obviously made contributions in other areas critical to the evolution of a public awareness of the valley's wine potential. Krug, who began so small as to be insignificant compared to all three, had goals which would eclipse everyone.

JUDGE CLINTON HASTINGS

JOHN C. WEINBERGER

W. SCHEFFLER

M. M. ESTEE

III. Wheat, Cattle, Quicksilver and Grapes, the 1870s

In the spring of 1870, when the ground had dried from the winter rains, Gottlieb Groezinger stood in the middle of Yountville and carefully selected the site for a winery he wanted to build. A half dozen workmen stood by as he paced off the size; one hundred and fifty footsteps to the west and eighty steps to the north. This building would take some time to construct, they all agreed, especially since it was to be two stories in height.

Groezinger was not finished, however, for at the north end of his winery, a wing would be added, eighty-four steps long and sixty wide with a full basement. When the foreman of the construction party had duly noted these dimensions on his note pad, the walking began again. Attached to this structure would be yet another, "the fermenting room" Gottlieb called it, of one hundred and five steps by thirty in width. All of this pacing was assumed to be at the rate of one footstep equalling twelve inches in length.

When the workmen had carefully pounded stakes into the ground to mark the three proposed buildings, Groezinger pointed to another site nearby where a temporary brick oven was to be built. He wanted his new winery constructed of brick and would have most of the bricks made right on the property. This would be the first brick winery in the Napa Valley and when finished, would dwarf every winery then in operation. As a matter of fact, there wasn't a wine cellar of this size anywhere in the state.

By evening, the talk in Yountville was only on one subject, the Groezinger winery. Within a few days, the news had spread from Napa City to Calistoga for it meant any farmer with a vineyard, had a new, wealthy buyer for his grapes. It also meant that viticulture and the making of wine would be the primary topic of conversation in the Napa Valley for months if not years to come.

Groezinger was not a wealthy San Franciscan, as were the millionaires of the rank of William Chapman Ralston (a recent founder of the Bank of California) who made their fortunes in Nevada silver. Groezinger had done very well in San Francisco providing fresh fish, fresh vegetables and well-made local wines for customers of his store. He must have borrowed heavily to finance this new venture; not from banks, but from good customers and friends who had been successful at speculating in mining stocks or the trading of real estate.

Groezinger, like Jacob Schram, Charles Krug (and Krug's newly hired wine maker, Jacob Beringer) was German-born. He had apprenticed in hotel-keeping, baking and picked up wine making along the way. At sixteen he moved to Switzerland where he worked as a waiter, an occupation he followed also in New York City after immigrating to America in 1848. It was not long before his customers' principal topic of dinner table conversation was the discovery of gold in California, and Gottlieb succumbed quickly. He arrived in San Francisco within months of Sam Brannan's public announcement on the subject.

One biography of Groezinger makes the claim that he returned to his homeland a half dozen years later and there collected "several thousand grape cuttings of best varieties" to be planted back in California.[III.1] This source does not state when he planted the cuttings but the next sentence reads: "In 1858 he turned his attention to the manufacture of wine in San Francisco, buying his first grapes of Colonel Haraszthy, and paying him for the same three cents per pound."

If Groezinger purchased grapes from Haraszthy, he also would have provided the Hungarian with some of the cuttings he brought from Germany. Haraszthy avidly sought new grape varieties for his Sonoma vineyardists. In 1861, Haraszthy advertised in the *Sonoma*

County Democrat, Santa Rosa, that he had 186 foreign vines. Some of these vines probably came from Groezinger. This was months before Haraszthy embarked on his own celebrated vine gathering tour in Europe!

Groezinger became a major purchaser of Napa Valley grapes and wines in the mid-1860s for it was here he believed the grape reached its peak of perfection. In the latter part of this decade he purchased his first land in the valley and with the financial backing arranged by 1870, began construction of his winery at Yountville. A portion of a description of the winery and its unique operation, as carried in Menefee's *Sketch Book*, is worthy of repeating:

> The roof of the fermenting room is nearly level, and comes up within six feet of the eaves of the main cellar. This roof is very strongly built, and is on a level with the upper story of the cellar. *On this is all the grape crushing done* [italics added], in the open air, skylights being fitted in directly over large fermenting vats below, into which falls the juice from the crushers. These crushers take a box of grapes, containing from 55 to 60 pounds, every seven seconds, and their capacity for juice is from 6,000 to 6,500 gallons per day. A platform leads from the roof to the ground, and one also from the upper floor of the cellar, and as a load of boxes of grapes is pulled up one platform by a horse below, a load of empty boxes goes down the other one. On this roof is also made all the Port, Muscatel, Sherry and Angelica. . . .
>
> Everything here, as in every portion of this vast establishment, bespeaks the tidiness of the Superintendent, Mr. F. Schweitzer, who has combined, all over the premises the three best elements of successful wine making: order, neatness and convenience. Everything that will take a polish shines, even the floors are swept clean enough to delight the heart of a tidy housewife, and all the casks are numbered.[*] The rubber hose and all the various implements in constant use in an edifice of this kind, are to be found in their appropriate place, and can be made available even in the dark.[III.2]

Behind the winery, spreading toward the west and north, a vineyard of 150,000 vines (roughly two hundred acres) had been planted, only one-sixth of which were the heavily bearing Mission grapes. Groezinger was a man of his word, he wanted wine quality

---

*Gustave Niebaum, who founded Inglenook ten years later, may have copied F. Schweitzer's cleanliness habits, almost making a fetish of his tidiness standards in the winery.

and he and many others felt the Mission grape produced a very inferior wine. The very first crush that fall at the Groezinger winery is described in detail in *Bancroft's Tourist Guide To California*, published in 1871.

Napa County began the decade of the 1870s with 7,163 residents, a gain in population of 2,291 individuals. New York and Missouri contributed the most former residents to the county's population, 446 from the latter state, 401 from New York. The total number of foreign born citizens constituted nearly a quarter of all the people who called this their home.

Napa's farmland was continuing to be broken up into smaller farms, dramatically so from only one decade earlier. The previous census gave the county 640 farmers. Now there were 620 farms of one hundred acres or less in size as the new decade opened, 77 farms of five hundred to one thousand acres in size, and 49 farms of above two thousand acres in size. A total of 746 men claimed to be engaged in agricultural pursuits, many growing grapes, of course.[III.3] There is no tabulation of the number of vines in Napa County in the census, and the figure quoted for wine production, 46,745 gallons, is grossly incorrect The *Transactions* of the California Agricultural Society for 1870 gives Napa a total of 2,172,900 vines; divided by an average of 700 to the acre this equals 3,104 acres.

The spectacular growth of vineyards in the Napa Valley over the past ten years cannot be credited simply to the energies of men like Crane, Patchett, Krug and more recently, Groezinger. This vine and wine boom was going on in many parts of California.

Bancroft's *Tourist Guide* in 1871 reported of Sonoma viticulture: "The number of vines now in cultivation is about four million, and Sonoma stands first among the wine producing counties of the state." Los Angeles County had finally been toppled from the front rank as the leading wine county in California. The Surveyor General of the state claimed there were now 22,402,850 vines growing border to border (32,000 acres, taking 700 to the acre).[III.4] Wine production had moved from about five hundred thousand gallons in 1859 to nearly four million gallons ten years later.[III.5]

One explanation for this heady state of affairs was the Civil War in the eastern states, the armed conflict lasting from the firing on Fort Sumter at Charleston, S.C., April 12, 1861, to the surrender of Gen. Robert E. Lee at Appomattox, Va., April 9, 1865. With so many eastern manufactured goods unable to reach California, a thriving home industry began in just about every consumer product.

French wines, which had such a strong foothold in the San Francisco restaurant business, became nearly unavailable because of the interruption in shipping. California vintners were delighted with the demand for "native wines," up until then a somewhat derogatory term in many restaurants or saloons. This was especially true on Dupont Street, the French quarter of the city (shortly renamed "Grant," honoring General Ulysses S. Grant).

Another explanation for the expanding viticulture industry in the Napa Valley by 1870, and in many other regions of the state, had to do with all of the publicity California wine making generated during the previous decade. In June 1867, the *New York Sun* carried its first California wine story. The reporter who wrote the article may not have heard of the Napa or Sonoma valleys, however, for he wrote:

> ... The whole southern part of the State is noted for its adaptability to grape culture. At that time the native grapes of Los Angeles arrived in San Francisco almost by the ship load, and in such profusion that during the season this fruit formed almost the common staple of food.

The *Home Journal* of St. Louis, Missouri was especially enthusiastic about the new California wine country as this excerpt shows from the fall of 1866:

> The opening of the California Wine region is most opportune. There, in the virgin soil and blander atmosphere of the sunny slopes of the Pacific, the vine flourishes in all its pristine health and vigor. It grows almost without human care, spreading its branches over the earth and bearing its rich loads of fruit every year, scarcely failing once in a century. California is unmistakably one of nature's most carefully prepared Wine Gardens.[III.6]

No single published source accomplished so much for California wines in the East as did Titus Fey Cronise's book *The Natural Wealth of California*. The 1868 book gave to the Eastern journalist for the first time a comprehensive overview of the new young wine industry, even listing the principal vineyardists in counties like Napa and Sonoma. Cronise's section on "Viticulture" begins:

> If there be any one vegetable growth which more than any other finds a congenial home over hill and dale and high mountain ranges in California, and which nearly every one plants, it is the grape vine. So general is the distribution that it is not easy to number the vines now growing. But there cannot be less than twenty-five millions of vines; and men of good judgement say at

least thirty millions. Two-thirds of these are the native Los Angeles grape. It is a good bearer and never fails. Its berry is the size of a large musket ball. From this hardy grape are made, by varied processes, White Wine of the Hock kind, Claret, Port, Sherry, Madeira, Champagne, Angelica and some others.

The "Los Angeles grape" was another name for the commonly known "Mission" grape, although there may have been two somewhat different clones or varieties of this grape, one more popular in the San Francisco region.

Cronise unknowingly touched on the point of most argument among wine makers—that the Los Angeles or Mission grape could be of universal use in wine production. Gottlieb Groezinger was one of the most vociferous opponents of this concept, blaming California wine's often poor ranking in the East among wine connoisseurs, on the source of it all, the Mission grape.

In his long treatment of the subject of viticulture, Cronise divided California into three grape growing regions:

First, the southern, or Los Angeles, making Port and other sweet wines, and white wines of much spirit and little aroma; second, the Coast Range, including Sonoma, Napa, etc., making white and red acid wines—Hock, Sauterne, Claret, etc.; third, the foot-hills of the Sierra Nevadas, in the gold mining range, including Folsom, Sonora, El Dorado, etc., making dry wines of extraordinary bouquet and aroma—Sherry, Madeira, Teneriffe, etc.; also, Port and German wines, the latter having a high aroma unlike any Rhine wine.

Napa was now ranked right beside Sonoma County, as the location for the best white and red acid wines (table wines), especially the popular Sauterne and Claret wines. Claret was a word given by the English to the red wines of Bordeaux, France, perhaps the most famous wines of Europe. This distinction between Los Angeles wine and Sonoma and Napa counties, was soon copied by other writers and accounts, in part, for the greater interest in the latter half of the 1860s in Napa County as a place to plant grapes.

Cronise noted that the East had a preference for sweet California wines. He claimed 150,000 gallons of Port was shipped from Los Angeles to New York in 1867 and that 80,000 gallons of Angelica was sent East. Claret was a good wine, no question of that admitted Cronise, "but not yet sufficiently tested in the Eastern markets."

There was a wine publishing milestone in 1863 in San Francisco, which may have been the original source for much of the background and statistics utilized in eastern newspaper wine stories. In January 1863 J.Q.A. Warren issued the first copy of the *California Wine and Wool Register*. This was the first wine publication on the West Coast.*

The first issue carried rather lengthy coverage of the first statewide wine convention, held in San Francisco in December 1862. Much of the attention of the delegates (including Dr. George Crane of St. Helena and Charles Krug), was on the varieties of grapes to be planted and many more problems besetting the novice wine maker. Committees were appointed to look into national tariffs on imported wine and those Eastern wine dealers who added fruit juice to California wine before selling the product to the consumer. Adulteration of wine was quickly becoming a common practice for it provided the wine wholesaler with seven gallons of wine for every five he purchased (depending upon how the individual "cut" the original).

The *California Wine and Wool Register* carried one curious remark made to the convention by R. F. Perkins, which demonstrated the increasing hostility between the farmer and gold or silver miner:

> The gold miners have passed over the earth, obliterating and making waste. But the vineyards have come, changed, and rendered green and beautiful the valleys and hillsides of our native State, making the abandoned soil valuable, and creating an interest which will live for centuries.

For two years, editor Warren kept up the struggle to survive the rigors of publishing in a city overrun with weekly and daily newspapers. He expanded the title to read *California Wine, Wool and Stock Register*. There were long articles on viticulture in the various growing regions of the San Francisco Bay, but in late 1864 the wine publication ceased.

It is somewhat uncertain as to what effect the opening of the first transcontinental railroad had on the state's expanding wine industry. For large bulk shipments, the railroad was not an ideal means of transportation as the high temperatures of the desert west in the summer could spoil wine. There is also a psychological factor here, which is not easy to assess. The East was now only a week's ride away, family and friends could be reunited quickly. California, which had sat sublime and alone on the Pacific shores during the American

---

*Actually the first two issues, for January and February, were published in Sacramento, then it was moved to San Francisco.

Civil War, was reunited with the nation. The vast wealth of California was the envy of every merchant east of the Mississippi River. In the euphoria brought on by the transcontinental railroad, California wine probably found a much more receptive consumer in the East.

It would have been impossible to determine just exactly what all of this meant to vineyardists of the Napa Valley by the 1870s if a local newspaperman had not gone out to see for himself in the winter and spring of '73. The journalist wrote for the *Napa Reporter* in Napa City and began a column January 4, which he called "Ramble Among the Vineyards of Napa." The columns were never signed, not even with the initials of the writer, although it seems likely it was none other than C. A. (Charles) Menefee, owner of the *Reporter*. Some of the material was reprinted word for word, later that year in Menefee's *Historical and Descriptive Sketch Book*.

Most of Menefee's columns began as he hitched up his horse and buggy and took one of the trails out of Napa City. Each farm was duly recorded with a brief few sentences about its products, especially grapes. If a winery was found on the premises, the attention of much of the column was on the subject of wine making. The first column, however, opens with a visit to Charles Krug.

The new Krug winery (completed the year before) was 90 x 104 feet with the central portion two stories in height of concrete. The upper room or second story was the press room, where all the grapes were crushed. Directly underneath, a room of 43 x 100 feet was for the fermentation of the must and was so constructed as to keep an even temperature throughout the year (this was achieved in part by surrounding it with smaller workrooms and the fact that the floor above would absorb most of the sun's heat).

"The very old wine ... will always be found in the pioneer cellar," wrote the reporter, which was that 14 x 20 foot, sunken cellar of straw roof dating to 1861. Krug had only made 58,000 gallons of wine in his new facility, the small amount being due to the late spring frosts which had badly hurt valley vineyards. His vineyard now covered sixty-eight acres, nearly half of which were foreign vines.

Dr. Crane had also just built himself a new cellar. "The first cellar was built in 1862," wrote Menefee. "It was of small dimensions, built of wood. The present cellar was built in 1870-1, of concrete, and is partly underground. It is 44 by 75 feet and, including underground portions, is two stories in height." His production was now 24,400 gallons annually.

Just south of Crane, a third new cellar had been constructed by the Giaque brothers. It, too, was of concrete, 100 feet long but only 26 feet wide. The brothers had made 24,400 gallons of wine the previous year. None of the three wineries just mentioned were operating at full capacity. There is some suspicion that cooperage was not available to meet the demands of the expanded wineries. More coopers were brought in only after the wineries were built and orders placed for more barrels, puncheons or tanks.

Down the road another half mile, Gordon Backus (a fortuitous name) had just completed his cellar, 80 feet in length by 30 feet and had only crushed 5,000 gallons. The Backus winery offers a good example of the advancement slowly coming in winery construction and architecture. Backus enclosed his concrete walls with wood, both inside and out. "The temperature is stated to be remarkably uniform." He used the concrete for insulation, and strength.

To the north of St. Helena, near the old Bale Mill, the new owners of the mill also had built a concrete winery.* W. W. Lyman, the son of the Reverend Theodore B. Lyman, rector of Trinity Episcopal Church, San Francisco, had invested funds from his mother in a business venture which was suppose to have a bright future—wine.[III.7] Built in 1871, the 30 x 50 foot, two-story building, yearly made about 12,000 gallons.

On Menefee's first outing he took note of five new wineries built since the decade began. Previously operating wineries included: H. A. Pellet and D. D. Carver, who had made 25,000 gallons of wine the previous fall; Gen. Heath, 11,000 gallons and Virginia Stratton another 5,000. "Besides the local consumption, about 400 tons of grapes were shipped to Groezinger & Co. of Yountville" concluded the writer, with wine being made by the giant firm in both Napa and San Francisco. The Groezinger winery at Yountville had produced 160,000 gallons of wine in '72, although it had a capacity to hold 400,000 gallons.

---

*The newspaper reporter refers to the use of "concrete" in the construction of many of these wineries, but it is highly doubtful concrete alone was used. Concrete had long been known and used as a mortar to build walls containing stones, as is the case with the Lyman winery. Solid concrete walls were not, as yet a part of such construction. It appears that when stones were gathered, as from a field and mixed rather indiscriminately with mortar, this was referred to as a "concrete" wall. When native stone was cut, sized and fitted neatly into place, then this was a "stone" cellar, as at the later Inglenook winery.

Three miles east of Yountville, the new Vine Cliff winery celebrated its second crush. Owned by George Burrage and George Tucker, it was tucked into the side of a hill somewhat like swallows fasten nests to the sheer rock walls of a steep canyon. In the *Reporter* column of January 25, 1873, Vine Cliff is described in this manner:

> One of the most romantic spots of Napa Valley is the same Vine Cliff Vineyard. A semi-circle of inaccessible rocky side-hills, in the cañon in which nestle the buildings, has, by the energy of man, been turned into a useful and picturesque piece of property. Hundreds of tons of rock have been patiently gathered off the hillsides, which now teem with grape vines, and hauled away. Truly does it look to one who saw it years agone (and not many at that) as though the finger of enchantment had been painted at its frowning, rocky surface and changed into a thing of beauty.
>
> The wine cellar is four stories high, the lower story of masonry, in the construction of which seventy barrels of cement were used. The stories above are built of lumber, 50,000 feet having been used in their construction.

Mention is made of grapes being crushed only the previous two years, which dates the winery to 1871.

An intriguing experiment was going on in the cellar. A redwood cask of 2,100 gallons had been built and was filled with Claret wine. "If the wine tastes of the redwood . . . then good-bye redwood for wine casks—an adieu we be sorry to extend to it, as it certainly is the cheapest material that can be gotten for that purpose." (Agoston Haraszthy had already proven redwood's value in the storage of wine—he had been using redwood tanks since 1860.)

At Oakville, the Napa reporter met Henry W. Crabb, more or less the founder of the new village of "Oakville." He retained title to the land on which the community store was located as well as a warehouse and the new depot. Crabb had one of the largest vineyards in the valley, seventy acres of Zinfandel, Muscat, Malvoisie, Rose of Peru, Golden Chasselas, Gray Riesling, Muscadelle, White Malaga, Black Hamburg and Black Frontignan.*

This reference to "70 acres" of vines signaled the beginning of a change in the reporting of vineyard size. Such vine statistics were always given in actual number of vines—that figure looked much

---

*The Robert Mondavi winery and vineyards now take up most of the original Crabb ranch.

more impressive! But Crabb had so many vines that he was proud to refer only to his total vineyard acreage.

Judge S.C. Hastings had three separate vineyards north of Crabb, one of thirty-three acres in size was so new it was not yet producing grapes. He had fifty acres abutting Crabb's land, which was being prepared for vineyard at the time of Menefee's visit in March 1873 and a third planting of forty-three acres several years old. Not far from it, brick was being accumulated on the ground at a railroad depot called "Rutherford Station." The brick was for a winery which was to be financed by a joint stock company of San Francisco and Bay Area investors.

Two days were required to visit and write an account of the new vineyards and orchards in Brown's Valley, west of Napa City. The first winery visited belonged to Theodore Sigrist and he and his brother John had been making wine for just about a decade. (Cronise in his 1868 book had listed the Sigrist brothers as owning the second largest vineyard in Napa Valley.) The Sigrists were making Brandy from excess wine during the reporter's visit, utilizing the steam engine of a wheat threshing machine for the necessary power. As with the larger wineries, there was also a cooper's shop on the premises which led to this observation:

> The casks are bought in New York, are set up and old casks repaired. In this connection, we would call attention to the fact that a cooperage started in Napa City with sufficient capital to compete with Eastern and San Francisco prices, would be certain to become a paying investment.

The Carneros region of the county, the last area visited by Menefee during his vineyard travels of '73, had as much frantic vineyard activity as any of the other areas in Napa. Taking the old Sonoma road out of Napa City, Menefee's first stop was at the farm of Bennett James. Here he found 18,000 vines, three-fourths of the Mission variety, the other foreign. Most of the grapes dated from the year 1861. This was the same age of Donald MacDonald's vineyard nearby, except the Scotchman had added four acres in 1869 and one more acre the previous year. Wrote Menefee:

> The road to Sonoma is dry, but in a terrible condition and shows signs of having been in a very bad state during our late rains. At noon reached Carneros Creek, where at its one hotel we were welcomed by the genial proprietor, A. R. Walden. Below the hotel is the shop of our old friend, Mont. Rose, the inventor of the

celebrated 'Mont. Rose' Vineyard Plow.
. . . They can be seen at the store of Allen, Parks & Kimball on Main street, Napa City.

Five miles beyond was William Winter's ranch, where grapes were planted in the late 1850s. One notable nineteenth century Napa Valley wine maker claimed that the Winter's ranch in '72 had the largest vineyard in the county, which would have been in excess of 100,000 vines, if true.[III.8] It is rather certain that Winter built his stone winery in the early years of the decade as well, though the only documentation to confirm this is a mention in Menefee's *Sketch Book* of wine making taking place in '73.[III.9]*

That Napa Valley wine was being shipped in carload lots to the East as early as '73 via the new transcontinental railroad, is documented in one of Menefee's country columns. In a second visit to the Pellet & Carver winery in St. Helena, Menefee was told that Pellet and Krug had pooled their resources and sent a full rail carload of wine directly to Detroit, Michigan. This could very well be the first such extensive shipping of wine from the valley to the East Coast utilizing the railroad.[III.10]

Six months after Menefee's wanderings and jottings among the vineyards of Napa, he combined all of this information with a good deal more he had been collecting assiduously and published his *Historical and Descriptive Sketch Book of Napa, Sonoma, Lake and Mendocino* counties of California. He added in the subtitle: "Comprising Sketches of their Topography, Productions, History, Scenery, and Peculiar Attractions." In three hundred and fifty-six pages he packed in many statistics on the economy of the four counties, portraits of many of the leading vineyardists and businessmen and brief but thorough biographies. It was the first history book on Napa Valley and County, a publishing milestone in the preservation of the details of the early years of the wine industry.

More than two-thirds of the Menefee book is devoted to Napa County and in a brief final chapter, he speculates on the future:

The pleasant climate in Napa Valley, and the facilities for travel, have already attracted many from the city [San Francisco], and we

---

*The U.S. Census for 1860, "Manufacturing," credits Winter with producing 20 gallons of wine. There is no other record of wine manufacture by Winter until the 1870s.

find the valley gradually being divided up into small tracts for homesteads, and elegant improvements being made. The wealth and culture of the city is in great numbers looking to this valley for a country seat, for a pleasant home where the substantial comforts of rural life may be enjoyed, and still the facilities of a rapid transit place them at the doors of the metropolis.

The Napa reporter and editor accomplished something else for the valley which he may or may not have had in mind. His book provided writers in the eastern cities of the United States with a ready reference source for the history of viticulture in California and particularly the details on one area in which the grape was booming, Napa Valley. The book gives the impression that the Napa Valley was quickly becoming the focal point of the state's wine industry; this was certainly true in the growing arguments about wine quality. There was nothing similar, as yet, for Sonoma Valley or any other wine area of the state.*

There was very little rivalry at this early date between Napa and Sonoma wine makers. A "Grape Grower's Association of Sonoma, Napa and Solano Counties" had been formed in the fall of 1871. (Note Sonoma is listed first.) These were meetings at which information was exchanged freely on methods of cultivating the soil, field grafting or bench grafting of vines. Everyone agreed on the need to obtain laws for the fencing of cattle and other farm animals. Too many cattle, horses and sheep roamed rather freely, doing a good deal of destruction to the vines.

In the spring of 1873, in early April, a heavy frost spread over most of the vineyards of the two counties and all the discussion at subsequent meetings of the vineyardists was on pruning or not pruning the injured vine and protection against the cold. Dr. George Crane argued that pruning the vine had absolutely no positive effect on the vine. John Sigrist went even further, claiming that the cane or spur which had been cut to remove injured growth, would leave "a sore, bleeding spot, and injured the dormant bud." He added that "one of his neighbors had burned brush freely, with a view to

---

*J. J. Owen published his *Santa Clara Valley* in the same year as Menefee. His fifty pages of text present a very clear word picture of the Santa Clara Valley but viticulture is treated in the most general terms with no statistics, not even names of wine makers.

influencing the temperature of the air [to combat frost], but the result was nil."[III.11]

The frost of April 5 and 6 was very capricious, ruining 50 percent of the crop at Sonoma city, but barely touching the vines up valley toward Santa Rosa. Charles Krug reported at an August meeting that 75 percent of the crop was lost in most of Napa Valley, the Mission grape suffering the most, the Zinfandel displaying the greatest recovery.

A large group from the Association traveled in September to Sacramento to attend the California Vine Growers and Wine and Brandy Manufacturers Association. Major J. R. Snyder of Sonoma made a startling announcement at the meeting:

> The phylloxera which made its appearance in Europe, has also been discovered in California. This may be owing to atmospheric influences, probably from the large amount of magnetism which has been thrown out through the solar system by the sun for the last two years past and this may have something to do with generating a particular class of insects. Accounts from France do not say so much about the phylloxera as they do about frost.[III.12]

France had also experienced a severe killing frost in April, only nineteen days after it hit in California. Snyder stated he thought the reports of injury to the vines in France from both sources, was exaggerated but did urge that a "good microscopy" be purchased by the organization for examining vines for the phylloxera disease. He had one more complaint: "We must have more life and activity infused into this Association if we expect to produce beneficial results." Too few grape growers attended county or state meetings.

It may have been Snyder's remarks about the insufficient interest of many in the industry which brought about the formation in December 1875 of the "St. Helena Vinicultural Club."* The three men most responsible for the new club were Henry Pellet, Charles Krug and a newcomer named Seneca Ewer. Krug was chosen the first president and within a short time a hundred names were added to the membership list. Meetings were held twice a month and by 1880 the club had its own Vinicultural Hall, a two-story building in downtown St. Helena.

---

*The Star thereafter used "Vinicultural" and "Viticultural" interchangeably in news stories, although Vinicultural seems to be the correct name of the club.

Krug was asked several years after the formation of the club to summarize some of its accomplishments:

> The vast amount of good the St. Helena Viticultural [sic] Association has done during the few years of its existence cannot be doubted. It has, by publication of its minutes and deliberations, spread a great amount of information among the grape-growers and wine men of this county and State. It has drawn the attention of many persons looking for vineyard land to this section, caused them to buy and settle among us, and to assist the building up of our county. . . .
>
> It has started an organization to keep the pernicious phylloxera from our beautiful vineyards, and you are well aware one man alone can do nothing in this line—only united action by all can ward off the dreaded calamity.[III.13]

Another goal of the St. Helena Club was the "collecting and publishing of valuable statistics showing the superiority of our climate, and the great fertility of our soil . . ." for the growing of grapes.

There were many wine men in the Napa Valley who were now firmly convinced that here was the most perfect spot in California, for the pursuit of viticulture. The cost of hiring vineyard workers became a major concern in the mid-1870s after the depression of '73 had made the selling of wine much more difficult. In order to cut the cost of producing wine, Napa Valley wine men began to consider much more seriously the use of Chinese laborers. The Chinese were available in large numbers. This kind of fluid labor force was the answer to a grape grower's prayer.

A letter sent down to San Francisco by train to a Chinese labor contractor, would bring as many workers as needed on the next day's passenger train up valley. The Chinese willingly worked for $1.00 a day and provided their own food and did their own cooking. A bedroll, also usually brought along, was all the Chinese worker needed for sleeping. The white laborer, on the other hand, expected his food to be prepared for him. In addition to his daily wage which was twenty-five to fifty cents higher, he demanded a roof over his head at night.

The nationwide recession had slowed the planting of grapes in the Napa Valley, but the young vineyards planted early in the decade came into full bearing just as the decline of wine consumption was becoming apparent. To Terrell Grigsby the overriding concern by 1876 was who would buy his grapes? He had listened to Krug and

Pellet and the other enthusiastic proponents of the grape, now he asked at a meeting of the St. Helena Vinicultural Club, who wanted his grapes?

Grigsby did not exactly attend the meeting expecting an answer to his questions so he had a suggestion of his own—why not build a series of large co-operative wineries in the valley. He urged three wineries be built, one at Calistoga, one at St. Helena and the third at Napa. Discussion on his proposal was enthusiastic, with the idea then put forward that a joint-stock company build at least one large winery.

The real culprit in this oversupply problem, claimed Krug, was that too many valley growers had planted the prolific Mission grape. He said the market was "glutted with inferior wines, made from the Mission grape" and that there were not nearly enough foreign grape varieties. If pressed, Krug would support one large co-op winery in a central location, but he also felt that the sixteen wineries in the immediate vicinity of St. Helena could handle all of the grapes there.

Grigsby may have been a little surprised to hear from Krug that St. Helena had sixteen wineries. He certainly knew the names of the oldest establishments, including Pellet & Carver, Schram, Crane and Krug.

The Yountville resident (eastern side of the valley) might not have recognized the Krug winery had he decided to visit the scene of so much up-valley wine making activity. Krug's winery had been gutted by fire in August 1874—not his original wine cellar half buried in the ground with a roof of straw but the 90 x 104 foot, two-story winery completed in 1872! He was not even able to save the contents, nearly 300,000 gallons of wine.

Krug did not wait for the embers to cool before he ordered lumber to rebuild the interior and must have hired an army of workers for he completed his annual crush almost right on schedule. He did move his distilling plant to a separate building the following year and when the machinery arrived from the East Coast, the *Star* had to use descriptive adjectives like "immense" and "the largest thing of the kind on the Coast."[III.14] The winery, whose foreman was Jacob Beringer, could now be described as the largest in the valley, perhaps because of the "immense" distillery.

In 1877 the United States Congress took action on a bill which helped Napa Valley vintners immeasurably, as well as those through-out the state. Considering the glut of grapes and wine on the market, the assistance could not have come at a more opportune time. The bill permitted the establishment of bonded warehouses for the storage of Brandy, that is Brandy could be made from excess wine and then stored without payment of federal taxes until the Brandy was sold.

Brandy was the perfect answer to every cellar filled with wine and no one to buy the product. Brandy could be distilled from the wine (five gallons of wine will produce roughly one proof gallon of Brandy) and kept almost indefinitely, especially if the price of Brandy happened to be too low. Since Brandy increased in price with its age, this was comparable to putting money into a savings bank. After 1877, many Napa Valley wineries added distilleries to their operations.

Three years before the Bonded Warehouse Act was passed another event occurred in the Napa Valley which in the long run, was to have a far greater impact on local viticulture. This was the establishment of a weekly newspaper in St. Helena, the *Star*, which from the first became a leading exponent in California for the cause of winemaking.

The *Star*'s founding editor was DeWitt C. Lawrence and the first issue published September 25, 1874 was sold for a twenty dollar gold piece to one "A. Clock, Esq." Almost nothing is known of Lawrence, even his reason for starting the newspaper except that he was more than likely an itinerant printer, one of hundreds that roamed the American West in the gold and silver mining era.

Less than eighteen months later, the *Star* was purchased by Charles Gardner and he not only rivalled Charles Menefee of Napa City in producing a word portrait of valley agriculture and wine making, he quickly became one of the chief spokesmen for local vintners. Gardner, energetic, almost to a fault sometimes, attended the meetings of viticultural organizations and then wrote and published lengthy accounts of the meetings, visited wineries and asked for personal opinions on the future of the industry. By the end of the decade, major newspapers in San Francisco were reprinting accounts from the *Star* on many wine subjects.

Gardner was born in Illinois in 1843, which made him thirty-three years old when he settled in St. Helena. He had been trained in the practice of law, being admitted to the bar in California at Los Angeles in 1870. Gardner never mentioned in his newspaper how or why he came to the Napa Valley, except that he had worked for a short period of time on the *Napa Register*. Soon he planted his own vineyards near St. Helena.

Many publications copied liberally from the *Star*, often without giving credit which irritated Gardner considerably. The *Pacific Coast Wine and Liquor Herald* in San Francisco relied on Gardner for many of its Napa Valley statistics and paid him this compliment in October 1876:

> The *St. Helena Star* is a strong, steadfast, and judicious advocate of the best material interests of Napa County, each successive number teeming with information of a local nature that is valuable to its readers everywhere. Its issue of Sept. 24th contains some carefully prepared statistics of the wine product of St. Helena, and a vivid description of its most important wine cellars.

Every year thereafter, for nearly two and a half decades, the *Star* carefully listed each winery in the entire Napa Valley (when the fall crush was completed) along with the amount of wine produced. That column was widely reprinted and in itself resulted in a vast amount of publicity for Napa's wine industry.

When the book *Illustrations of Napa County* was published two years later, the publishers acknowledged that they had borrowed liberally from the columns of the *Star*. Three years later when the publishers of the *San Francisco Call* newspaper compiled a guide to the state, *California As It Is*, Gardner wrote the chapter on Napa County. His bias toward wine was barely disguised in this statement:

> **Productions.**
> The great product of the county—and almost the only increasing one—is wine. A brief review of the others will tend to a consideration of this. The latest county statistics are the Assessor's of 1877, and the grain yield showed therein is probably as large as it has been since, or ever will be.

Gardner acknowledged the county had produced 545,000 bushels of wheat but neglected to state that they came from more than 25,000 acres. The total acres devoted to grapes was a mere 3,360! Some writers traveling through the valley barely noticed the vineyards in the 1870s, whereas Gardner had eyes only, it would seem, for the grape.

Publications like *California As It Is*, printed in a handy 5½ x 8½ inch size, with a full color cover (somewhat gaudy but eye-catching nevertheless), had wide circulation throughout the eastern portion of the nation and no doubt even in Europe. The counties are not listed alphabetically but seem to be arranged in some sort of ranking by economic development. Napa County follows Sonoma County, about one-third of the way into the 178 page book. The final five paragraphs which Gardner wrote under the heading "Productions," deal almost exclusively with wine and the grape. There is the possibility that some readers might come to the conclusion that the soil here was, indeed, best suited to vineyard cultivation.

Clarence Smith and Wallace Elliott's *Illustrations of Napa County*, published in 1878 brought to the outside world for the first time, lithographic reproductions of many of the major vineyards and wineries of Napa County. Charles Krug was given (or he paid for the insertion) a double-page spread with the winery and neat rows of wine barrels or casks, clearly shown. C.J. Dyer was the artist. He may have had some eyesight problems for he shows an "1868" founding date on the main winery building, but nowhere to be seen is the original straw-roofed winery. Krug's original winery, completed in 1861, may have burned in the fire of August 1874.

The dominance of viticulture and wine making in the county might again be wrongly surmised by looking at the Smith and Elliott book. There are fifteen lithographs showing farms which included vineyards and/or wineries. Several of these cover double-pages, such as the wineries of Charles Krug, the Beringer brothers or Terrell Grigsby. Less than half a dozen lithographs depict the growing or harvesting of wheat, and most of these are in the Berryessa region.

Shortly before the artists for Smith and Elliott (of Oakland, California) began tramping about the Napa Valley for the best views, Miss Hannah Millard of San Jose visited the region to "faithfully" reproduce by watercolors, some of the local grape clusters and leaves. She had been selected by the State Vinicultural Society to undertake watercolor studies for a book of reproductions to be published by the Society. H. W. Crabb was one of three committee members to oversee the project with Charles Krug in charge of negotiating the details and cost of publication.*

---

*The Society originally planned to publish 500 copies of the book. It is doubtful this goal was met for a hundred years later in 1978, the book had its first republication, with only a half dozen copies of the original known to exist. The price of an original was placed at twenty-five thousand dollars by one book dealer. See *Grapes and Grape Vines of California*, San Francisco: Edward Bosqui & Co., 1877.

Gardner at the *Star* saw the new book coming at precisely the right time for the vineyards of France were being devastated by the phylloxera. With the French industry nearly gone, the great wine men of Europe could come to California. He also saw the book bringing a good deal of attention to the wine industry, attention it needed if the current wine glut was to be alleviated.

> The association should be assisted and encouraged by all the winegrowers in the State, and we know of no enterprise so worthy the assistance and encouragement of the State itself.

added Gardner.

Gardner also appears to have been the author of forty-eight pages on "Viticulture in Napa County" in the *History of Napa and Lake Counties, California*. Published in San Francisco by Slocum, Bowen & Co., in 1881, it has over nine hundred pages with Lyman L. Palmer credited on the Preface page as the historian-in-charge. Gardner's contribution to the book is acknowledged in the Preface but not defined.

In addition to a lengthy background study of grapes and wine making in California since the Catholic missions were founded in 1769, there are pages of statistics on production and long lists of vineyardists—just the kind of material Gardner liked to gather and publish frequently in his own newspaper. No other single individual had such an excellent overview of the county or valley's developing wine industry, by virtue of the fact that he wrote about it constantly. Even Charles Krug probably did not visit every winery, at least once a year, as Gardner did to gather his material for the weekly *Star*.

One of the subjects carefully avoided by Gardner whenever he wrote for publication outside the valley, was the use of Chinese laborers in Napa vineyards. He did not side-step the subject in the columns of the *Star* but had to tread carefully when the prospect arose of attracting the sandlot rioters of San Francisco to the Napa Valley.

Unemployed white workers in San Francisco, and perhaps some laborers who preferred not to work but enjoyed a good public fracas, began congregating in open sandlots south of Market Street where they listened daily to anti-Chinese rhetoric. Out of this came the Workingmen's Party in California, which by 1878-79, was strong enough to elect city mayors, legislators and rewrite the state constitution. Several sections of the constitution with strong anti-Chinese language, were shortly declared illegal by the Supreme Court.

Chinese workers began moving into the vineyards and wineries of Napa Valley in large numbers by the late 1870s, in part because they worked for lower wages than white laborers but principally because they were more reliable. C. A. Menefee put the problem in perspective in his *Sketch Book* when he wrote:

One of the most important questions presented to the agriculturist is that of labor. The farmers frequently find it impossible to get laborers to perform their work. A great portion of the labor employed during the vintage in picking and shipping grapes is Chinese. People are not favorably disposed to these Asiatics, but often find themselves reduced to the necessities of accepting these or none.

There is no State in the Union where the laborer has so easy a time as in California, but this very fact has an injurious effect upon the laborer. It is harder here to find good and trustworthy laborers than elsewhere. Few think farther than the best means of shirking responsible labor, of getting the largest sum and making the least return therefore. Many, after the week's work is over, stroll away to dens of vice, and crime, to come away, by no means benefited (pp. 217-218).

Menefee was not alone in such editorial opinion, the same strong anti-labor statements could be found in the columns of many weekly newspapers. One of the worst problems in the 1870s resulted whenever news of a new gold or silver strike spread through the countryside. The white laborers would abandon hoe or spade in the middle of a vineyard and take off for the mountains. The Chinese who had good jobs, rarely did this. (Unemployed Chinese in the cities succumbed to the temptations of a gold strike, just like the white males.)

Napa Valley newspapers were not adverse to carrying advertisements for the Chinese labor exchanges. "CHINESE HELP FURNISHED" reads one ad in the *Star* of July 27, 1877, "San Sing, at Ginger's China Store, St. Helena, will furnish all kinds of help, for cooking, railroad work, chopping wood, etc., at Yountville, Oakville, Rutherford, St. Helena, Calistoga, Pine Flat [Sonoma County], or any of the surrounding country. Good [work] at cheap prices."

In San Francisco, "Crosett's & Co." furnished workers, although their advertisements in Napa Valley publications left out the word "Chinese." Since their address was 623 Clay Street, right in the heart of Chinatown, the type of worker provided was clearly understood. "Quong Goon Loong," dealer in "China goods" in St. Helena's large Chinatown "across the bridge," was another clearinghouse for vineyard labor. If Quong was typical of his time, all wages were paid directly to him, then after deducting his fee, and advances for food, *he paid* his fellow Chinese whatever remained.

The Chinese pursued a wide variety of tasks in the Napa Valley besides vineyard work. When the first road between Calistoga and Pope Valley's quicksilver mines was opened in late 1873, the *Napa Reporter* could record that "twenty-seven Chinamen and three white men" were doing all of the work. John Lewelling used Chinese to build fences around his vineyards and fields but lost a large pile of fence posts when Chinese workers burning grass, set fire to the fence posts. Simpson Thompson at Soscol used Chinese in his nursery, losing his work force when he reduced their wages to five dollars a week, but he found replacements without any problem.[III.15]

The Chinese were used to dig tunnels into the rock hillside for C. Lemme when he built his winery west of St. Helena in 1877. The *Star* of June 8 reported: "A Chinaman was killed yesterday at Mr. Lemme's place near town, by the caving in of a bank where they were cutting into the hillside for a cellar."

They were used too, in the construction of the huge Occidental winery in 1878 of Terrell Grigsby on the east side of the valley, a half dozen miles north of Napa City. Grigsby used Chinese workers almost exclusively on the ranch for cutting hay, harvesting grain and whatever other tasks were needed on a daily basis. Grigsby, however, paid a dear price for his actions. Not long after the winery was completed, his barn was burned down by someone who left a note warning further fires would follow if he did not discharge his Chinese workers.[III.16] Fires broke out mysteriously in wheat fields of other farmers in the valley and for several years it was an unpleasant hazard to be lived with for anyone who used the Chinese.[III.17]

It was not long before the Workingmen's Party had organized a Napa chapter and in June 1878 the famous orator of the Party, Dennis Kearney of San Francisco, came to Napa for a picnic. (It was Kearney who finally convinced a group of sandlotters in San Francisco to march up Nob Hill and set fire to the mansions of Mark Hopkins, Stanford and other wealthy men. The police prevented any fires from actually breaking out, but on numerous other occasions Kearney's spellbinding speeches set off riots in many cities in California.)

All of Kearney's oratory had little effect, at least after 1880, on the wholesale hiring of Chinese in the vineyards and in the wineries of Napa Valley. They soon constituted the majority of all such workers, perhaps governing 75 to 80 percent of the labor force in all of California's vine growing and wine producing counties.[III.18]

The Chinese found employment in another aspect of Napa County's economic development which was burgeoning too, in the 1870s. This was in the mining and reduction of cinnabar ore into the metal quicksilver. No appreciable amounts of gold or silver had been mined in the county up until that date, but quicksilver gave the local residents some reason to hold up their collective egos whenever California's mineral wealth was discoursed upon or described in print. Hundreds of thousands of dollars in quicksilver wealth was produced in the county, yet no single person or even group of individuals seems to have become what might be classed as "wealthy," from it.

The first cinnabar discoveries came in the 1850s with new ledges periodically uncovered in the 1870s. This prompted great excitement for a few weeks, then faded into oblivion. When a major discovery of the ore was made at the Geysers, in nearby Sonoma County in the summer of 1873, the resulting quick-silver fever spread into Napa. Much like the silver mining fever engendered by the Comstock lode in Nevada, wealthy San Franciscans by the score wanted to invest in this newest bonanza, or what they hoped would be a sure new source of wealth.

Pope Valley was the major location for most of the Napa mines, although others were opened at widely scattered localities. The Phoenix mine was first located in 1861 in Pope Valley and was operated without much success until the early 1870s. Up to forty-five men were employed at one time in the mine. Many woodcutters were needed to supply the furnaces needed to heat the red cinnabar clay to the point where the quicksilver ran free. Anywhere from fifty to seventy-five thousand pounds of quicksilver were produced annually, returning forty to fifty thousand dollars to the mine owners.

It was expensive to operate a quicksilver mine, most being located high in the hills and far from nearby towns or railroads which could bring in the necessary furnaces, boilers, condensers, hoses, lumber and other necessities. Few mines survived longer than a half dozen years, the price of quicksilver always fluctuating dramatically and the cinnabar ledges were rarely very extensive.

One unusual mine was the Summit mine located in the Mayacamas mountains west of Yountville. It was discovered by the

Whitton brothers, Green and John. The Whittons sold their rights to the mine for $45,000* in the early 1870s to J. Pershbaker with this description in Menefee's *Sketch Book*:

> The claim is very extensive, and there are attached to it 160 acres of timberland. The Summit is one of the most promising quicksilver claims in the county. The surface prospect is very extensive. The surface ore is found on the west side of the mountain for a distance of over 1,000 feet, and can from its favorable position be obtained to a great depth, at moderate expense, without tunneling or blasting. The underground work consists of three main tunnels with seven branches. The main working tunnel is 400 feet in length. The mine is worked upon two levels connected by a shaft. There is a substantial railway track in the main tunnel and chutes from the upper to the lower level . . .

Pershbaker built new roads from the mines to the furnaces, about a mile to the east; the Whitton brothers transported all of the ore by mule to the furnace site. The mine, incidentally, employed twenty-four white workers and eight Chinese. Several miles north of the Summit was the Oakville Quicksilver Mine which at its peak employed thirty Chinese and half that number of white miners.

The quicksilver mining "era" in Napa County is generally thought of as occurring in the 1870s and 1880s, but a number of the mines continued operations well into the next century. Other mines included the New Burlington, west of Oakville; Red Hill mine, Pope Valley; Silver Bow, Pope Valley; Overland mine, near the Summit mine west of Yountville; Mutual Quicksilver mine, Oakville; Valley mine, Pope Valley; and a half dozen mining companies which seemed to take turns buying each other out or operating mines. Much of the money made in quicksilver in the county was in such paper transactions, the last stockholders being left with empty pockets.

One quicksilver mine which generated a great deal of excitement in St. Helena was the "Esther," located two miles southwest of town. It was discovered by a gentleman named Langely who was digging a well by hand when the ground suddenly darkened to a deep red color. The first assay carried out on the soil in San Francisco suggested a return of forty-eight dollars per ton. When tunneling

---

*It is doubtful the Whittons were paid the full amount before the mine closed down. This was the pattern in many similar transactions.

began, the ore quickly turned much richer and St. Helena had its own quicksilver mine.[III.19]

At one point the quicksilver excitement even pushed the news of wine making off the front page of the *Star*, right in the height of the crush. The issue of October 29, 1874 carried this story:

Cinnabar and Silver Excitement. Well it has come to pass. They have it; we have it; everybody has it—the fever we mean—not that of the aches and shakes, but of the cinnabar, silver and gold.

It is raging, the acme, the tip-toe of an old fashioned '49 excitement is reached. We look for depopulation and population. By depopulation we refer to the amount of stampeders from town, to the mountains three miles East and West of us and by population to THE RUSH, that is just commencing from other parts. During the past week the excitement has been so furious as to start prospectors out with lamps, and the cold drenching rain had no effect in quenching the fire of the thirst for the almighty rock that produces THE ALMIGHTY DOLLAR.

Anyone who would think that the valley's vintners were still crushing grapes instead of prospecting for cinnabar under such stimulating conditions, would be quite wrong. Many of the investors in the various mines or miners themselves were well-known wine makers as this story demonstrates, under date of March 18, 1875:

According to notice a miner's meeting was held at Jacob Schram's on the 8th day of March at 9 a.m. for the purpose of organizing a mining district. Joseph Mecklenburg, J. Schram, C. T. McEachran, Peter Conter, John Head and L. Beyersdorf, assembled at the appointed place and time and organized the miners meeting by electing McEachran, President.

Although the quicksilver excitement continued to renew itself in sporadic bursts of enthusiasm, the vintage was never again affected quite like the year of 1874. A few days of digging for an elusive ledge of red clay, which might disappear with the next shovel full of earth, usually sent most vintners and grape growers back home, satisfied. Making wine was never such hard work and at the end of the day, instead of a shovel full of useless dirt, the result was a cask of new wine. There was an almost constant debate in the Napa Valley over what varieties of grapes to plant, whether for wine making, table use or raisin production. The wishful thinking seemed to be that one variety could fill all purposes. Many vine growers had the experience of the farmer near Rutherford who admitted to planting forty different types, then spent years trying to select the best, never satisfied with his choices.[III.20]

One vineyardist wrote to the *Star* in November 1875 that he found the Black Malvaisia to be the best grape:

> We have tried to get all the points possible, on the subject, pro and con—and we would advise all vine growers to put in the Black Malvaisia. Our reasons are these. It will make No. 1 Red wine and it has been proved by our young wine maker, Mr. Richard Heath, to make a No. 1 White Wine—Now if the wine market calls for a white wine, you can make it from your Malvaisia, and on the other hand, if Red wine be the saleable article, you can make a first class article from the same grape.

Judging from the number of vines planted in the entire county to that grape, most people agreed with the writer. Just a year earlier, someone who liked the non-de-plume "Vitis" (there was one for nearly every weekly published in the state) agreed, and recommended as well the Zinfandel, Burger, Muscat and Chasselas, plus the Rieslings.[III.21]

The Mission continued to be the most popular grape among all growers, in every county of the state, plus such varieties as the White Muscat of Alexandria, Flame Tokay, Black Malaga, Black Hamburg, Rose of Peru, Royal Muscadine, White Malaga, Red Frontignac and several varieties of Chasselas. Some of these doubled as table grapes, wine grapes or for the making of raisins. Curiously, cuttings of the great wine grapes from the Bordeaux or Burgogne regions of France had been brought to San Jose in the early 1850s and planted extensively. Since there was no market for these shy bearers because quantity was what the grower needed, the price of grapes per ton was nearly equal.

A farm of thirty-six acres in size, with two-thirds of the land planted to grapes, sold in the central Napa Valley for $6,500 in the late seventies. This included dwelling houses, barns and a well. That worked out to $180 per acre.

One individual who was planting the finer varieties from France was Henry Crabb of Oakville. In the latter part of the decade he set out 36,000 vines on thirty-six acres, giving him 1,000 vines to the acre. This was the practice rather routinely followed in Los Angeles but not in the San Francisco region. His vines included "Burgundy" (no further specification given), "Charbaneau [Charbono?]" and "Tintoria [Teinturier]." He would shortly have more varieties of grapes growing in his Oakville experimental vineyards than anyone in California.[III.22]

One reason most growers declined to follow Crabb's lead was that wine grapes simply were not in large demand, and neither, for that matter, was California wine. To survive, viticulturists had to diversify, and raisin grapes could bring in more income, for example, than the wine types.

John Lewelling of St. Helena was considered the local pioneer raisin grower and producer, at least production in commercial quantities. His first raisins were offered for sale in 1872 in fifty, twenty-pound boxes. They were Muscats, dipped in boiling lye water, then dried on scaffolds rather than in the sun. The experiment worked well, the raisins bringing 12½ cents a pound in San Francisco, some as high as 14 cents.

Lewelling's main grape was the Malaga, although he used Feher Szagos, Muscats, Malvoisie and even something he called "La Falle." In 1876 he began shipping raisins to New York, probably the first such shipment ever sent from the valley.

There were three other major producers of raisins in the valley by mid-decade. James Crewey, who was located just south of Lewelling and like him, first dried his grapes on hillside scaffolds. He could report that early rains did little damage to the lye treated grapes. J. H. Post and J. M. Cushing depended more upon artificial drying.

The *San Francisco Bulletin* reported that by 1876 the United States was the world's largest consumer of raisins, taking about half of all those exported from Spain, for example.

"The California raisin producer has a market in his own country that will take all he is ever likely to produce," stated the *Bulletin* and the growers of Napa Valley did not miss the point.[III.23]

About this same time, a German immigrant named John Weinberger introduced the concept of selling just plain grape syrup with a Napa Valley label.

Weinberger had been a grape grower since the early part of the decade and suffered the indignity once too often, apparently, of having no one who would buy his grapes. In 1876 he built his own winery but then went his neighbors one better by ordering from Cincinnati, Ohio the various copper kettles and other equipment needed to make grape syrup from fresh crushed grape juice. The process was described in detail in the *Star:*

Juice from Mission grapes is expressed in the ordinary way, a ton yielding about 120 gallons fit for syrup making. After the grapes have been through the crusher, the juice is drained off, all that will run freely, when the pumice is thrown in a press tub, and all the juice that will run white pressed out—about a couple of hours pressing will accomplish this. When the juice begins to be colored, it should no longer be used, and all the rest of the pumice may be thrown back into tanks and fermented for common wine, or sent to the still, or fed to hogs, for which latter purpose it is very good.

The juice then ready, should, before it undergoes any fermenting process—that is, within a day,—be placed in what is called a clarifying tank, holding not less than 150 to 200 gallons, and made of planished (tinned) copper. The copper is to enable it to be heated, and the tinning to keep the acid of the juice, when cooled, from forming verdigris.

This clarifying tank is over a fire, and the juice is heated up just enough to bring it to a boil. Just before this point a process is gone through to neutralize the acid and separate the starch (or albumen) contained in the juice. This consists in the use of lime.

Three pounds of "unslacked" lime was mixed well with a gallon of water and a small portion of the now hot grape juice, then dumped quickly into the clarifying tank. The natural starch in the hot grape juice separated immediately to the top, like "particles in curdling milk." This was quickly skimmed off the top and discarded.

The final step in the process of making Napa Valley grape syrup required pumping the hot grape juice to "Cook's Patented Evaporator," which came from Cincinnati and cost Weinberger $163.75. It was in essence, a table nine feet long by four feet wide and about four inches deep, divided into many small compartments. The juice enters the table, runs over the heated surface and some evaporates as the compartments are alternatively opened and closed, to move the juice along. Two hundred fifty gallons of juice could be processed in twelve hours, each three gallons of juice giving one gallon of syrup.[III.24]

One side process which came rather unexpectedly, was the formation of grape sugar. It was available in at least one St. Helena store by Christmas, '76, although the store's proprietor warned it was not candy but made a very useable sugar for cooking purposes and sold for considerably less money. The sugar resulted from utilizing too high heat on the evaporating table.

Two years after Weinberger began his grape syrup enterprise, he constructed a separate stone building just for that purpose and sold his entire output of 1,500 gallons without having to peddle it from store to store. Stories of the unique syrup plant north of St. Helena were published in various California magazines and Weinberger soon found he had more competition than he might have wished. Nearly every new idea was regarded by some individuals as the road to a fortune, especially if they had missed it digging for gold or silver.

This was an era for much experimentation, especially since so few knowledgeable individuals were available to give expert advice. Frank Schleiter of Napa decided to try making Champagne in the fall of 1874. Press reports called the end product remarkably like that beverage made in France. Whether this qualifies as the first real Champagne made in the Napa Valley is questionable, especially since he used the Muscat grape, a fine table grape but one with usually too much sugar for Champagne.[III.25]

> Dr. Crane is just now engaged in an enterprise that is new to this part of the country; the building of a house especially for the manufacture of sherry wine,

reported the *Star* in early January 1877. Sherry was one of the most popular wines in California, as well as in the eastern states. The newspaper erred in crediting Crane with being the pioneer Sherry maker in Napa Valley, that honor went to two Portuguese immigrants, John Ramos and Joseph Mathews. The process also was not the true solera-oven method followed in Xeres, Spain where Sherry (an Anglicized word) originated.

Crane was the first to make Sherry in the St. Helena area, his oven being a stone building 28 x 32 feet "with 16 foot thick walls" (which surely was a misprint in the newspaper!). A furnace provided a somewhat constant temperature of 150 degrees for the baking of wine into Sherry. Only eleven months after the Sherry oven was opened, Crane sold his production to S. Lachman & Company of San Francisco.

The first Sherry-type wine produced in Napa Valley came about at William Woodward's ranch northeast of Napa City. The *Napa County Reporter* described the process (similar to Crane's) as early as November 1872:

> We next crossed the road, and entered a house containing 7,500 gallons of that never to be forgotten sherry. One end of this building is the bake oven, 17 x 30 feet, which was filled with pipes of the new-made-sherry, and in which it has to be baked for six months

a fire being kept up under it, day and night. John opened the oven door for us, and we saw the casks inside with the 'green' oozing out of their seams. This 'green' is just like the grease one can find on the hubs of a buggy wheel, and it is the purging of this stuff from the Sherry by its six months' 'heated term' that makes it not only so palatable, but frees it from that horrible adjunct to so many vintner's vintages, the headache.

The "John" referred to here was John Ramos, but another worker present was Joseph Mathews who later produced Sherry in the basement of his stone and brick home in Napa City. In 1882 he constructed the Mathews or Lisbon winery on Brown Street and added a Sherry-baking oven.*

The terror of the grape grower, spring frost, struck the valley twice during the decade of the 1870s. Both frosts occurred during the month of April, resulting in severe damage to vineyards over most of Northern California. There was one major difference, however, between the '73 and '77 frosts, in that some growers began to understand the use of smoke pots and the role heavy layers of smoke could play in keeping the cold away from the tender vines.

Gottlieb Groezinger of Yountville must have read of the experiment of John Sigrist's neighbor in using smoke to combat the frost in '73 but with no beneficial result. Groezinger made elaborate preparations in April 1877 to fight the cold temperatures, his workmen setting out 200 piles of "combustible" materials. As the thermometer moved slowly downward and the danger point was finally reached, he ordered one pile of flammables after another set fire. A newspaper account said the smoke was so dense that long after the sun came up, "it could not for a long time penetrate it."

In the 1870s, any geographical description of Napa County or Valley inevitably went to some length to describe the special relation-

---

*The winery functioned intermittently to the 1950s and has recently been reopened, the Sherry oven rebuilt as a restaurant. Many in the wine industry did not regard this quick-method as real Sherry. Charles Wetmore wrote in a "Treatise Concerning the Principles Governing the Production of Distinct Wines ...," published in 1891 by the State Viticultural Commissioners: "The so-called sherry taste, ... is greatly increased and hastened by subjecting white, or even red wine, to a high temperature in specially arranged baking houses, called here 'sherry houses.' Such wines, suitably fortified and agreeably sweetened, are the ordinary sherries ... The peculiar qualities of genuine natural Spanish sherries, are, however, not even approximated by such methods."

ships that existed. *The Resources of California* newspaper provided this account of Napa in October 1874:

> NAPA VALLEY is the largest and by far the most important of all the county valleys. It is some 35 miles in length from the southern boundary of the county to its head, three miles above Calistoga. In width it varies from one to five miles, and at the junction of the numerous small valleys which join it from the mountain range on either hand it often swells to a greater width. Berryessa, Pope and Brown valleys are next in importance, and may be considered tributary to the main valley, as they all have their outlets through the mountains into it. Of the varied productions of Napa county, grape culture is by far the most important. . . .

There was so much public confusion as to the precise boundaries of Napa Valley that Gardner in the *Star* at last felt duty bound to explain it in some detail, and this peculiar story appeared January 16, 1883:

> WHAT IS NAPA VALLEY? 'Inquirer,' San Francisco, writes, 'To solve a question, please kindly state in your valuable paper what portion of Napa county is known as Napa Valley, and which are its boundaries?'
>
> ANSWER. Napa Valley is that portion of Napa county which is included in the Valley of that name. It heads above Calistoga, about Mt. St. Helena, (at the Northern boundary of the county), and runs in a Southwesterly direction, almost to the Southern line of the county, below the City of Napa. It is about 35 miles long, by one to 5 miles wide, and contains about 87½ square miles. The area of the whole county being about 800 square miles, it will be readily seen what proportion the one bears to the other in this respect.

To understand the ratio in size of the many valleys of the county, the square miles of land in each helps clarify the situation: Napa Valley, 87½ square miles; Berryessa, 10¼; Pope, 8; Chiles, 5; Wooden, 3; and Conn, 3 square miles.*

Conn Valley especially is rather difficult to separate from the larger Napa Valley, being in essence an arm of it but since historic times has been given the full status of a "valley." It lies in the hills forming the eastern flank of the Napa Valley, almost directly east of the town of St. Helena. Grapes had been grown there since the boom

---

*A large portion of the arable land of Berryessa Valley is now covered with the waters of Lake Berryessa, formed when Montecello Dam was completed in 1957.

years of the decade's opening, M. Kaltenbach being the first vineyardist. Kaltenbach was also the first wine maker though by mid-decade Everett Musgrave was producing about ten times as much wine as Kaltenbach's yearly five hundred gallons.[III.26]

A year later Fred Metzner began the third winery in the valley, a small structure capable of producing only a few more gallons than Musgrave. In the last year of the 1870s Louis Corthay built Conn Valley's first winery of any size, a 28 x 45 foot building capable of holding 75,000 gallons of wine. The first story was of rock, the upper of wood.

Chiles Valley, like Conn just a few miles to the north, is located in the folds of the hills on the eastern side of Napa Valley. The principal entrance then was a road just east of Rutherford which wound its way gradually to the higher elevation of Chiles. The low and irregular hills which separated Chiles from Conn or Pope Valley, made it rather difficult to ascertain exactly when the traveler had left one valley and entered another. Local residents did not feel that way at all and were intensely proud of the distinct place they held in the county's geography and history.

Col. Joseph B. Chiles arrived in Napa County in the early 1840s, long before gold had been discovered in California. He was granted the Catacula ranch by Mexican officials in 1844 which included what soon became "Chiles Valley." After 1844 when he constructed a much needed grist mill, farmers for many miles around regularly traveled to his farm to grind corn and wheat.

There was a small vineyard in Chiles Valley by '77 and it likely had been there for decades, dating to the 1840s when Chiles built his home. Alfred Boothe, a local resident gave this brief description of the valley in June 1877:

> The whole valley is about eight miles long, by an average width of half a mile, and contains 20 or more families, with two schools. The well known Chiles mills are situated about the center, and makes a market for all the wheat raised in the vicinity. These mills are among the oldest in the State, built in 1848.*

The *St. Helena Star*, from which this story was taken, ran another brief description of Chiles Valley in the same issue which shows how

---

*The Chiles Grist Mill site is now a State Historical Landmark. The mill is believed to have been erected in the years 1845-46.

differently two farmers viewed the development of agriculture in their area. C. D. Hughes told the editor:

> The canyon proper, from Dinning's up to the mill, a distance of seven miles, contains about ten ranches. . . . They are mostly devoted to grain, stock raising and vineyards. Ewbank has the biggest piece of grain, about 25 or 30 acres, besides hay land. Kaltenbach and Ewbank have the most vineyards, about 5 acres each.
> . . . There is no wine cellar yet in the canyon, though Kaltenbach talks of one and will undoubtedly have one. He is a thorough wine man.

The final sentence indicates that Kaltenbach, who had a small wine operation in Conn Valley, was planning to build a winery in Chiles. Chiles, Kaltenbach and Ewbank were growing grapes by '77 but no wine was yet being produced.

Pope Valley was the best known of Napa's tributary valleys because of the quicksilver mines which began operating there about the time of the American Civil War. Many San Franciscans had traded in Pope Valley mining stocks without being too sure of how one traveled to the mines. The valley lies east and northeastward from St. Helena and could be reached by two roads; the road up over Howell Mountain and back down, one of the steepest in all of California's coastal region. A second road could be taken from Calistoga to the valley.

Pope Valley has a higher elevation than the lands in Napa Valley, receives slightly less rainfall and was home for many centuries, to hundreds of Indians. George Yount told in the *Hesperian* magazine of his difficulties with the Pope Valley Indians, having to engage them directly in battle on at least one occasion. William Pope obtained a land grant for the area in 1841 from the Mexican government but it was Col. Joseph Chiles who planted the first vines in the year 1851.[III.27]

William Haug began the first modest winery (for which documentation exists) in the valley in 1880, producing one thousand gallons. Considering the numbers of miners employed by the quicksilver mines and the fact that cinnabar was being dug out of the hillsides many years before, Haug's winery may not be the earliest.

The *San Francisco Call* in January 1884 carried a brief description of the valley, with special emphasis on the vine potential:

The hillsides are well adapted to the growth of the vine, but viticulture, which has become one of the chief industries in other portions of Napa County, is as yet in its infancy in Pope Valley. It is, however, enjoying the attention of some who have been and are preparing to plant vineyards of considerable extent, among the number being the farm of the late Dr. Maxwell, which has a vineyard of choice vines under cultivation; also T. H. Ink is preparing to plant a hundred acres of vineyard the coming spring. . . . The nearest railroad at present is at St. Helena, eighteen miles distant, where grain and all kinds of farm produce are hauled.

For some time in the mid 1870s, St. Helena and Calistoga were rivals for the Pope Valley trade with the outcome dependent upon a good road. Gardner, at the *Star*, rather frequently urged St. Helenans to build a good road over Howell Mountain to connect with the road maintained by Pope Valley residents. Most of the time his urgent pleas went unheeded.

There were three general stores at different locations in the mid-70s in Pope Valley, a blacksmith shop and miles and miles of wheat fields. The wheat was hauled in sacks on very sturdy wagons pulled by six to ten pairs of horses or mules. From Pope Valley it was a very precipitous climb up over Howell Mountain, then a steep descent on the other side to the railroad in St. Helena. Old-timers recall it was a toss-up as to which part of the journey was the most difficult, the heavy wagon of wheat being potentially very dangerous on the descent if the braking system failed. Grapes and puncheons of wine shortly became a common sight on the road, as well.

There were few vineyards planted as yet on Howell Mountain, although Edwin Angwin was being urged to open a resort considering the natural beauty of his farm:

We all agree that Mr. Angwin has a beautiful place situated in a little valley on the top of the mountains, the land is very rich, an abundance of water, mountain springs, running streams and the healthiest place in the county. Mr. Angwin should make of it a resort for health and pleasure for others and profit to himself.[III.28]

Berryessa Valley was totally devoid of vines in this period, as most of the land being farmed, was devoted to wheat. Berryessa had a much more serious problem than Pope Valley when it came to its semi-remote location. A local correspondent named simply "Mallie" once described the travel situation for anyone who called Berryessa home:

The export and import business troubles us not a little. Along those drowned plains in the lower valleys, our neighbors wishing to visit San Francisco or go back East, can step aboard a train without any disagreeable prelude to their journey.

It is very different with us; we have 'to wait for the wagon' or about the same thing, the rumbling old stage-coach, which is worse, and then be driven and jolted and mutilated over a road of thirty miles that just begs description. Webster hasn't coined the word descriptive of the condition of the Napa grade during the long and rainy weather. And as for the Win-ters' road, its condition has been impassable and the Berryessa people are perfectly disgusted with it. . . .

During the long rainy season we live here 'hermetically sealed,' even the schools were closed, but with the appearance of spring, two schools have opened in the valley, and another soon to commence.[III.29]

Calistoga, like the outlying valleys of the county, was often over-looked in all the viticultural excitement around St. Helena and between there and Napa City. The oversight could be traced in part to the lack of an aggressive newspaper, like the *Star*, to publicize the town.

A weekly newspaper was founded in Calistoga in 1871 which ran rather fitfully for two years. A second journal was established in 1874 only to close after a few months. In '76, *The Calistogian* appeared, with the owner, J. H. Upton, carting off the presses to Hollister within the year. J. L. Multer finally remedied this unhappy situation with *The Independent Calistogian* which debuted the day after Christmas 1877. Multer more closely followed Gardner's enthusiasm for local events than any of his predecessors.

An explanation in part for the comings and goings of journalists-printers at Calistoga was the economy of the town. It had gone through a recession with the collapse of the fortunes of Samuel Brannan and the closing of his health resort. A Sacramento savings bank held title to all of Brannan's property. The hotels and bunga-lows, where the rich of San Francisco once promenaded, were closed and unkempt. "The 'Springs,' so long the glory of Calistoga are now, we are sorry to say, in a sadly dilapidated condition," stated one newspaper account.[III.30] But the town was being put back on its feet by quicksilver, or rather the earnings from supplying quicksilver mines. Two new hotels had just been built, the Magnolia and Cosmopolitan. The town's first brick structure was under construc-tion on Lincoln Avenue by J. B. Brown.

The nearby Petrified Forest was of so much interest to scientists and the public alike that a "Prof. James" of San Francisco spent a week making stereopticon slides. He planned to show the slides of the unusual forest at the Centennial Exposition of the United States at Philadelphia. There was a firm belief in Calistoga that this would bring many visitors to the town and might become an attraction some day rivalling the Geysers. After the Brannan debacle, the town needed some new focus of public attention.

Several small vineyards had been planted near Calistoga in recent years, but the most ambitious project was that of Judge Evy, three miles north of town. Dr. R. Garnet had recently taken over the vines, which included Missions and foreign varieties. Evy had even erected a small wine cellar and made small amounts of wine, but Garnet did not continue the practice.

Despite the fact that wine making and viticulture were to be found scattered across the length and breadth of Napa County in the 1870s, the center of the industry was clearly in the town of St. Helena. No other portion of the county gave itself so completely to the grape. Editor Gardner in the *Star* put it precisely in those terms when he wrote an editorial called "Our Chief Interest" and ran it in his March 11, 1876 issue:

> The chief interest of St. Helena is the vine. Her soil and climate are especially adapted to it, years of labor and enormous sums of money have been expended in the pursuit of its culture and attendant industries. It is our great preponderating interest—so much so that to take it out of the calculation we have little else to sell and bring an income.

To back up his statements on this exclusivity, Gardner and friends undertook a private census of the vineyards located in the "upper valley," that region lying north of Oakville and including the "small valleys adjacent to Napa Valley." There were 2,054,000 vines, planted about 700 to the acre or three thousand acres of grapes. Gardner insisted that although the figure of three thousand acres appeared large, he had contacted the vineyard owners for the exact count. He estimated that 150 separate individuals owned vineyards. Gardner concluded:

> Our design now is to call attention to the magnitude of the interest in question, and its importance in revenue, both direct and indirect, to local, State and general governments, which should impose

upon it as little burdens as possible, and in every way foster and
encourage an enterprise that has called to its advancement so large
a share of the energies and resources of our people. . . .

It was not just the acreage in vines that was increasing rapidly
either, for Gardner discovered to his surprise the next year that the
number of wineries had doubled between Calistoga and Oakville.
Where there had been fifteen cellars, now thirty or more could be
counted. Over the succeeding weeks Gardner took his readers on a
tour of these wine cellars beginning with the "dean" of all local
vintners, Charles Krug.[III.31]

Krug's efficient crew had only produced 210,000 gallons of wine
in '77, down one-quarter from the previous year. Jacob Beringer was
still the major domo, the man "who has long graced that position and
whose judgement of the business is among the best in the country."
Across the street, Jacob and his brother Frederick had their first crush
as well, in the Beringer winery—40,000 gallons, "a good amount for
the first year's work."

Besides the old-timers now like Schram, W. W. Lyman, or
Laurent, Gardner discovered a long list of first-time wine producers:
Conrad Wegele, east of Krug; Frank Staetzel, in the hills southwest
of St. Helena; Charles Trumpler, on Pope Street right in St. Helena;
W. P. Weaks, two miles south of town; and at Oakville, two French
immigrants inaugurated the "Brun & Chaix" winery with ten thousand gallons of new wine. Southwest of Oakville, John Benson began
making wine in a small wooden building, but he had plans for a much
larger stone structure a few years hence.*

All of these wineries were producing far below capacity due to
the effects of frost that spring. Especially hard hit were the Napa City
wineries, which either did not own vineyard or owned small acreages.
They were dependent to a much greater extent on grapes purchased
from local farmers.

There were three wine cellars in Napa City, the largest being the
"Uncle Sam," founded by Peter van Bever and W. W. Thompson.
New owners had just taken charge, C. Anduran and another young
Frenchman named Charles Carpy who was foreman. (Some consid-
ered the Uncle Sam the "state-of-the-art" in wine production: an
elevator hoisted the grapes to the roof for crushing. Steam engines

---

*Benson's magnificent stone winery, "Far Niente" was not built until 1885.

everywhere sped up each step in the wine making process, especially for steam-cleaning tanks and pumping the wine from fermenters to storage, etc.)

The cold weather and frost of that spring were not the only reasons so many wineries were falling below previous production figures. Gardner in his survey added a brief footnote in one of his December columns:

> The reason of its diminished product [Uncle Sam Cellar], as well as for that of many others, is that while the vineyards have not of late years increased to any great extent, the cellars have multiplied largely, and divided the grapes among a great many more than there formerly were to take them.

This problem of producer outrunning the supply of grapes had been more or less common since the wine industry began in Napa. For two or three years a flurry of vine planting would result in far too many grapes, then with falling prices or no market at all, vine planting would nearly cease. With the construction of a number of new wine facilities, the price of grapes would start rising, attracting the planting of more vines. Unfortunately, no one seemed able to foresee the needs of the young industry and bring about a more stable pattern of growth.

Giacomo Migliavacca, the Italian immigrant grocer and fish peddler who established his business in Napa City in 1866 and made wine in his back room, finally built a separate winery in 1874. Located near the river at Fifth and Main streets in downtown Napa, he could make about 45,000 gallons of wine annually, relying in part on a huge 5,000 gallon wine tank he had imported from Italy.

Joseph Matthews was Napa's third wine maker, operating a small cellar under his home on Main Street. He had crushed no grapes this year (perhaps because he could find none to buy), but was planning the construction of a large cellar for next year in the city.

Three miles south of Napa City, John McClure founded *his first winery* that year and gave the Carneros a new wine cellar. It was a very small affair, like most cellars in the county, and he crushed enough grapes to make 13,000 gallons of wine.

Charles Lemme was a wealthy San Franciscan, like millionaire John Benson, who became intrigued with raising grapes and then the making of wine. He ignored the rich bottomlands and climbed high into the hills, emulating Jacob Schram and cleared off forty acres of land, planting twenty-five to vines in '74. He brought in Chinese workers to construct his stone winery, 40 x 75 feet, with a vaulted ceiling. He completed only one story of the cellar in time to have his first crush in '76, 5,000 gallons of wine. Lemme had no intention of selling his wine immediately and did not need to because of his wealth. He would age it properly before releasing it for sale in San Francisco.

Although Gardner's wine survey appears to be quite accurate, he did miss two or three wineries operating in the county. For example, William Winter's cellar was not included. This would have been about a half dozen miles west of McClure on the road to Sonoma. Charles Menefee in his *Sketch Book* credits Winter with initiating wine making in '72. The Sigrist family is also overlooked in the Gardner survey.

Napa Valley's growers and vintners found the time every month to sit down and spend hours arguing and debating and telling each other about the lessons to be learned from practicing the growing of grapes. At one meeting in February 1877 they listened to Capt. James Sayward describe seeing vineyards in Italy being covered with smoke when there was a danger of frost. He noted they used coal tar burned in small iron pots.

Dr. George Crane thought all the pruned cuttings, etc., from the vineyard should be saved and then burned on the needed frosty mornings. John Lewelling insisted this would be a waste of time unless the bundles of faggots or straw were first soaked in coal tar. Charles Krug read an article translated from German of how brush burned on cold nights had a "salutary" effect on the vines. He warned, however, everyone had to participate or the effect would fail. (Only a few vineyardists, like Gottlieb Groezinger, took all this advice and saved their vines from killing frosts in early April.)

Late in December that same year, the St. Helena Vinicultural Society appointed H. A. Pellet as their delegate to the Paris Exposition planned for 1878. Almost everyone was in agreement that California wine should be liberally represented at the Exposition, and offers of cases of wine came from John Thomann, Jacob Schram, H. W. Crabb, Pellet and James Sayward.

In the spring of '78, the club began serious discussions on building a warehouse which could be bonded under the new Brandy Bonding Act recently passed by Congress. A separate "St. Helena Warehouse Association" was created to construct an 85 x 102 foot stone building near the railroad. The site had to be moved several times due to conflicts and finally construction began in June on a large lot not far from the Baptist church. Dark-colored stone was used with white stone for decoration. The warehouse was ready by time the fall crush began.

Politics as it concerned tariffs on foreign wine, took up more time at vinicultural meetings then any other subject. Resolutions were constantly being written and rewritten by the Society before being adopted and forwarded on to Congress in Washington, D.C. One such resolution quickly followed the adoption by the San Francisco Chamber of Commerce of a petition to Congress to lower the tariffs on all imported wine so as to stimulate the wine and liquor importing business. It came as a particularly cruel blow to the California wine industry to find the businessmen of San Francisco quite willing to virtually endorse French wines over the local product.

The Chamber may not, of course, have understood the deleterious effect of their action on fellow Californians. Fortunately, the wine industry did not need to fret long over the issue for most Congressmen still believed in high tariffs to protect America's young industries, including wine.

The vine disease phylloxera was being discussed increasingly among all wine men in the northern portion of the state. Charles Kohler told a state meeting that he had been sent a substance from Germany (composed largely of nicotine) and his vines in the Sonoma Valley, affected by the disease, seemed greatly improved after treatment. No one had yet seen the vine louse in Napa Valley and it was hoped that Sonoma would be the only place of contamination.

Most valley vintners who had been making wine for several years slowly came to realize that something had to be done to increase the sale of wine outside California. The "Napa Valley Wine Company" was one result of all the discussions and was formed early in the decade by Charles Krug, Jacob Beringer and M. G. Ritchie.

These three men may have taken this action as a direct result of a story carried some months previously in the *Curtis Quarterly Wine Circular* of San Francisco. In a study undertaken on the distribution of wine during the year 1872, the *Curtis* investigators found that only about one-tenth of the state's annual wine production was being sold outside California. About the same amount was consumed inside the state. One-tenth was used in making Brandy; two-tenths were carried over in storage and could not be sold; one-tenth was lost by evaporation and other storage problems; the same amount went into sweet wines; and two-tenths were wines not merchandisable. (The remaining one-tenth is absorbed by rounding off all figures given in the study.)[III.32]

These figures must have astonished any serious vintner. Out of 7,000,000 gallons of wine produced in the state, only 900,000 gallons were exported to the eastern states or foreign ports for consumption as wine! To correct this situation as rapidly as possible, Krug, et al decided to set up branches of the Napa Valley Wine Company in major eastern cities, the first one to be in St. Louis. George Fagg was appointed the agent and within weeks succeeded in planting a very pro-California wine story in the *Western Watchman* of St. Louis. One line of the story reads: "In the interest of patriotism, health and temperance, the production of the choicest Wines on the American soil should be encouraged." Missouri's own fledgling wine industry made the city rather more partial to anything fermented on American soil.

By mid-decade, the Napa Valley Wine Company expanded to Kansas City. Later the same year, Krug shipped thirteen barrels of wine to Thompsonville, Georgia. Thereafter it became difficult to keep track of who was forwarding wine and to what exotic locations. W. W. Lyman had found a distributor in North Carolina, Krug had one in New York City.

John Lewelling and H. W. Crabb pooled resources and had two railroad boxcars filled alternately with table grapes from their vineyards and ice. The destination was New York City and the shipment in October 1876 must have been the first such consignment of grapes to the East Coast from the Napa Valley.

The following year John Lewelling read a letter before a meeting of the Vinegrowers of St. Helena from a Philadelphia firm asking him for much more wine than he alone could supply. The firm was taking the unusual step of wanting to deal directly with the producer rather than buy from a San Francisco wine agent. The reason for this action may have been some dissatisfaction with the quality of wine received for the Philadelphia firm expressed a willingness to pay a higher fee for "pure California wines."

All of this activity was paying off rather well by the end of the decade as is indicated in a story which appeared in the *Wine and Liquor Trade Circular* of New York City. Wine shipments from California to the Atlantic coast of the nation had reached 1,243,241 gallons, a respectable increase in only two years.

Much of the credit for this expansion in the East Coast wine market belonged to Charles Krug. He was an individual with limitless energy, traveling frequently, even to Washington, D.C. when it became necessary to oppose or gain support for a law which affected the making of wine. Krug was at every meeting of valley growers or wine makers and went to many state wine meetings. He had an opinion on every subject, which may have made him disliked by some fellow wine makers.

Gottlieb Groezinger topped Krug in one sense, when he shipped samples of all of his wine directly to London. The English were true wine snobs, taking only the best French Claret, Burgundies, Champagne or Sherry from Spain. There is no record of Groezinger making a sale in London but maybe he did not expect to do so. At least, not immediately.

The wine boom of the mid-1870s saw the establishment in the Napa Valley of several wineries to rival Krug or even Groezinger. Jacob Beringer's winery was one of these, although it would take some years to complete the winery buildings, all of the tunnels and a mansion for comfortable living.

Jacob Beringer did not have quite the colorful background of Charles Krug, although he was probably a much better vintner. The evidence to support such a statement stems from the fact that when Jacob arrived in the Napa Valley in 1870, Krug hired him to be his winemaker.

Beringer had apprenticed at the age of fifteen in the Berlin, Germany wine firm of Tim & Kloske. After several years with a winery at Mainz, he immigrated to the United States, arriving in 1868. He obviously knew something about wine, even the importing of it for he opened his own shop in New York City. An older brother, Frederick, already in New York, probably helped him establish the small business.

Jacob never explained why he suddenly put all of this aside after only two years and headed directly for the Napa Valley of California. If he did reminisce about it to friends or descendants, the story was never recorded in print and the details have been lost. It is possible that Krug and the Beringers became business partners when Krug shipped some wine directly to New York City. Jacob may have preferred the making of wine rather than the selling of it and took up Krug's invitation to come to the Napa Valley and help him out.

Three days before Christmas, 1876, Jacob Beringer and a crew of workmen began excavations for the first Beringer winery. Jacob and his brother had purchased the land just north of St. Helena from William Daegner, perhaps selecting the site for its view or because the hillside behind the Daegner home seemed to be solid rock, excellent for building tunnels to store wine. The cornerstone for the winery was not laid until the following March, the year Jacob reached his thirtieth birthday.

The Beringer winery was the object of considerable public interest even before it had its first crush of grapes. Jacob had bought himself one of the most beautiful stone hillsides in the valley, the rock was high and wide and deep and perfect for tunneling. His announced plans dwarfed anything similar in the valley and would rival those of Buena Vista in Sonoma. The *Star* in March of '78 declared:

> Through the back wall is pierced one archway, pointing straight into the hillside, and already extending 16 feet in. At the end of this archway work has begun, and is to be pushed forward until a depth of 50 feet, by 17 wide is reached,

In another twelve months, the tunnel reached a depth of one hundred feet, due to the fine continuity of the stone. This gave the Beringers one tunnel, a hundred feet long by seventeen wide and since it appeared more could easily be built, two more were ordered, one on either side of the original. Toward the back of the main tunnel, two shafts were dug to connect the three solid rock wine cellars. All of this was not completed for several years, digging straight into such solid rock took time.

The first crush of grapes at the winery did not come until the fall of 1877 and produced only 40,000 gallons of wine, rather modest considering the scope of the planned winery. Jacob actually must have done the work at night considering the fact that he was still in charge of wine making at the Krugs. Two years later 100,000 gallons of wine was fermenting in Beringer tanks.

The Beringer's New York connection helped establish it immediately as this story demonstrates from the *New York Retailer* of December 4, 1880:

> ... To New Yorkers, the most interesting chapter in this native wine literature from the California press is what is said of the house of Beringer Brothers, of St. Helena, Napa County. As we have seen, Napa County has become the most productive of the vineyard counties, and Sonoma now ranks second. This is partly true of the

quality of wines, as well. There are none of more exquisite taste than those of the Napa Valley. In this valley the Beringer Brothers rank first among the vintners in very many respects. Mr. Beringer of 40 Whitehall street, the President of the Arion Society, is the head of the firm.

A number of Jacob's vintner friends would dispute or politely argue the point as to whether the Beringers ranked "first among the vintners," but no one paid any attention to such squabbles in New York.

The first Beringer winery was a stone structure 40 x 104 feet, three stories high and each story a large single room. The construction superintendent must have been a builder of ships, judging from one description of the time:

> The ground floor is of cement, and has a slight pitch for drainage. The second floor is built like a ship's deck, regularly caulked and watertight. It is laid entirely of 3 x 3 stuff, cut so as to leave the edge of the grain up, and thereby prevent splintering. It has also watertight baseboards, so that it could, if necessary, be filled with water to a depth of several inches. The third story is where the crushing is carried on, the cellar standing against the hillside and a road leading around the back, so that wagons can unload their grapes upon the third story. Eight hatchways provide openings for conducting the juice into tanks below.[III.33]

Most wineries built thereafter in the valley, were constructed in a cutaway hillside so the grapes could be hauled by horse and wagon directly to the top floor for crushing. The gravity flow of the juice to fermenters and finally to the bottom floor for aging, prevented any use of pumps. Jacob did not originate this concept, but his winery was the inspiration for others to follow suit. (If the winery was on the valley floor, an artificial hill was sometimes created against one side of the winery; or a loading device was required to bring the lugs of grapes to the top story. Nearly all grapes as picked were piled into lugs– boxes – from 20 to 40 pounds when full, and transported to the winery.)

Terrell Grigsby may have been attempting to overshadow the Beringer winery when he began construction of his "Occidental" winery in 1878. It was 58 feet wide (compared to Beringer's 40 feet) and 112 feet long (Beringer's was only 104 feet). Both commanded sweeping views of the valley, almost at opposite ends, for Grigsby was located a few miles north of Napa City and on the eastern flank. The

Occidental Cellars may have just nudged out the Beringer winery by a small percentage when it came to architectural beauty.

Grigsby had arrived in the valley in 1852 from Missouri, with a wife and seven children. His vineyard was planted in the early 1870s and within a few years he was urging the construction of three centrally located wineries to serve the entire valley. No one took his advice so he determined to build a winery approximating the concept he espoused at a St. Helena Vinicultural meeting. The stone walls were two feet thick, the doors eight feet wide so horse and wagon could transport grapes directly inside. Thirty-three windows let in sufficient light and the highest point of the structure towered 54 feet above the landscape. The stone was the best thus far located in the valley, from a quarry near Napa Soda Springs:

> In color it is white and gray, with greenish and reddish shades, and when first taken from the quarry it cuts nicely with an axe or saw. But when exposed to the atmosphere it becomes quite as hard as other stone.[III.34]

Grigsby never explained the meaning of the name he chose, the "Occidental." He held such strong convictions about the word that he had it cut into the stone on the front of the winery. "Occident" means "of the West, western culture, European and America." There were Occidental hotels, restaurants, even a small town in Sonoma County carried the name. Since Grigsby hired Chinese laborers almost exclusively, and had one barn burned down by anti-Chinese individuals, he seems to have wanted to stress the point that he was of American stock, born in Tennessee and like many of his neighbors, partially a product of Missouri.

One mile north of the Beringer winery, John C. Weinberger caught winery building fever too. He had built a very modest structure for that purpose in '76, 42 x 62 feet and of two stories, of stone. A wooden third floor gave him the then customary space for crushing the grapes with a hillside created on the north end for bringing the grapes directly to the crushers via horse and wagon. Three years later, he added another structure alongside the first and slightly offset which was nearly a duplicate, although of different proportions, being 28 x 80 feet. The two units could handle 180,000 gallons of wine. The two foot thick walls were of red lava rock quarried on the property and the heavily timbered interior (of redwood) meant that it was to endure a long time.*

Almost directly across the road, Jean Laurent built a new winery for himself in the same month and year as Weinberger added his second addition. By the time he was finished he could store almost as much wine, too, in a two-story stone cellar much different in looks. Laurent had one long building, one hundred feet, by sixty feet in width.**

In Brown's Valley, the Sigrist brothers had sold their property to Gordon Barth the previous year and Barth quickly announced he had very ambitious plans for the pioneer wine making establishment. Barth had discovered a quarry on the property and set about building a stone building of somewhat generous proportions, 120 feet on the side facing the valley. This made the building appear much larger than might otherwise have been the case. Together with the original stone winery, Barth could now boast of a place to age 300,000 gallons of wine, surely this made his winery the largest in the valley.

If Barth did actually boast to friends that his was the largest cellar in the county, his pride received a jolt when he read in Napa Valley newspapers of the extent of recently completed work on the Uncle Sam winery:

> It has a frontage of 146 feet on Main street, and 120 feet of it runs thence back to the river, a distance of 160 feet. The other 26 feet run back only 56 feet. These lines, it will be seen, give a very large area, but besides this is a part of the back end, equal in size to 60 x 160 feet, has two floors, adding one floor of that size to the capacity of the cellar. The entire area of floorage is 30,256 feet, and the estimated capacity, 400,000 gallons. If all goes well, another floor is contemplated next year which will raise the capacity to an even half a million.[III.35]

The reporter's description may have left quite a few readers confused, the building appearing to have a very strange configuration. If it could handle cooperage of nearly half a million gallons, the Uncle Sam winery was Napa County's largest, by far, as the decade of the 1870s came to a close.

---

*The winery was converted to a private home by William and Alice Gonser in the 1940s. It has stood the test of time and is in nearly perfect condition .

**This is now the Markham winery, and is also as sound as when it was built over a century ago.

There was one surprise statement related to the expansion of the Uncle Sam winery. Giovanni Bustelli, superintendent of the entire plant, warned that unless local grape growers made some plans to expand their acreage, Uncle Sam would plant its own vines and possibly ignore the local grower. His statement is worthy of quoting verbatim for it provides another clue as to why the county's wine industry in that decade centered around the town of St. Helena:

> The farmers of the vicinity of Napa, says Mr. Bustelli, are planting no new vineyards, and do not even take creditable care of what they have. This is a discouraging fact for winemakers there, for it gives poor promise of a supply of grapes to work on.[III.36]

Henry W. Crabb of Oakville not only operated a large winery, capable of holding 300,000 gallons, but his winery was by far the most unusual in the valley. Reflecting perhaps the strange character of the man, his first winemaking facility, of wood, had been completed in 1872 and was 56 x 110 feet, one story. Seven years later he completed another building almost identical in size but separate from the other, 58 x 124 feet, one story and of wood. Between these two buildings stood a fermenting cellar, 40 x 60 feet in size and not far away was the distillery, of the same size. He used no stone, but all buildings were carefully painted and well maintained.

Crabb was much more interested in growing of grapes than he was in the making wine, though he excelled in the latter as well. It was impossible to ascertain how many varieties of grapes he was growing, but in 1876, the *Star* reported he had a collection of 183 separate grape varieties. Two years later, in a biography on him in the *Illustrations of Napa County*, this count had climbed to 250! Perhaps Crabb did not have an accurate count himself; he was just determined to surpass Agoston Haraszthy, late of Sonoma, in the total varieties of grapes and extent of his experimentation. In the biography of Crabb in the 1878 *Illustrations . . .* , there is a flattering indirect comparison made between the two men.

Since Crabb always attended the meetings of the St. Helena Vinicultural Association and every other county or state group with an opinion on growing grapes, he was asked to contribute to a new book on the subject. The editor and author of a large portion of *American Grape Growing and Wine Making* was George Husmann of Missouri. The second edition, published in 1883, carried Crabb's theories of viticulture in the Napa Valley. He planted his vines 1,000 to the acre, pruned with low heads and short spurs with two fruit buds each. He gathered five and one-half tons of grapes per acre only three years after planting one large vineyard.

Crabb reviewed the decade of the 1870s at some length ending with a very enthusiastic future outlook:

> In 1876 the business dragged heavily, nearly bankrupting numbers. Wines were in large stock, and had to be sold to distillers and vinegar factories, at 10 to 15 cents per gallon.
>
> ... There was no market for our wines. They were in bad repute, due mainly to adulterating processes which were carried on to a very great extent in the interest of importers, and for the purpose of crushing the wine and brandy industry here. But since that time the business has greatly increased. The report of the Surveyor General of the State for the year 1876 gave 35,000 acres of vineyards; the next year 41,000; the next 77,000; and this year may be estimated at from 85,000 to 90,000 acres, making an average increase of about 35 per cent for the last four years (pp. 171-172).

Other wine men, notably Charles Wetmore, would shortly dispute these figures but not the grape planting boom which was occurring. Crabb alluded to the reason when he mentioned that the vine disease, "phylloxera" was not found outside Sonoma Valley. It was devastating the vineyards of Europe which gave California wine men shivers up and down the spine thinking the state might replace France as the great wine *entrepot* of the world. Crabb may have been shivering, too, when he wrote the concluding lines of his chapter on "Viticulture in Napa County, California":

> If the industry be not stifled by Congressional legislation, whoever lives a half a century hence, will find the grapes of California in every city of the Union; her raisins supplying the Western Hemisphere; her wines in every mart of the globe, and then, with her golden shores, her sunny clime, her vine-clad hills and plains, will California, indeed, be the Vineland of the World.

IV. Phylloxera and the Viticultural Boom of the 1880s

ne week before Christmas, 1880, Professor Eugene Hilgard of Berkeley boarded the San Francisco to Vallejo ferry for a quiet trip to St. Helena. From Vallejo he traveled by railroad, enjoying the trip with several friends and colleagues. He was the first faculty member of the University of California assigned to the teaching of "viticulture" and was to be a special guest that afternoon of the local Vinicultural Club.

Eugene Hilgard's remarks later that day were to seal the destiny of the Napa Valley and helped precipitate a wine boom of such proportions that it would not be matched for many decades.

Distinguished men of Hilgard's stature did not often visit the small town of St. Helena and this occasion quickly became a major event. Even the wives of Vinicultural Club members came to hear what the learned professor had to say. Possibly the only individual in the entire surrounding area who did not attend was Charles Krug, who was too ill to leave his sickbed. Krug was the perennial host of most notable visitors therefore, he must have been seriously indisposed to miss this special visit.

The *Star* devoted more than half of its front page the following week to the coverage of Hilgard's reception and his remarks. This was an historic occasion, wrote editor Gardner in the opening paragraph:

> Saturday last was a day long to be remembered in the history of St. Helena; a day of profound gratification to the friends of her one great interest [wine], the occasion of an exposition of the science on which her prosperity rests that is already the earnest study of viticulturists and is destined to become a permanent contribution to the literature on the subject. Professor Hilgard arrived on the morning train, accompanied by R. B. Blowers, of Woodland, one of the State Viticultural Commissioners, and other gentlemen.

Hilgard was in St. Helena to deliver an address which was required by an Act of the State Legislature when it created the new Board of State Viticultural Commissioners. An appropriation had been made by the Legislature to cover the expenses of annual lectures in each of seven grape growing regions. Hilgard's speech, in keeping with the manner of the time, required about two hours to deliver. He covered many topics but one statement stood out above everything else he said:

> The turning point of the tide [in California] was at the time when the havoc carried by the phylloxera into the European vineyards, created a panic as to future supplies; so that those who had thus far turned up their noses at the nameless and fameless American wines, were led to reflect and at least try what could be made out of the promiscuous material, in case there could be no other available source.

Hilgard's remarks in St. Helena, rather widely reported thereafter in the state press, indicated that the phylloxera just might destroy completely the vineyards of France and elsewhere in Europe. What had been considered rumor and exaggeration before, was now reality—in part because Hilgard said so.

A new type of fever spread across the California landscape, this one caused by the Vitis vinifera grape of Europe. It was nearly as contagious as the gold mania of 1849.

Charles Wetmore, the Chief Executive Officer of the State Viticultural Commissioners, attempted to convey what was happening when he wrote in his *Second Annual Report* "about one hundred thousand acres of grapes have been planted" in the past four years.[IV.1] He expected 30,000 more acres of new vines in 1884. It was his considered opinion that the entire state had no more than 50,000 acres of grapes prior to the start of the vine boom.

The Napa Valley itself had only 3,500 acres of grapes when the new decade began. Within two years there were nearly 12,000 acres in vineyards![IV.2] There was no returning to wheat or cattle raising in Napa County for the vine was nearly the only topic of conversation.

No one quite understood how the phylloxera vine louse traveled to France from America or when. A story published as early as 1873 in the *Napa Reporter* claimed it had been first discovered nine years earlier near the city of Avignon. In a decade it had cut in half the wine production in many districts. It was claimed the famous "Hermitage" wine cellar would not produce another vintage—at least with its own grapes. The same was true for Chateau Margaux and Chateau Lafitte.

"It is certain," stated the Reporter, "that if the insect plague continues and increases at the same rate for the next five years, as it has for the last five, California grape growers will have nothing to complain of on account of cheap French wines."

Two years later, *Scientific American* magazine reported that M. Dumas had discovered a compound of sulpho-carbonates that was a certain remedy for the new vine disease in France.[IV.3] Other scientists came forward with blends of chemicals to make the same claim, but like Dumas, all of them failed. Often the cure was worse than the original disease. The French government appropriated 20,000 francs as a reward to the first person to come up with a phylloxera remedy.

Napa Valley growers had received a direct report from France in 1877 on the disease, from General E. D. Keyes, founder of the Edge Hill winery south of St. Helena. (He sold the property to Richard Heath shortly before going to Europe.) Keyes disclosed that the French government had awarded a medal to one of its citizens for "discovering" that the phylloxera could be eradicated by flooding the vineyard with water. Subsequent tests proved this was not a solution.

By the late seventies, American envoys in France were reporting the rather widespread acceptance of American vines as being resistant to the phylloxera. Eastern America was pinpointed as the source of the disease where the vine and the dreaded insect lived in harmony. American vines were tougher than the European counterpart, and secreted a substance which surrounded and isolated the phylloxera. The solution was to graft onto American rootstock, the fine noble grapes of France, Germany or Italy.

Since the eastern states of America grew a wide assortment of grapes, conditioned by many centuries of growth to distinct climate and soil, the next step was to find resistant roots adaptable to the various soils and climate of France. Unfortunately, no single vine suited all conditions. The specifics of plant growth were little understood and when vine after vine failed to meet the great expectations of the French, the reports again increased that France's wine industry would soon be a memory.

Harper's Weekly in March 1879 surveyed the grape situation in France and America and hinted that salvation was to come from the Pacific Coast:

> The fact that two hundred and eighty tons of California grapes were received weekly and sold in the markets of Philadelphia during the past season, shows that this interest is an important one, especially as the American grapes are little liable to the attacks of phylloxera, which has caused so much devastations in France, and the approach of which to other countries in Europe is looked upon with so much alarm.
>
> Professor Riley [U.S. Department of Agriculture] some time ago pointed out the comparative immunity of the American grape, and the fact is so well appreciated that enormous importations are now being made from America to Europe, and a special periodical, called *La Vinge Americains*, has been commenced in France.
>
> The method adopted now is to use American roots as stalks on which to graft the regular wine grape.

By Christmas, the New Orleans *Picayune* was reporting that "not a drop of [French] champagne wine will be made this year" even though some grapes were being picked in the Champagne district. The grapes were in such bad condition that the leading producers announced there would be no purchases for production of the effervescent beverage.[IV.4]

In reporting on the failure of the grape crop in Germany, the *San Francisco Chronicle* editorialized:

> The important bearing of these circumstances upon the welfare of California is obvious. Here the vintage is plentiful, the wines are always good and pure, the future is full of promise. Already the consumption of California wines in the East and Europe has reached respectable proportions. . . . California has every right to

become the leading wine-producing country of the world. Let our fashionable and wealthy families set the example of using none but native wines . . .[IV.5]

Newspaper after newspaper carried long stories on the bright future of wine and grapes. The *San Francisco Post* castigated the wealthy local investor for not putting his money into grapes, particularly in the Napa Valley: "Now that the destruction of the French vineyards is a fixed fact . . . The eyes of the world will be turned to our valleys in tremulous hope and anticipation of good wine."[IV.6]

In nearby Sonoma County, the wheat fields were disappearing just as fast as grape cuttings could be obtained for replanting. A Healdsburg newspaper in a story called "The Boom in Vine Planting" listed seventeen local farmers who were expanding or planting new vines.[IV.7] In December 1880 the same publication reported that Alexander Valley farmers were being "awakened to the possibilities of our future industry" in the vineyard.

In early January 1882 Arpad Haraszthy, President of the Board of State Viticultural Commissioners issued a warning that vine planting was moving ahead much too rapidly. Reports reaching him suggested that "200,000,000" grapevines (surely a typographical error, 20,000,000 or 25,000 acres) were readied for planting statewide. The high prices paid for grapes in recent years cannot continue, he advised in the strongest terms possible.[IV.8]

No one paid the slightest attention to Haraszthy. The *Healdsburg Enterprise* even hinted that "Possibly Mr. Haraszthy looks upon the matter from a dealer's standpoint, and that his fears of over-production of wine and low prices for grapes [and wine] are groundless."[IV.9]

There was good reason to ignore Haraszthy and the few other timid voices of gloom over the widespread plantings of vines. Rural weekly newspapers like the *Star*, *Russian River Flag* or *Sonoma Index-Tribune* joyously reprinted every positive story carried in eastern journals on California's wine future. The *New York Grocer* for example, observed:

> The barriers of prejudice against California wines and brandies seems broken down at last in the Atlantic States, and not only have prices appreciated here, but the demand is greater than the local dealers can supply. . . . The future for California winemakers and distillers seems to be a bright and lasting one.[IV.10]

There had never been such words of encouragement before for Napa Valley and California vintners! The entire country would soon be drinking California wine if the situation was not altered by any drastic changes. No one, of course, expected the dreaded disease would seriously harm the Napa Valley. A chemist for the Department of Agriculture in Washington, D.C. even made an official report that there was no apprehension in California that the disease would spread beyond the few isolated places it had been found.[IV.11]

One more indication of the wine boom in Napa County could be seen in the vast numbers of new residents settling between Soscol and Calistoga. The county's population doubled in the ten years separating 1870 from 1880. The official United States Census taken in the summer of '80, gave Napa County 13,235 residents. Napa City had about 5,000 of these inhabitants; St. Helena, 1,500; Calistoga, 800; Yountville, 300; Monticello (Berryessa Valley), 200; and Knoxville, 300, a quicksilver mining town in Pope Valley.

There was a radical change in the occupations of many of the residents. By the year 1881, over 500 individuals listed themselves as farmer-grape growers. Dozens of the vineyards were large enough to be the sole interest of the owner, there being little time left after cultivation, pruning, sulphuring or picking, for any other agricultural activity.

The area stretching from Yountville to St. Helena, known as the "St. Helena district" contained by far the most vines in Napa County, nearly 7,000 acres. Napa City and surrounding region had 3,300 acres in grapes and the upper valley region with Calistoga as center, contained 1,100 acres in vines.

A thorough canvassing of the production of wine in 1880 at Napa County's wineries came up with a total of 2,857,000 gallons.

There were fifty-two wineries in the county as the new decade opened. Only nine of those wineries could handle over one hundred thousand gallons of wine. H. W. Crabb was listed as the largest though this was inaccurate. On the next page is a list of all wineries in the entire county:

Name	Gallons	Name	Gallons
Beringer Bros	145,000	Lemme, C	13,000
Beretta Bros	5,000	Leuthold	11,000
Brun & Chaix	115,000	Medeau, J	12,000
Barth, G	120,000	McEachran, C	3,500
H. W. Crabb	300,000	McCord, J	49,000
Crochat, G	35,000	Migliavacca, G	65,000
Corthay, L	2,000	Pellet, H	25,000
Degouy, N	58,000	Pettengill, Dr	5,000
Debanne & Bresard	36,000	Reed, W	14,000
Dorr, L. (Grigsby)	65,000	Rosenbaum, F	5,000
Folger.	10,000	Rossi, A	10,000
Fountain, G	18,000	Schram, J	20,000
Gila Bros	45,000	Scheffler, W	250,000
Gaique, T	52,650	Schultze, 0	10,500
Groezinger, F	275,000	Sciaroni, F	10,000
Heyman, E.	19,000	Schranz, A	60,000
Hagan, H.	35,000	Salmina, F	20,000
Haug, G	1,000	Simonton, J	25,000
Jeanmonod, A	25,000	Semorile, B	15,000
Knief, J	2,500	Tossetti, B	20,000
Kortum, L	38,000	Thomann, J	100,000
Krug, Charles	280,000	Van Beaver & Co	200,000
Krug & Smith	76,000	Weinberger, John	75,000
Kalthenbach, M	400	Wegele, C	10,500
Lyman, W	4,000	Woodward, E. W	4,700
Laurent, J	60,000	Weaks, W	1,500

The creation of the Board of State Viticultural Commissioners in the spring of 1880, is one more reason the planting of grapes flourished in the Napa Valley. This Legislative Act was recognition by the state that viticulture was becoming a major industry and required its own governing board. There was little money in the original Act to fund its activities, but this was corrected a year later.

The Board was composed of nine members, all appointed by the Governor (this was plain politics, to ensure the Governor's signature). Seven of the members were active growers coming from one of the following districts: First, the Sonoma District, composed of the counties of Sonoma, Marin, Lake, Mendocino and the remaining coastal counties stretching to the Oregon border; second, the Napa District, composed of Napa, Solano and Contra Costa; third, the San

Francisco District, of San Francisco, San Mateo, Alameda, Santa Clara, Santa Cruz, San Benito and Monterey. The other four districts were: Los Angeles, Sacramento, San Joaquin and El Dorado (taking in the Sierra foothills counties).

The fact that Sonoma was listed as the "First District" may be attributable to its higher public recognition as a fine wine region or that Sonoma County Assemblyman Capt. James Adams introduced the bill into the State Legislature. Charles Krug was one of a dozen wine men to address the Legislature on February 3, 1880 to urge creation of the Board. It was approved April 15, 1880.

Section 8 of the Adam's Bill instructed the Board of Regents of the University of California to "Provide special instruction" pertaining to viticulture and wine making, to examine soils for grape growing, to test wines from the various districts and even to examine California trees for the best wood for cooperage. The reports of the "Professor of Viticulture" were to be published and disseminated to the state at large. This Act brought the University into viticulture for the first time, officially, although the study of grapes, like other fruit, had been a part of the Agricultural Department since its founding.*

Actually the real motivation for the founding of the new State Board was the growing threat of the phylloxera vine disease. Krug and other wine makers, knew some systematic approach was needed to combat the vine louse and "state authority" was essential to force growers to follow the decisions of the Board regarding eradication of the pest. A Viticultural Health Officer was appointed in 1881 to oversee the fight against the disease. French language publications on "Phylloxera" were translated to English and distributed.

Arpad Haraszthy, who was named President of the Viticultural Commissioners declared at the end of the first year in his Report to the Governor of California, George C. Perkins:

> One of the most important labors accomplished by the Board has been the discovery of the phylloxera in Napa, Solano, Yolo, El Dorado and Placer [counties], whereas, before the Board began its labors, this fatal pest to the vine was considered to have existed only in the County of Sonoma. The danger is imminent; it is only

---

*Dr. Eugene Hilgard began teaching classes in viticulture as early as 1876-77, one of the first such courses offered in the United States.

through State legislation and assistance that the continued spread of its ravages can be checked, and one of the future grandest resources of the State saved.[IV.12]

Haraszthy's disclosure to the general public that phylloxera had been discovered in Napa County must have rankled many Napa grape growers and land speculators. There had been the hope that the disease might not invade the valley, confining itself for some peculiarly unnatural reason to the neighboring valley to the west, Sonoma. Three years earlier the Star had carried an angry denial of any phylloxera in Napa County after the San Francisco Chronicle made the claim.[IV.13]

Where the phylloxera first attacked Napa Valley vines is not quite certain, or what year the pest crossed the Sonoma County boundary. It was in the valley certainly by 1880.

Treatment with bisulfide of carbon was begun in December of that year on vineyards belonging to John Weinberger, just north of St. Helena. Gottlieb Groezinger had the disease in his vineyards at Yountville by the spring of 1881. The phylloxera louse probably invaded the lower end of the Napa Valley the Carneros, first, well before the decade began. It was thriving in the vineyards of the Buena Vista Vinicultural Society in the early 1870s and these vines were just over the hill, literally, from the Carneros region.

Two or three isolated pockets of phylloxera did not constitute an outbreak of the disease in the minds of Napa Valley growers and there was no alarm over its presence. It had progressed extremely slowly in Sonoma Valley, taking fifteen years to infect scattered vineyards throughout the area, so there was seemingly no great fear of it. Everyone expected a cure would be found for the disease, if one did not exist already in the bisulfate of carbon.

Judge Clinton Hastings of Rutherford declared much of the Viticultural Board's hysteria over the phylloxera to be unfounded and that it could be prevented "by good sanitary conditions." His opinion carried more weight with local wine men than state officials. The disease could be ignored, at least for the time being.

There was plenty of other evidence that the public did not take the phylloxera threat seriously in Napa Valley. "The land 'boom' still continues, and property is changing hands," wrote the Rutherford correspondent to the Star in January 1881. O. S. Sargent had just purchased 50 acres of the Ross family east of town and 20 acres were being planted to grapes. The Harris ranch in the same vicinity had been sold with 75 acres set aside for grapes.

Precisely one year later the weekly journal listed 597 land or property transactions that had occurred in Napa County during the previous twelve months!

One acre of Napa Valley vineyard then sold for about $170! This is what Charles Scott paid when he purchased the Conrad Wegele farm of 22 acres—16 of which were in vines. Scott, originally from Berkeley, had operated a winery briefly in Healdsburg. Wegele took his gold coins and headed for Dry Creek Valley northwest of Healdsburg and opened a winery.

Scott, incidentally, also received a small ten thousand gallon winery with his purchase and a house. A new home in St. Helena then could be had for $1,500. One advertisement for such a home on Kearney Street described it as one and a half stories, seven rooms with hardwood floors throughout and completely landscaped. The lot size was almost big enough for a mansion, 240 feet by 60 feet.

A growing acre of Napa Valley grapes did not remain below $200 for long. Three years after the Wegele farm and winery sale, Oscar Schulze began advertising his farm and vineyard of only 16 acres combined, for $12,500. That price was nearly four times what Wegele had asked. Schulze also had a modest wine cellar on the property.

Charles Wetmore, the chief executive officer of the Board of State Viticultural Commissioners found himself innocently drawn into a controversy over the relative merits and value of Napa soils for grapes in the summer of 1884. He had attended a meeting in July in the valley and during his remarks, made the statement that the value of vineyards also depended somewhat on location. The proximity to a railroad, a town with laborers, nearness to the market, and *one's neighbors*, had something to do with it all:

> For instance, to be a neighbor of Mr. Krug of St. Helena, or such men elsewhere in the vine growing communities, would add at least $100 to the value of land.

Wetmore's kind remarks about Charles Krug would not have escaped the notice of San Francisco investors. Alaska fur dealer Gustave Niebaum probably had already made up his mind to spend a portion of his fortune on vines and a new winery in the valley, but Wetmore's statements were the kind of assurance he needed to go forward vigorously.

Niebaum was unknown to most local residents in Napa Valley when the *Star* brightened everyone's hearts with this brief item in late November 1880:

A big land sale has been made at Rutherford, the particulars of which are not accurately informed of; but understand that a member of the Alaska Commercial Company has bought Mrs. Ruhlwing's farm and the Nook Farm property of Judge Hastings for $48,000.

Niebaum's name was linked to the sale in subsequent issues and the newspaper let it be known he was a millionaire. He quickly became the "man of the hour," someone of substance, as it were, to attract other wealthy San Franciscans to invest in the Napa Valley. Although he would later build one of the best quality wine reputations in California, his contribution to the valley is much more important for what he then represented to others!

Niebaum (or more accurately spelled in his native Finland, Nybom) was born in Helsinki on August 30, 1842. His father was an official with the local police and earned a sufficient income to educate his son well, although this did not include attendance at a university. Niebaum late in life claimed to speak five languages fluently: Russian, German, French, English as well as Finnish. Some of the basis for learning these languages must have been obtained in the schools he attended.

Language study may have been a part of the curriculum at the Finland Nautical Institute which Niebaum attended and there earned his master's papers and the right to command a cargo vessel. At the age of 19, he was on the high seas and within a short time was sailing the inland waterways of Alaska. His ship traded at Alaska ports for furs, especially the seal, which were highly prized in Europe.

After Alaska was sold to the United States by the Russians in 1867, he sailed to San Francisco, looking for some opportunity to link his knowledge of the north with a new American commercial enterprise. Here he met Louis Sloss, Lewis Gerstle, John F. Miller and others who were forming the "Alaska Commercial Company." In January 1868 he became a partner in the business which quickly came to dominate both the fishing and fur industry of Alaska.

Niebaum saw little of San Francisco for the next decade, for he was in charge of the Alaska operations. He made many trips to Europe to sell furs, especially in London or St. Petersburg. His proficiency in Russian and French languages probably made him the most important member of the Alaska Commercial Company for he was in effect, the chief fur salesman. The company prospered and so did Niebaum, far beyond what he had ever imagined.

By the late 1870s, Niebaum's counsel was needed far more in San Francisco, at the headquarters of the Alaska Commercial Company, than in the outpost to the north. His wife may have been of some influence in this decision, too, for after their marriage in 1873, she was alone much of the time. Louise Shingleberger was a next-door neighbor of the Sloss and Gerstle families and they no doubt played cupid for the sea captain—already thirty-one years old when he married.

If Niebaum's youth was spent in very modest surroundings, he did not let that influence him when he began building his Napa Valley estate. Perhaps he had acquired a strong competitive instinct in his personal as well as in his business life and wanted to build a showcase in Napa Valley to match the grand San Francisco homes of his business partners.

As soon as the purchase of the Ruhlwing and Hasting's farm had been formally sealed with signatures and payment in gold, he hired a large work force to begin planting new vineyards, constructing barns, houses, waterways—the orders flew so fast that local newspaper reporters could not keep up with all the changes. He must have had in mind also the building of the most magnificent winery in California, but that he decided to do one section at a time (which made Inglenook an architectural puzzle for later historians).

The name "Inglenook" had been applied to the ranch for some years before Niebaum arrived. W. C. Watson who planted vines as early as 1871 on one of Niebaum's purchases, gave his farm the Inglenook name. Niebaum could see lithograph drawings of Watson's "Inglenook" in the 1878 published *Illustrations of Napa County.*[IV.15] Curiously, Judge Clinton Hastings called his small Rutherford vineyard "Nook Farm" as well.

Niebaum and Louise may have spent their first Christmas in the Napa Valley in 1880 for the year had not ended before he was out overseeing the clearing of sixty acres for vineyard. In the first week of February, Sauvignon cuttings (probably Sauvignon Blanc) arrived from San Jose. Within weeks a new distillery was under construction, and then a stable for his finest horses.

Judge Hasting's modest wine cellar was next dismantled and a new winery reconstructed of the old materials increasing it to 55 x 120 feet in size.[IV.16] Cooperage for 100,000 gallons of wine was in place by July. That it did not suit the sea captain is evident from a statement in the *Star*, which claimed another cellar would be built alongside the first in the future. Niebaum did not care a whit either about the growing anti-Chinese movement in California for the newspaper recorded that 17 white men and 8 Chinese were doing the construction work.[IV.17]

In early November, the *Star* took note of Niebaum's first crush, some 61,000 gallons! Few of the grapes were his own, they came from such neighbors as Charles Thompson, John Dent, David Doak and William Dinning.

It is conceivable that within two years of Niebaum's arrival in the valley, some neighbors began to think of him as "peculiar" or at least, "strange." In his '82 crush, he hired men to stand alongside a conveyor belt (taking the grapes inside the winery) and snatch away any grapes that appeared unripe, as well as to remove all unnecessary leaves, stems, etc. He was fussy, obviously, when most growers were just happy to get the grapes picked and to the winery.

"This is something of an experiment as yet, but it seems reasonable that the quality of the wine should be improved by it, and we hope that Mr. Niebaum may so find his very commendable care rewarded," observed the St. Helena newspaper.

Besides these points, the proprietor is paying particular attention to grape varieties—not only those which are esteemed the best here, but which most nearly answer the demands of consumers and will thus make the wines of Napa Valley acceptable to those before whom they must come for a market. It is gratifying to thus see not only money but brains put into the business . . .[IV.18]

The following summer, Niebaum invited his ranch foreman Hamden W. McIntyre, to sit down over lunch and discuss the new winery he wanted built at Inglenook. He had seen a castle or wine cellar along the Rhine in Germany, and several others, which attracted his attention and this is what he planned for the Napa Valley. McIntyre agreed to draw up the general plans, incorporating a number of innovations.

McIntyre was Vermont born, in 1834, and later trained in civil engineering and mechanical drafting. He was not an architect but that did not matter to Niebaum, he wanted someone who would follow his orders. McIntyre became acquainted with Niebaum about a dozen years before when he accepted work on St. Paul's Island, Alaska with the Alaska Commercial Company. Niebaum discovered his talents with the drafting pen and brought him to the Napa Valley.

The new winery which began to take shape through McIntyre's artistry, had one immediate innovation. There were to be distinct compartments within the winery for the storage of each variety of wine. Most wineries were one large room with puncheons of wine of the Zinfandel grape stored alongside a white variety like the Burger. The majority of wineries, which were no more than ten to twenty thousand gallons in size, often blended everything into just two types of wine—red and white. The wine consumer purchased wine in bulk, red or white, and when in a restaurant, the wine came in a large pitcher.

Niebaum decided it was time to change all that. Or at least, he was not going to sell to the average working class wine drinker. He planned to bottle all of his wine (that was unheard of, besides being frightfully expensive) and offer the varieties more or less standard in England: Claret, Burgundy, Sauterne, Chablis, etc. The wine stored in each of his "vaults" or compartments would rest in twenty, one-thousand gallon "ovals" or ten, five-hundred gallon barrels. The four wine vaults were housed in a building approximately 70 x 40 feet in size with a flat roof—a second story would be added later.

Work on this new winery was begun in June 1883 and was completed in time for the fall crush. Niebaum did not see much of the vintage that fall; he was taken ill in September at Lake Tahoe with what was described as "congestive lungs."

Nothing more was done to the winery for nearly two years. Niebaum's health may have been part of the answer, but he also left in early '84 on a long trip to Europe. While in St. Petersburg, Russia (selling furs), he was made a vice president in the Alaska Commercial Company. The trip must have been unusually successful.

In July '85 workmen began excavations for the foundation to another portion of the Inglenook winery. It was necessary to excavate down to "hardpan" (a solid rock-like layer) and here McIntyre and his laborers found a surprise: hardpan under the winery ran at least twelve feet deep, when it could be found. For this and perhaps other unknown reasons, construction came to a standstill.

McIntyre's drafting pen was not idle that year. A neighbor at Rutherford had heard of his special talents and asked if he would design a stone winery for him. Seneca Ewer had purchased land right in the heart of the village and wanted something more modest than Niebaum's, but nonetheless noticeable. What he got was a design for a 100 x 126 foot, two-story winery—to be built with Napa Valley sandstone from Howell Mountain.*

There is good reason to believe Niebaum and railroad magnate Leland Stanford may have been friends for that same summer Stanford came to Rutherford to have a talk with Hamden W. McIntyre. He wanted a winery designed for his new Vina vineyards site in Tehama County. McIntyre could not refuse the richest man in the country (or close to it), and this winery design was slightly different—it was to be built entirely of brick and wood, a massive 300 by 60 foot wide. And that was only the start, there would be more structures on the ranch and an elegant home.

The Vina-Stanford winery may have been the only winery design drawn up in a railroad dining car. Stanford traveled by private car or private train, in company with an entourage of assistants. His visit to Rutherford was in May with the car pulled off on the siding for the day. He, obviously, would have viewed the construction completed at Inglenook and may have even dined at Niebaum's house, but the business dealings usually took place back on the train.

Another participant in the Stanford-Niebaum lunch with McIntyre that day may have been wealthy San Franciscan John Benson. He owned a large producing vineyard just southwest of Oakville and needed a modest little three-story winery, too. He had made wine on a very small scale previously at his country ranch, but now he wanted something more imposing for a small hillock a mile north of his home. McIntyre drew up plans for three stories, all of Napa Valley stone, with cupolas on the roof—it was almost a scaled down version of what Niebaum had in mind.

McIntyre may have stayed up nights thereafter drawing plans for wineries all over California. There was no one with his expertise in the entire state, indeed *he seems to have become the first winery architect in the entire United States!*

---

*This is now the center core of Beaulieu Vineyards winery. Georges de Latour purchased the winery in 1923.

By the spring of 1886 Niebaum had become impatient with his uncompleted winery. A trained San Francisco architect named William Mooser came up to the valley to offer assistance—suggesting that some serious problems had been encountered with construction. Certainly the grand central core of the winery, designed by McIntyre, had to have solid footing or the vast weight of three stories of stone rising to 90 feet, with tower, would sink into the earth.

The arched ceilings in the ground floor wine vaults may have caused some of the delay. The ceiling was composed entirely of concrete and this type of construction was so new that there was much experimentation required. Iron pillars were needed for additional support. The cement itself was in the process of development and not always available. The *Napa Register* claimed in October 1887 that the shortage of cement was one of the primary causes for delays in completing the winery.

By that fall, Inglenook, which had began to take shape three years earlier, included a three-story central core and a one story southern wing. Its appearance may have given some hint of future glory, but at the moment the winery seemed slightly undressed.

It is doubtful the formal "sampling room" at Inglenook, which really set it apart from every other winery in the state, was finished before 1890. The state's leading viticulture newspaper, The *San Francisco Merchant and Viticulturist*, offered this description in a January issue:

> The sampling room, on the right as the building is entered, undoubtedly represents a small fortune in its cost. The walls and every piece of furniture are of solid oak—the chairs, tables, sideboards all being made to order in Germany. The walls are adorned with costly pictures and plaques of bronze and porcelain. Near the ceiling, shelves project from the wall and these are lined with unique and vari-colored bottles, glasses, vases and ewers, held in place by a railing.
>
> The ceiling is frescoed in appropriate designs and the windows are of stained glass. The goblets, wine baskets and articles of virture [sic] that complete the appointments of this room are all of rare design, costly manufacture and in consonance with the other features of the cellar. When last in Europe, Capt. Niebaum made a selection of rare ornaments and other bric-a-brac including some old but expensive lanterns. . . .

There really was nothing like this in the wine industry in California. Niebaum intended to entertain in the grand style and influence his visitors and members of the press. With Inglenook, Napa Valley winemaking advanced a giant step from not only producing grand wine, to how wine was to be marketed and sold.

Two individuals probably played a major role in this activity for which no published credit had been given. Niebaum was a seafaring man until he retired to San Francisco and his duties at the Alaska Commercial Company.

It seems rather unlikely that Niebaum would have had time while traveling in Europe to attend to the buying of "bric-a-brac" or costly bronze and porcelain plaques. Would he even have sought out an artist to paint frescoes on the ceiling? Louise (Shingleberger) Niebaum may deserve the credit for all of this, despite what the *Merchant and Viticulturist* states.

Additionally, Niebaum knew nothing about the promotion of wine. He certainly never spoke on the subject and even openly avoided newspaper reporters. The genius behind the wine image Inglenook was fast acquiring, belonged to Ferdinand Haber. He was a member of Alfred Greenbaum & Co., a San Francisco company which distributed Inglenook wines. (He would soon make Rutherford and Inglenook his home.)

With Niebaum's grand castle Inglenook, finally completed in 1888 (at least as far as wine making is concerned—some aspects like the sampling room took longer), the question arises as to what year should be considered the "founding date" of the winery. Very shortly, Niebaum began advertising in the *Merchant and Viticulturist*, "Inglenook Vineyard—Established 1880."[IV.19] Niebaum did not buy a winery or vineyards in the Napa Valley until after the fall crush that year so obviously he could not have made wine. *His first wine efforts came one year later.* The first portion of the present grand Inglenook winery dates back to the crush of '83.

He did, however, purchase a winery as part of Nook Farm, which was in operation as early as 1879. The *Star* for January 21, 1880 verifies wine making there the previous fall of 76,000 gallons by E. B. Smith and Charles Krug working together. There is no evidence of wine production in an earlier year! Niebaum should have used "1879" instead of starting it all over again with his purchase.

Somewhat before Niebaum drew his checkbook from his desk drawer to make the first purchase of land in Napa Valley, various San

Francisco publications sent writers to report on the growing vine excitement to the north. Sallie R. Heath provided the finest eyewitness description of the valley yet published, in the *Californian* of September, 1880. She reported on everything from valley Indians to Soda Springs, but her central theme was viticulture and wine:

> Let us turn to the interest at present paramount—grape culture. This is a subject of more than passing interest to the world at large, for the day is not distant when California will claim her right to stand upon equal footing with the European wine States. She will undoubtedly rival, in maturity, those with whom she now, in infancy, competes.

Heath points out that some of the Napa wine cellars were of considerable architectural beauty, especially those constructed of stone. These cellars were beginning to attract tourists, especially young men on spirited horses/ who sometimes tried to visit all forty in one weekend.*

National attention came too in a story published in *Frank Leslie's Illustrated Newspaper* of New York. It was one of the most widely read publications in the country, although the particular story in question, "Our National Industries—The Vineyards of Sonoma Valley, California" relegated Napa to a second place. Still, it helped to have compliments such as this opening paragraph:

> General as has become the use of California wines, not only in this country, but in England, France, China, Japan, Australia and the Sandwich Islands, to which places regular consignments are now shipped, it is believed that the industry of viniculture has not yet passed out of the experimental stage. The gifts of nature are so vast in that section of our country, and the energy of man so tireless, that the possibilities of the future are scarcely comprehended.

Leslie's publication listed three major grape-growing districts in California: Sonoma, Sacramento and "the St. Helena district." The word "Napa" was used several times later in the story so there was no confusion as to St. Helena's location. The story in the Christmas issue of 1880 was not long, but the compliments on Napa grapes and wines were enough to generate much more interest in the subject.

---

*To Heath's credit she recounts the unjust treatment of valley Indians, most of whom had been driven out by white settlers. She mentions six different tribes and their location. Few writers of the time on Napa Valley even mentioned the subject!

By the following spring, the *San Francisco Chronicle* editorial-ized that the Napa Valley would soon be one big vineyard. Tourists' publications as *California and the West* were going out of their way to include descriptions of the Napa Valley.

To devote over six hundred pages to a rural county history may have seemed excessive and nothing approaching that size had been done before in California until the *History of Napa and Lake Counties* came out in late 1881. The chapter on viticulture and wine making required almost fifty pages and biographies of leading wine men take several times that number. Charles Gardner, editor of the St. Helena weekly newspaper, no doubt wrote the viticulture history but L. Vernon Briggs wrote many of the other chapters.

Many of the publications which followed about Napa Valley, liberally copied from the above book, often without acknowledging this source. The county supervisors did some of that for *Resources of Napa County*, which devoted much space and photographs to Ingle-nook. F. L. Jackson borrowed statistics for his *Napa County and Its Many Great Resources* as did K. F. Kettewell for the *Napa County Land Registers*. A San Francisco publication called *Resources of California* lifted whatever it wished from all these sources during its frequent stories on Napa Valley in the 1880s.

George Husmann who had recently settled in the Napa Valley at the Simonton "Talcoa ranch" in the Carneros, hurriedly put together a new edition of his book *American Grape Growing and Wine Making*. H. W. Crabb of Oakville submitted the chapter on Napa Valley. His contribution was pallid considering all the excitement going on around him but this minor complaint is far overshadowed by the fact that the most popular viticulture book then available in the country was out in a new edition, inscribed "Talcoa Vineyards, Napa, Cal.; Nov. 9, 1883."

The effect all of this publicity was having on the valley can be measured by the growth of new wine cellars. At the beginning of the decade, the number had been forty-nine. Another 14 were added in the following three years but then the figure jumped dramatically to 97 wineries in '84, 112 the following year and 175 by 1886! The *Star* announced it would no longer survey each winery for their annual fall crush—the list was too long.

Wine production doubled in the same span of six years, from 2,910,700 gallons to 4,800,000. It is not clear in which year another milestone happened (because such figures always varied from one source to another), but *Napa County became the leading producer of dry wines in California.* Los Angeles held that honor until the early 1870s, then Sonoma took over and finally about 1884 Napa seized the banner.

Many if not most of the new wine cellars were being constructed by longtime residents of the county, such as Chris Adamson whose vineyard was planted almost a decade before all of this recent wine excitement. Adamson's Rutherford cellar built in 1880 could hold half a million gallons and within a few years every drop he produced was shipped directly to Bremen, Germany. His Napa Valley Brandy began replacing French Cognac as the phylloxera destroyed French Cognac vineyards.

It seemed that nearly everyone building a new home in the valley designed it so that the basement could be a wine cellar. Frank Sciaroni built a home in St. Helena 30 x 35 feet, two stories over a stone basement which was his first winery. Frank Kraft did the same thing the first year of the decade, crushing and fermenting outside and storing 8,000 gallons below the house. A gentleman named Croft did the same thing, but the Baretta brothers were satisfied with a small wooden winery 46 x 26 near the John York ranch north of town.

In Calistoga, a relative newcomer named Kortum decided to keep the wine tradition of the small village alive by reviving the town's only winery, built by Julius Fulscher. Louis Kortum soon acquired a significant reputation for high quality wine.

Two miles east of Oakville, at his Mt. Eden ranch just taking shape, George S. Meyers of Oakland, completed his winery in 1883. His premier crush was at first listed in local newspapers as 2,500 gallons, then corrected the following week by adding another number 2 which gave 22,500 gallons. His favorite grape was the Charbono. Neighbors who dropped in to see the new winery, noted the double-wall construction and other indications that this winery was built to last.*

From across the bay in San Francisco, Henry Hagan caught a ferryboat almost the same day as Meyers to the Napa Valley, relinquishing his position with the state's oldest wine firm, Kohler and Frohling. He did not wish to build a cellar but instead was

---

*The winery did indeed survive for more than a century and was recently reopened by Jim and Anne McWilliams.

pleased to buy the ranch and winery known semi-affectionately as "Bill Woodward's whiskey ranch." It was in the hills northeast of Napa and included a long winding entrance lined with cedar trees. Hagan promptly renamed it "Cedar Knoll Vineyards."

From Vallejo, Alton L. Williams left his position with the railroad and followed Gustave Niebaum to Rutherford where he soon hung a sign on his vineyard which read "Inglewood." He constructed in 1884 a modest wood frame wine cellar 24 x 60 feet and put in enough cooperage to hold 15,000 gallons. His heart may not have really been in wine making for he spent about twice or three times as much money building an elegant Victorian home and landscaping the grounds into a country estate.*

Sometimes precisely the reverse psychology seemed to be at work as was the case with the pioneer Napa banking family, the Goodmans. They founded in 1886 the "Eshcol" winery with an architectural assist from Hamden McIntyre. Although an all wooden structure, it quickly became the prototype for all wooden wineries to follow, at least wine cellars built with more than modest means. It was constructed like an icehouse, utilizing the latest techniques to keep the interior cool no matter what the outside temperature. Some of McIntyre's ideas were truly revolutionary for the time.

The Goodman brothers, James and George, had settled in Napa Valley in the mid-1850s, turning to banking for their livelihood almost immediately, although George served for several years as county treasurer. The early stability of the bank may have been tied to his position since county funds deposited with the bank were often crucial to survival.

George's interest in viticulture and wine making is easier to understand than his brother James, who spent more and more of his time in San Francisco tending to investments. George ran the Napa bank but found time to serve on the board of directors of the Napa County Immigration Association and may have helped write the enticing pamphlet published in 1885, *Napa County, California*. Napa needed more settlers and the bank needed more clients. He assisted also in a colorful pamphlet published the following year called *Napa County and Its Many and Great Resources*.

---

*The Inglewood winery has long since been dismantled but the home has been faithfully restored by new owners in 1965, William and Lilia Jaeger.

James, on the other hand, sat on the board of directors of several major San Francisco businesses where lunch or dinner talk probably was the boom in Napa Valley vineyards. He was manager of the Safe Deposit Company in San Francisco, on the board of the Clay Street Savings Bank, and one of the "scoundrels" often vilified by the San Francisco press for controlling the city's fresh water supply through the Spring Valley Water Company.

The name given the property, "Eshcol," made it stand out like "Inglenook" or "Inglewood" or "Far Niente" (Benson's place). "Eshcol" caught many residents off guard, they not only could not pronounce it, no one knew whom to ask for help. They should have started with one of Napa's most prominent citizens, the honorable Judge Henry C. Gesford. The word is Hebrew and means somewhat liberally translated, "valley of the grape." Gesford, though not of the Jewish faith, suggested the name to the Goodmans.

Anyone passing under the large wooden sign over the entrance to "Eshcol" would have been surprised to see how differently the vineyard was laid out compared to neighboring farms: long narrow blocks of 1,160 vines each, separated by avenues sixteen feet wide in precise measurement. It may have reminded one of a military drill field. At the corner of each block, white posts were driven into the ground with the name of each variety of grape growing therein. Eshcol gave the appearance more of a huge nursery than a practical vineyard.

In July 1886 the Goodman brothers accepted the bid of Napa carpenter J. L. Robinson to build a 125 foot by 60 foot all-wood winery. He was to receive $1,500 for his efforts, all lumber and materials to be supplied by the owners. The winery was to be three stories high in the central portion with two wings—it bore a slight similarity to Inglenook but on a much smaller scale. Even the cupolas on the roof matched what McIntyre had drawn for Niebaum. The *Napa Register* of July 16 claimed:

> The building will be constructed of wood and heavy tan paper, the latter being used for lining and diaphragm between the studding, to form two dead air compartments in the walls, to insure a suitable and even temperature. Thorough ventilation and drainage is secured. Capacity of the winery, about 175,000 gallons,

McIntyre was trying something quite new to the wine industry—he was attempting to provide insulation between the double, heavy timbered walls and with the dead air space control the temperature inside the winery! The timbers used for the frame were so heavy a small railroad engine could have traveled over the second-story flooring with no visible sagging. "The best features of the other cellars have been incorporated into it," noted the *Register*.*

Since winery architect McIntyre was drawing plans for at least three to four wineries at once, and overseeing construction of them all, it is difficult to document where each of his architectural innovations first appeared. A year before he began work on the Eshcol winery, he was working on the Ewer winery at Rutherford and a few miles to the south at Oakville, demonstrating to John Benson the ideas he had for his Far Niente winery.

The actual construction of the Far Niente winery began in March 1885, according to the *Napa Register*. Stone masons at the Ewer winery in Rutherford began work in May. (Even Morris M. Estee's new stone winery called "Hedgeside" got underway in April, probably before Ewer's cellar.) With Eshcol coming a year later, it appears Far Niente was where McIntyre actually put into practice most of his new concepts in winery architecture.

The roof of the winery had to be McIntyre's single most important contribution—indeed the problem of leaking ceilings may have triggered McIntyre's involvement in the first place in this innovative field.

Because so many fires began in roofs of homes and commercial buildings in California, especially in San Francisco where major portions of the city burned regularly in the 1850s, insurance companies required metal roofs where and whenever possible. This was "corrugated" iron, which by the definition of the term means folded or alternative ridges.

On wineries, a light wooden understructure was built and the large sheets of corrugated iron laid on top. In fall and winter, moisture condensed on the underside of the roof and dripped on everything below. In summer, the heat penetrated to make the floor below uncomfortably hot.

---

*The winery has suffered through many years of rather fitful operation by differing owners. In 1968 the Trefethen family, including son John and wife Janet, began restoration to its former grandeur.

McIntyre pondered the situation carefully and came up with an easy solution:

> To avoid this, it occurs to me, that change might be made without any material addition to the cost [of a winery]. It has been customary heretofore in the use of iron plates, to place the rafters quite a distance apart, say eight feet and across these to lay horizontally purlins [wood cross beams], on which the iron should be laid—the purlins to be set three feet six inches or three feet four inches between the centers, or nearer if required.
>
> Abandoning this construction, I laid a roof with timbers, as for shingles, with about two feet and half to three foot between centers of the rafters, and then covered with boards, laying them close together, edge to edge, and on this covering laid the corrugated iron. I laid the iron the full width of the sheet. . . .
>
> To my great delight, not altogether surprise, I found that this obviated the difficulties named. Since the roof has been constructed, there has been no condensation of moisture shown.[IV.20]

McIntyre's remarks came before the Sixth Annual Viticultural Convention in San Francisco in March 1888. He pointed out additionally that the space created between the now solid wooden underlining and the iron provided for the free and rapid movement of air from the edge of the roof upwards (hot air rises) and kept the iron from sweating. The problem was solved. It is a wonder no one had thought of it before!

McIntyre also argued successfully at the convention for the concept of building multistoried wine cellars. On hot days the heat always penetrated the top floor to some extent, but the strong construction used between floors prevented the hot air from going any further! Again the idea was simple, not earthshaking.

McIntyre probably was the first to use concrete in the building of the floor in a winery.

All of these concepts McIntyre incorporated into the construction of Far Niente at Oakville.

The discussion on winery architecture at the Sixth Annual Viticultural Convention took for granted the concept that all crushing was carried out on the top floor of the winery. The movement of any large volume of wine within the winery was a serious problem made simple by allowing gravity to move the wine.

There was yet one other aspect of winery design quite taken for granted. Whenever possible, a winery was located *abutting a hillside*. Actually a large hole was excavated for the first floor into the hillside, which put the second or third story firmly against the hill. This was done so that a road could be constructed from the valley floor along the hillside to the top floor—which gave direct access to the crushing equipment.

Wine cellars located away from such hillsides required transporting the grapes to the top floor by conveyor belts, of some type. To avoid this problem, artificial hills were often created just for the benefit of a winery!

Incidentally, John Benson who hired McIntyre to design his new winery was another of those wealthy San Franciscans who invested lavishly in the Napa Valley but never called it home. He had been born at Boston, Massachusetts in 1824 and on April 1, 1849 he was in California to join the Gold Rush. Benson never admitted to having found any gold in the Sierras, rather he began buying and selling city lots in San Francisco and made a small fortune much easier that way. City directories often listed him as a broker of real estate, or as many wealthy men then preferred to be called "capitalist."

When the transcontinental railroad was completed in 1869, he took long trips to New York and then sailed to Europe for the summer. His fortune continued to accumulate so fast that by 1871 he purchased 306 acres of George Yount's Caymus Rancho Mexican land grant. He set forty acres of it to the Muscat of Alexandria grape—primarily a raisin grape (although every grape was used in wine making or Brandy when no other use could be found for its juice).

Benson was attracted to the Mediterranean coasts for his vacations, particularly Italy and Spain. On one trip abroad he brought back the Carob bean and planted 25,000 of them, hoping to make a special distilled liquor popular in some Mediterranean countries. He introduced the European Messina Quail and planted young cork trees from Portugal. This was not the first planting of the cork tree in Napa Valley, but his plans were more ambitious than predecessors.

Benson's country home and ranch was about a mile and a half south of the site he wanted for his winery. As a matter of fact he had a small wooden winery in place near his home by 1881 or '82, but he did not apply the name "Far Niente" to it. He picked out the knoll northwest of his home for his new winery .

The 60 x 100 foot winery of native stone was to be built by San Franciscans "Ranson and Hill." Only a small portion of it was completed when a dispute erupted between the stone mason and Benson. Such men were not accustomed to taking direction from an "architect" like McIntyre (it was a new profession, certainly) and Benson fired them. 20,000 gallons of wine were produced, nonetheless.

St. Helenans J. Delucchi and Mixon and Son were given the job the following spring of completing the winery with the central portion being raised to three stories and increasing the capacity to 175,000 gallons. The total cost would come to $8,000. Three years later a local newspaper reported: "He does not sell in quantities but bottles and disposes of to clubs. Makes only a wine of the first quality."[IV.21]

If anyone asked Thomas Williams the foreman of the winery and ranch what the formal name of the place, *In Dolce Far Niente* meant in English, he may not have been able to answer the question. Like Eshcol, there was no simple definition and "In dolce far niente" depended upon the meaning desired by the speaker. It was Italian, of course.

The phrase had become very popular with English poets like Lord Byron, who vacationed in Italy frequently and even with America's premier poet, Henry Wadsworth Longfellow. He once wrote in a letter to a friend:

> Your letter was just what I wanted. That is, it was a letter which gave me a graphic picture of yourself and your situation. I could see you at your study window, enjoying Narragansett and Mount Hope a delightful (certainly a very faint) reminiscence of Naples and Vesuvius. It is there Tasso and Ariosto sound sweetest to your ear, that the *dolce far niente* of a summer evening is most heavenly.[IV.22]

Benson could be a dreamer at times, despite his harsh business exterior required for San Francisco. The phrase he adopted means "sweet doing nothing" or simply, sweet nothing.

There was one small fly in the ointment to the Napa Valley viticulture and wine making boom. With over one hundred new wineries opened within five years and 12,000 acres of grapes planted in the first three years of the 1880s, there was a very serious shortage of labor—both in the vineyard and in the winery. The Chinese were the most dependable workers and easily available overnight from San Francisco or St. Helena agents. But growing numbers of vintners feared the consequences if and when they did bring the Chinese into a vineyard for pruning or picking grapes.

S. A. Scott, Brandy gauger for the U.S. Treasury Department, reported letters being received in the Calistoga area threatening to burn buildings of anyone who employed the Chinese: "The men who would maliciously . . . fire another's property is not the one to supersede the Chinamen in the vineyard, on the farm or elsewhere," he angrily exclaimed.[IV.23]

The *San Francisco Chronicle* on October 2, 1883 sent shivers down the spine of many vintners when in an article on the Napa Valley the writer added:

> On the other side of town [St. Helena], toward the South are several vineyard and wineries in easy reach which are worth inspection if one has the leisure. Just on the outskirts of the town you come on the trail of the Chinese, which is over all this paradise, as over every other winery in California.

Riots or something akin to mob violence broke out in many cities in western United States and by May 6, 1882 the United States Congress bowed to pressure and passed the so-called Chinese Exclusion Act. The bill provided for a ten year moratorium on all Chinese immigration into the country (exempting students, teachers, merchants and travelers passing through the United States), and it prohibited the naturalization of Chinese.

It is rather surprising that it took four years before individuals holding anti-Chinese feelings in St. Helena organized to remove its Chinatown. The *Star*, of course, sent a reporter:

> Four o'clock Tuesday was signalized by the tooting of whistles and ringing of bells, and a large crowd soon congregated at the Town Hall. W. T. Simmons took charge of the company and formed them in line. He told them before starting that the demonstration was expected to be quiet and orderly and that one man should do the talking. If anyone couldn't submit to this he had better stay behind. The company then marched to Chinatown to the sound of the drum, beaten by W. D. Ayers. Arriving there, not a Chinaman was to be seen; the doors to their shanties were closed and bolted, shutters were up at the windows and the town seemed deserted.

Police officers Allison, Spurr and Fee had arrived before the marchers and stood their ground on the warm February 1886 day. Several Chinese shop owners were finally induced to come out and listen to the complaints, then everyone marched back into the gathering twilight, perhaps because the man who owned most of their "shanties," John Gillam, was a fighter too.

Gillam explained in a long letter to the local newspaper that the first Chinese in St. Helena arrived about 1868 when the railroad was under construction. Housing was needed and he supplied it, supposedly on a temporary basis. Eighteen years previously, St. Helena residents found the Chinese amusing and enjoyed watching them work, then eagerly hired them to undertake all sorts of tasks. (Chinatown was just across the first stone bridge, heading south toward Napa.) Now that the tide had turned the other way, he was willing to ask the Chinese renters to leave if someone would buy the houses or replace the expected loss of revenue. He had no takers.

There was no question in the minds of most Napa residents that the Chinese were critical to the health of the wine industry.

Large numbers of field workers were needed in early spring to prune the vines, then later in the spring the hoeing of weeds from around each vine—something no machine could do. In the fall, only the Chinatowns of large cities could supply the pool of men needed for picking the grape. They were even extensively employed in the winery itself, in part because the Chinese were far less inclined to drink on the job!

As late as the year 1889, Edward Roberts in Harper's Weekly estimated California employed 30,000 to 40,000 men in the production of wine.[IV.24]

Roberts, too, explained why so many Chinese were hired in preference to white laborers:

> Grape varieties in California, with the exception of a few foreign varieties, are pruned very low, the stem being only about a foot and a half high. . . . Gathering the grapes is laborious work, the picker being obliged either literally to kneel or to bend his back to a painful angle. . . . Chinamen are generally employed as pickers.

Controversial issues such as the Chinese were easily put aside when embarking on a journey to town. County roads from outlying area barely existed. The first road from Berryessa to Rutherford was completed in 1886. The new wagon road covered 22 miles, cost $1,000 per mile, excepting stone bridges and gave residents of the eastern portion of the county their best access to the county seat.

This new roadway was open year-round with the main problem being the frequent flooding of portions of the east side of the valley by the Napa River. No road had been built the entire length of Napa Valley's eastern flank because of the periodic flooding. The State Legislature had authorized the county to raise the funds necessary for an east side road as early as 1881, but the problem was containing the Napa River and that was another subject entirely.

One milestone transpired toward the end of the decade that caused a tear or two to well up in the eyes of old-timers: In June 1888 the Napa-Sonoma Stage Line was discontinued. It had covered the route for thirty years or since 1858. With the new railroad completed that year from Vallejo to Santa Rosa via Sonoma, Napa residents took the more convenient, gentler means of travel.

For many Napa residents who had arrived in the valley before the Gold Rush, even for many who had been residents only a decade, the booming 1880s was not to their liking at all. With more than fourteen thousand residents and dozens of new arrivals each day the serenity of the place was seriously disturbed.

One of the principal objections to the Chinese, for example, was not the difference in color or even that they were not Christian (although this was a grave charge for old-line Southern Baptists from Missouri), the objection was simply they came in too large numbers. When a down valley train arrived at Rutherford or St. Helena, a hundred Chinese sometimes disembarked amid considerable noise and confusion. They were whisked quickly away to nearby vineyards but the intrusion was inescapable.

It was not only the Chinese, however, who brought forth scowls of displeasure from local residents. Almost as many young white laborers found the locals hostile and uncaring. When young white males traveled to the vineyards for field work, they demanded a roof over their heads at night and prepared meals. What they found were barns and often haystacks as a place to sleep and the meals varied not a little from ranch to ranch.

In January 1888 the Independent *Calistogian* began urging local ranchers to build permanent homes for their white workers as one inducement to overcome the tendency to fall back always on the

Chinese. This labor question was discussed and argued so frequently at St. Helena Viniculture club meetings that some members may have stayed away to avoid the rancor it caused among friends.

If anyone needed solid evidence that the problem was very serious, they found it in the murder of wine maker John C. Weinberger in March 1882. No man had been more active in the local wine industry. Weinberger was the first to publicly state he believed the phylloxera disease had invaded Napa Valley and in his vineyards. He imported the first equipment to produce concentrated grape syrup—an alternative to wine making when the prices fell too low. His large stone winery on the hillside a mile north of St. Helena, built in 1876, was as conspicuous and attractive as any in the valley.

Weinberger was shot three times at the Barro (Lodi) train station near the Krug winery by a twenty-nine year old former employee named William Gau. Gau, also from Germany as was Weinberger, had fallen in love with his boss's daughter and when that fact became known any cordiality between the two men because of nationality, disappeared. Weinberger had not explained to anyone why he opposed marriage between the two young people.

Weinberger died within minutes of the shooting which occurred at noon time. When the required coroner's jury assembled the following day to bring a verdict on the cause of death, the jurors were a list of Who's Who in Napa Valley wine making: Charles Krug, Jacob Beringer, C. T. McEachran, John Thomann, William Castner, Ed Heymann and others. The verdict was murder. There was however to be no trial for Gau, he committed suicide.

Later that same year in the Metzner winery, two employees became involved in a fight which one lost and the other won—at least temporarily. The loser went to San Francisco, borrowed a pistol and returned several weeks later and killed his adversary. The young murderer was sent to San Quentin prison for life.

Sometimes there was no making sense of the conflicts that arose in a small supposedly quiet wine making town like St. Helena. As the *Star* editorialized May 12, 1888:

> The lynching of an eighteen year old boy by the citizens of St. Helena last Saturday night will forever remain a blot on that town.

The deed was carried out under a bridge crossing a creek near the Beringer winery. The youth's name was John Wright.

According to eyewitness testimony given at the coroner's inquest, a local resident named Budd Vann had become slightly intoxicated before deciding to visit a local house of "ill repute."

His entry was refused at the door by Wright, a brother of the woman inside. Vann, whose courage was considerably enhanced by his condition, forced his way inside where he was shot by Wright and killed.

Vann's large number of friends were outraged by the act, somewhat justifiable so since Vann's condition should have been taken into consideration and assistance summoned to remove him. The brother acted impulsively, they claimed and without just cause. Wright was brought to trial rather quickly and he angered Vann's friends even more by refusing to testify in his own behalf. He had no attorney present as the speed with which he had been brought to trial did not allow time for the family to arrange any defense.

Perhaps it was young Wright's silence on the matter that resulted in his lynching—in a bizarre sort of way. The refusal of one man to fight another has been known to rile troubled waters even more, something which goes deep into the primal instincts of man. Wright's refusal to defend himself verbally may have been interpreted as arrogance which needed punishment. No charges were ever brought against anyone for the lynching.

Despite the image which might be conveyed by the lynching or even the attempt of a gang of men to rid St. Helena of its Chinese citizens, this was an area of country gentlemen—the wine and grape boom of the 1880s made this a reality. Not only had a great deal of wealth come to the town and vicinity, many men were earning handsome incomes, building expensive large homes and spending much of their time at viticultural meetings. St. Helena grape growers were fascinated with the subject of the grape and always were willing to talk about it. No city in the state sent larger contingents to wine conventions or district meetings sponsored by the State Viticultural Commissioners.

This explains why Santa Clara vine grower J.B.J. Portal told a meeting of his county vine club that St. Helenans were "one of the most unified and best organized associations of this kind on this coast."[IV.25] Santa Clara would do well to pattern itself after their aggressive neighbors to the north.

Even the residents of the city of Napa realized that St. Helena had something very special going for itself and Napa appeared to be left out! "Why should St. Helena, an obscure village of the valley, enjoy greater thrift according to its population than Napa City, the shire town of the county, the Oxford of the Pacific, the most favorably situated place in California?" asked the *Register*.[IV.26]

The editor placed the blame and credit on one group—the St. Helena Vinicultural Association. Whatever they said or did seemed to end up in the newspapers:

> Their talk at these meetings, and every item of interest with regard to their individual success in the business, is given to the local press, the metropolitan press copies it and everybody reads it.

Whether Charles Gardner, as the editor of the *Star* deserved this praise or Gardner as secretary for the St. Helena Viniculturalists club, the end result was still the same. St. Helena wine making was drawing an increasing amount of attention from all over the state.

This condition just could not go on, the city of Napa had to share in some of the press attention and to achieve this desiderate the "Napa Viticultural Association" was established. There may be some measurement of the power of the press here for the organization followed by only one week the stinging editorial in the *Register*.

Thirty-eight members signed the enrollment petition the first night including St. Helenans Charles Krug, E. W. Woodward and Chris Adamson. Nothing serious in viticulture transpired in Napa County which did not involve Krug.

"Of the other signers a very large proportion are not only not vineyardists, but not even farmers in any sense," observed one reporter in attendance.[IV.27] This sounded suspiciously like sour grapes since the Napans who joined that night included just about every important businessman in the town: George and James Goodman, F. L. Coombs, George Cornwell, W. F. Henning and many more.

As the decade of the 1880s progressed, more and more time was spent arguing about the phylloxera. About the vine pest, everyone held a strong opinion; first, that the disease was not going to be serious in Napa Valley then second, it could be overcome with good animal fertilizer, mercury treatment, electric shocks, or with this or that resistant vine.

The Zinfandel grape probably caused as much heated debate at these meetings as all the other grape varieties combined. Everyone grew the grape because it was a quantity producer and that earned growers the most money, yet any reputable wine man denounced the Zinfandel. Krug said at a Napa District Viticultural convention in 1883:

> Among the claret grapes we have abundance of Zinfandel, and we commit a great blunder in planting Zinfandel as we have done. Instead of planting the Zinfandel on the hills, where their proper home is, in warm, loose soil where they make a splendid A. No. 1 noble wine, we have committed the blunder of planting in rich, adobe soil. I myself confess to have committed that blunder.

If Napa vineyardists listened and heeded Krug's advice on most aspects of grape growing, they paid absolutely no attention to his remarks on the Zinfandel. Four years later the *Annual Report* of the State Viticultural Commissioners showed that the Zinfandel far overshadowed every other grape in the valley, even surpassing in acreage many other varieties combined. Nearly 6,000 acres were planted to the Zinfandel while all Riesling types came to 2,636 acres, the Chasselas, Palmino and Burgers amounting to 2,597 acres and even the still popular Mission and Malvoisie, 2,031.[IV.28]

There was even a boast that the popular Zinfandel originated in the Napa Valley, at least in so far as California was concerned.

In June 1885 William Boggs published a long letter in the *Star* describing his early years at Sonoma when Agoston Haraszthy had been his neighbor. Contrary to the claims being loudly disseminated about the state by his son Arpad, Boggs remembered being told that John Osborne of Oak Knoll ranch, north of Napa, had cuttings available for a number of unusual grape varieties. Boggs was on the Board of Directors of the Sonoma Horticultural Club, with Agoston as President, and recalls:

> Many thousand were planted from them [cuttings] the same season in the nurseries of the Horticultural garden under my supervision. Among them were the Zinfandel. Prior to that time there were no foreign vines introduced into Sonoma, excepting one or two varieties of the table grape, Black Hamburg, and another grape that resembled the Zinfandel. . . . Black St. Peter, a few white Sweet Waters and the Catawba and Isabella.[IV.29]

VARIETIES OF GRAPES PLANTED.

Post Office	Acreage 1881	Acreage 1887	All Riesling	Chasselas Font., Palomino, and Burger	Sauternes, incl. Sauv. Vert	Cab. Sauv., Fr. Merlot, Verdot, Malbec	All Reds, except Zin., Miss., and Malv.; all Pinots, Ch. Noir, Alicante, Petit, etc.	Zinfandel	Mostly Miss. and Malv.	Table and Raisin	Tons of Grapes—1886	Gallons of Wine made—1886	Gallons of Brandy made—1886	Resistant Vines, Acres—1887
Conn Valley	223	657	32	112	3	5	60	390	53	1	1,300	150,000		
Spring Mountain	55	355	11	58	5	10	20	216	32	3	400	21,000		
Pope Valley	20	165	2	29		1	1	36	85	4	156	4,000		
Beryessa	18	33		5				12	16		150			
Childs Valley	13	129	15	16	8	5	10	55	20		196	6,000		10
Howell Mountain	100	690	85	110	20	65	150	215	45		390	40,000		20
Calistoga	250	1,710	254	243	25	119	160	522	275	12	2,000	646,000		72
St. Helena	1,611	5,246	963	797	83	255	551	1,831	694	17	14,387	1,777,000		49
Rutherford	721	1,527	200	213	55	45	191	452	94		4,611	404,000		20
Oakville	429	1,085	317	144	33	54	89	433	99	11	4,032	800,000		30
Yountville	585	1,674	264	339	43	28	117	582	195	12	3,960	212,000		25
Napa	1,260	3,340	433	531	137	192	259	1,000	423	50	7,303	348,000		425
	5,285	16,611	2,636	2,597	412	779	1,008	5,744	2,031	109	39,595	4,468,000	102,322	651

(From the Annual Report of the Board of State Viticultural Commissioners, for 1887 (published in 1888). "Varieties of Grapes Planted" in Napa County.)

Boggs' memory may be slightly flawed in that Haraszthy did transfer to Sonoma in 1857 many varieties of grape he was growing in San Mateo County near Crystal Springs. Boggs' claim covers the year 1859, and his long letter is extremely detailed which adds something to its credibility.

Haraszthy could add no proof to the claim his father imported the Zinfandel from his native Hungary except an obscure entry in a daybook kept at Buena Vista—which does not name the variety made reference to. Arpad, by the way, was in France during the late 1850s studying wine making and was not an eyewitness to such events as Boggs describes.

Boggs' letter is noteworthy for another special reason—he included the "Catawba" grape among those being grown in Sonoma before the American Civil War. Catawba is, of course, a major eastern American grape variety *and more than likely carrying on its roots, the phylloxera vine louse.* The disease could easily have been imported into California during the Gold Rush decade and then spread to the major European vines as they were introduced.

Had there been more French immigrant wine makers in the valley grapes like the Zinfandel would not have been so popular. San Jose was the center of the French colony as far as viticulture was concerned in California, but their numbers were increasing very slowly in Napa Valley.

The first French immigrant may have been one "L. Roux" who established his "French Restaurant" on Main Street in Napa in 1862. The question immediately arises as to whether he opened a French style food emporium to meet the needs of his countrymen or was he the first Frenchman who needed some type of employment? One could eat three solid meals a day, seven days a week for $6—about 30¢ a serving.

French operated schools were always popular in small towns in California and Napa had the Paccaud School, on old Sonoma Road in the early 1870s which advertised: "English, French, Music, Board and Washing . . . $30.00."

Henry Pellet, who began making wine in 1859 for John Patchett was often referred to as the first French vintner in the valley, but he was Swiss-born (with good French ancestry, obviously). Bordeaux native Jean Laurent who began making wine in 1874 opposite the Weinberger winery north of St. Helena, must have been the first

Frenchman to own his own cellar in the valley. He had so much competition for this honor that it may never be possible to sort out who came first.

Laurent was born in 1837 and by the age of fifteen was panning for gold near Tuolumne in the Sierras. That he found little of it, or lost it perhaps, somewhere along the way, is evident by his opening a small vegetable farming business near Napa a few years after the American Civil War had ended. (He may have taken his meals at Roux's French Restaurant.) In the early 1870s he abandoned his vegetables for the vine, purchasing land between Krug and Weinberger.

Laurent did not like to work alone during the early years of his wine endeavors, he either had a French partner or had French laborers working with him. A gentleman named Jean Pierre Pichon assisted for several years. Another Frenchman, only identified as "Ferand," worked with Laurent in the early 1880s in making cream of tartar from the deposits which lined all wine barrels and puncheons.

One year before the monumental decade of the 1880s began, Laurent hired more of his fellow countrymen to assist in building a stone cellar 60 x 100 feet in size and two stories. He probably directed the construction himself for it had none of the distinctive qualities that McIntyre incorporated into valley winery design. Nonetheless, it was functional and could hold two hundred thousand gallons. By virtue of the winery's size and Laurent's knowledge of viticulture, he quickly became one of the prominent figures in Napa Valley wine making. Most accounts of St. Helena Viticultural Association meetings carry some reference to him.[IV.30]

About the time Laurent was scurrying about St. Helena planning his wine making, two French brothers named Giaque began modest wine making two miles south of St. Helena. Charles Menefee claimed the brothers had built a winery in 1871. This cellar burned a few months after the crush, and they rebuilt the following year producing 24,400 gallons. At one point the *Star* stated of the brothers wine cellar:

> This large establishment, now under a cloud in a revenue point of view, was yet closed and in the care of a keeper.[IV.31]

Next to Jean Laurent, the most famous French names in the valley were Jean Brun and Jean Chaix who after their first wine making in '77 were referred to forever after simply as "Brun and Chaix."

Two rather novel and pioneering aspects of their viticulture work set Brun and Chaix apart from everyone else in the Napa Valley and earned them considerable enduring notoriety.

Jean Chaix was one of the first advocates of planting vines on Howell Mountain. He liked the intense red volcanic soil and suspected the grape might rise to new heights of perfection when stressed by the hillside gravels and intense sunshine. In early 1880, the first twenty acres of grapes were planted. William Woodward had set a half acre in vines nearby five years earlier and a neighbor, Higinson, also had an experimental patch of 200 vines but Chaix's planting was the first serious commercial vineyard on the mountain.

It was the 50 foot signal tower next to the Brun and Chaix Oakville winery which caught the imagination of everyone for miles around.

The two French immigrants had started their wine making in 1877 in a tiny 20 x 34 foot wooden winery southeast of Oakville. In August construction began of a 160 x 34 foot winery next to the railroad making it possible to produce more than one hundred thousand gallons per year. They had imported nine grape varieties from the Medoc region of France—preferring not to rely on local rootstocks.

Brun and Chaix quickly realized they had a problem communicating between their Howell Mountain vineyards and the Oakville winery. It took too much time to send a horse and rider back and forth, up and down the mountain. They ordered the construction of a water tank building which would reach 50 feet into the air. An inside stairway led to the roof which was surrounded with a high railing:

> But the principal point of the item is that their mountain vineyard about 10 miles to the north, on Howell Mountain is within range of vision, and they first propose to establish a system of signals which will be seen by the aid of telescopes, to communicate whatever is desirable from cellar to vineyard and the reverse. This will be equal to a telegraph while daylight lasts and no doubt a system of flashing lights might carry out the project in the night as well.[IV.32]

To the top of the structure, they added a fifteen foot high windmill with a "12 foot wheel" which made the entire edifice a prominent feature of the landscape. A well bored inside, fed water into a ten thousand gallon tank, whenever the wind was strong enough to turn the huge wheel.

There is some indication the signaling device did not work well or perhaps the men at either end misread the other's frantic arm movements. Six years later Brun and Chaix built an elaborate three storied, 60 x 60 foot stone wine cellar on Howell Mountain.

Much of the interest in the Chaix vineyard experiment on Howell Mountain stemmed from the fact that in 1882 there was a severe frost on the valley floor while high on the hillsides, the cold did little or no damage at all. This may have been Chaix's original motivation for climbing to the 1,400 foot level on the mountain, especially after the hard frost of '77 and the damaged vines of '79.

French immigrant Charles Carpy had arrived in Napa City shortly after the Civil War (probably ate too, in Roux's French Restaurant) and worked in the Uncle Sam Cellar. A year after Brun and Chaix founded their small winery, he and another French partner, C. Anduran, purchased the Uncle Sam winery and began expanding it to 146 x 120 feet with a capacity of nearly half a million gallons. Carpy soon became a major figure in the Napa Viticultural Association as well as involving himself in anything having to do with wine in the valley or San Francisco.

There were many other lesser French names involved in Napa wine making. Emil Bressard and Louis Debanne built a small wine cellar at Oakville the year after Brun and Chaix got started. August Jeanmonod (or Jeanmond) began crushing grapes the same year and, of course, chose Oakville as his place of business. R. Chabot had his stone cellar completed nearly a decade later near Crystal Springs with the name "Villaremi" cut into the stone above the entrance. Vincent Courtois made wine in several valley cellars including operating Larkmead for several years in the 1880s. There was also a Franco-Swiss winery in Conn Valley owned by G. Crochat, Christian Volpers and Fred Metzner.

Despite their collective years of experience in viticulture, the French immigrants did tend to exert less influence than other nationalities because of one basic flaw—few spoke English well enough to converse in technical terms. Typically, the French immigrant was far less interested in dropping his own native tongue in favor of English and resisted that necessity until the bitter end.

There was an attempt in the mid-80s to use the French language in some meetings of the State Board of Viticultural Commissioners and especially at wine conventions. In May 1885 a wine convention in San Jose held an evening session in French.

Charles Wetmore, who was the first Chief Executive Officer of the Viticultural Commissioners was such a Franco-phile, having studied and traveled extensively in France, that he often took the French side in any argument. His impact on viticulture in the nineteenth century was more important than any other individual with the possible exception of Arpad Haraszthy, son of the Hungarian count.

One area of controversy in which the French definitely could offer no advice was the best spacing between vines. In France, where the soil had nurtured grapes for centuries, it was common to plant as many as 2,000 vines to the acre. In California where the soil was virgin, the common spacing was no more than half that amount and usually considerably less. To the French immigrant this was a contradiction for the better the soil, the more vines should have grown per acre. The catch was the lack of rainfall in the summer.

Henry Crabb who contributed a chapter on viticulture to Husmann's 1883 edition *American Grape Growing*, advocated 1,000 vines to the acre. Charles Krug wrote in 1884 that the "most common system of planting adopted in California is that of squares with the vines placed at seven feet apart."[IV.33] This would have meant 889 vines to the acre. The *Star* estimated in 1876 that vines in Napa Valley were planted 666 to the acre.

When the St. Helena Vinicultural Association gave up on vine spacing they were confronted with the height of the vine and whether to stake or not to stake. Agoston Haraszthy was responsible in large part for introducing the concept of keeping the vine close to the ground. San Francisco's *Daily Alta California* reported October 1, 1859:

> Col. Haraszthy does not train his vine in a strong trunk three feet high, as was the old Spanish custom, but he cuts off the stock about ten inches from the ground.

Husmann's *American Grape Growing* confirmed that this was still the case in the 1880s with Gustaf Eisen writing of the Fresno area:

> The trunk of our vines is generally kept to 2 feet. . . .

and Julius Dresel of Sonoma added:

> the vine stem is commonly 18 inches to 2 feet high.

This, of course, was the explanation for so many Chinese working in California vineyards as they did not mind the stoop labor as much as white field hands. Charles Krug may have been the individual who changed all of this almost single-handedly. In July 1886 Krug made public his findings on training vines to grow much higher and along wire supports strung through the vineyard. He claimed he got longer canes from vines whose trunks were trained to a "head" about waist high. With the vines higher off the ground in spring, frost damage was reduced. In the summer heat, the grapes suffered far less than when close to the hot ground.

It was also at this time that French immigrant Eugene Morel convinced William Scheffler at Edge Hill Vineyard that he could make a far superior wine to that of his neighbors by not crushing the grapes at harvest. Instead, Morel had 1,200 and 1,500 gallon fermenting tanks filled with grapes until their weight accomplished the task. Each grape quickly burst and fermentation began.

Scheffler liked innovation. When a man named John L. Heald demonstrated his latest machine for crushing the grape, Scheffler purchased it on the spot. Heald had his shop in Vallejo and quickly gained such an enviable reputation for his work that he could not fill the orders fast enough.

Heald was the first person to offer Napa Valley wine makers a machine which combined several tasks into one: his crusher provided for the emptying of lugs of grapes directly into it at one end and from which a conveyer device moved the grapes into the crusher. It was all operated by steam power and could handle 100 tons per day. Krug had purchased one of the first prototypes built by Heald, then the Beringers ordered one, Henry Crabb bought two, Isaac DeTurck in Santa Rosa purchased one and Heald was, as the saying goes, "in business."

Krug, Pellet, Seneca Ewer, John York and a dozen other wine growers were on hand in July '82 to witness the first public trials of the "Stockton" gang plow near St. Helena. It, too, was a major change in vineyard work for Stockton had come up with the idea of linking together two standard iron frame iron plows. As the *Star* reporter observed:

> In this operation was sounded the death knell to all single plows in the future, for it was demonstrated that a man riding on the seat can drive with more precision than when walking and holding a plow, and can plow two furrows easier than one by the old system.

For the first time in history, vineyard workers stopped walking behind the horse-pulled plow.

There was one universal problem facing Napa wine makers which came up for discussion every time two or more of them got together for longer than five minutes. What could be done to halt the practice of diluting or adulterating California wines, particularly on the East Coast, or selling it with a foreign label on the bottle?

Gottlieb Groezinger stepped off the train in Napa in the fall of 1888, after a wine selling trip to the East and in descriptive phrases laced with unprintable four letter words announced it was "next to impossible to obtain a good glass of [California] wine anywhere in the East."

Jacob Schram had earlier told the *Napa Register* the same thing after an eastern trip in 1886. He discovered that most of the California wine being sold in New York, St. Louis or Boston, was sold with a foreign label on the bottle: "Competition compels us to sell California wines under foreign labels," claimed eastern dealers for they felt the consumer was not educated as yet to drinking wine from America's West Coast.

The eastern newspapers had begun sensing some sort of scandal even earlier and the *New York Post* in the spring of 1883 wrote:

> The trade journals are again directing attention to the fact that a large portion of wine sold in this country as foreign wine is produced in California and sold in bottles labelled with imitation foreign labels.[IV.34]

Every sort of trick possible was resorted to in perpetrating this deception because California wine could be purchased at a far lower cost than French wine and if sold with French labels, retailed for a much higher price. Unfortunately, some or perhaps many bottlers of West Coast wine also "cut" the beverage by adding fruit juice or even water—hence Groezinger's complaint that he could not find a good glass of California wine anywhere. The blame was not entirely on eastern dealers, however, pointed out the *Post*:

> Even in San Francisco, where some local pride might be expected to help the sale of native wines, they are bottled and sold largely with French labels, some being imitations of labels of celebrated

houses, and others being more innocent of deception because they do not steal trademarks."*

Newspaper publicity such as this helped bring about the passage in the State Legislature in spring of 1887 of "The Pure Wine Law." The law declared in Section 2:

In the fermentation, preservation, and fortification of pure wine, it shall be specifically understood that no materials shall be used intended for substitutes for grapes, or any part of grapes; [and] no coloring matters shall be added which are not the pure product of grapes. . . .

This was the first time in California, and probably in the entire country, that a law had been enacted which guaranteed the purity of wine. Wine and, indeed, most alcoholic beverages had been abused and tampered with since Colonial times.

Not everyone was pleased with the new law for it appeared to place the burden of proof of purity on the wine maker and not the dealer.

The only solution to the problem was bottling at the winery of all wine but this was an economic impossibility. A wine bottle (all were hand blown) was far too expensive for general use. Most wine was sold directly from barrels stored in saloons, in cellars of hotels, stores, wherever wine was retailed. The customer usually brought his own container which could be refilled time after time.

Gustave Niebaum attempted to circumvent wine adulteration by bottling all of his wine—but then he had the wealth to afford glass bottles and supposedly his customers could pay the higher cost. The *Star* of August 31, 1888 claimed he allowed "no wine to leave his cellar under two years old, and then only in bottles."

Foreign labels on wine, the phylloxera vine louse or even spring frost did not deter the continued investment in Napa Valley vineyards by wealthy San Franciscans. When Morris M. Estee purchased land northeast of Napa City and announced plans to build a large winery, designed by none other than Hamden W. McIntyre, the entire valley rejoiced. He was the most prominent Californian to

---

*Most wine was sold in bulk, directly from the barrel in California so this statement was gross exaggeration although still pinpointing a problem.

recognize the valley's wine future, eclipsing even Niebaum or Samuel Brannan.

Estee had come to California in 1853 when 20 years old and grabbed a gold pan and shovel and headed for El Dorado County. He had been a school teacher in his native Pennsylvania and returned to that profession to make a living when the gold nuggets proved too difficult to find. Because he had a gift for oratory, a friend suggested he study law and by '59 he was admitted to practice in Sacramento and elected three years later to the State Assembly. Thereafter he won election to one position after another in the state or was named to political jobs by friends "in high places."

He had become a resident of San Francisco by the time he became the secretary of the state Republican Party and Speaker of the Assembly at Sacramento. He was chosen by his party on two occasions to be United States senator, but the Republicans failed each time at the polls and likewise Estee. In 1882, only a year after purchasing land for vineyard in Napa Valley, Estee was nominated for Governor of California by the Republican Party.

Estee had been named President of the newly formed Napa Viticultural Association just the year previously. Would it be possible that the new governor of the state would be a Napa Valley resident? The concept was so exciting that "Estee Clubs" were formed in most towns. It seemed obvious that the gods were smiling down on the valley, first with the grape and wine boom and now Morris Estee.

Estee made one tactical error which may have contributed to his defeat in November. He began passing himself off as a gentleman farmer, even appearing at a state Grange meeting in disheveled clothing, from dirty boots to an old felt hat. The Grange could deliver a large solid block of votes and Estee thought he would win those votes by dressing down to the common man.

The California press quickly took note of his new appearance and as the *Healdsburg Enterprise* put it September 30:

> When he addresses his San Francisco and Oakland audiences he assumes the dress of a fastidious man of fashion. Perhaps, he occasionally takes a harlequin character for political purposes.

Estee also had problems walking the political tightrope in Napa Valley between the many foreign-born residents and those whom considered themselves natives. This undercurrent of hostility toward primarily European immigrants made itself known in a letter to the *Napa Reporter* just before the election. The writer wanted to know why Estee spent so much time with Krug and Scheffler and Pellet and the Beringers rather than American-born citizens like Lewelling, Crabb, Ewer or William Bourn. Krug responded with a Letter to the *Star* denying the allegation and pointing out that Estee was the best friend the vine grower ever had in California.

The charge did not make sense since Estee had visited the home of the Lewellings, the Bourn residence and others just before a grand pre-election torchlight parade in St. Helena. He had eaten dinner with the Schefflers instead of with a native American. Could the irritation have derived from the fact that Estee was accompanied from San Francisco by another friend, named Emmanuel Goldstein? Estee lost the election by 67,175 votes to George Stoneman's 90,694.

At the Republican National Convention in Chicago in 1888, Estee was elected chairman and he helped guide the name of Benjamin Harrison through the political process until he was the party's standard bearer in November for President of the United States. Estee's reward, two years later was being named United States District Judge for Hawaii, a surprise to most Napa residents and probably even to Estee. Estee did run again for Governor of California in 1894, and lost by a slim margin to James H. Budd.

Estee hired architect McIntyre to draw up plans for an elaborate stone winery on Atlas Peak Road in 1885. It was to be 125 feet long, 60 feet wide, two stories of stone and one of wood. Stone tunnels to be carved into a wall of stone half the height of the winery, would provide the most attractive tunnels in all of California!*

----

*The winery is in perfect condition even now but has not been used for wine making since Prohibition. Quail Ridge winery leases the stone tunnel for aging and a retail outlet. Dale and Delores Buller purchased the property in 1954 and live in the elegant stone house next to the winery also built by Estee. Estee entertained frequently here his Republican party friends from all over the state. No doubt some of the decisions were even made here to support Benjamin Harrison's candidacy for President in 1888. At the national convention of the party that year, Estee was elected chairman and guided Harrison~s candidacy through the entire political process with Harrison winning the presidency, of course. No doubt many other political bargains were concluded in the Estee/ Buller home which determined who ran for U.S. senator or congressman, governor of California and even state assembly or county offices. The site should be a state historic landmark and it certainly is of historical significance in and for Napa Valley and county.

HANSEN/LEWELLING PHOTOGRAPH ALBUM

HARVEY J LEWELLING   HANS HANSEN

HOTOGRAPHY was so experimental in the 1880s that only the boldest individuals took it seriously, even as a hobby. Portrait photographers, most of them itinerant working out of studios rented for brief periods, were slowly becoming accepted by society, with their heavy cameras, tripods and sinister black hoods.

Harvey J. Lewelling (1855-1939) of St. Helena was in his twenties when he learned the camera, although his wealthy family had another career for him in mind, such as bank president.

Harvey liked to photograph the family's trotting horses and other subjects close to his Sulphur Springs avenue home. He did, however, capture most of St. Helena's Fourth of July parade in 1885. New wineries fascinated him. They were cropping up at the rate of nearly fifty a year in the Napa Valley and became one of his favorite subjects.

Some three decades later in Oakville, a youthful Hans Hansen (1874-1942) took the same interest in his family farm. He had one of the new hand-held cameras and sent his film to San Francisco for processing. Lewelling had developed his own film in a studio located where the *St. Helena Star* is now published.

Hansen was most interested in capturing "moments" in time such as the first replanting of a vineyard decimated by phylloxera. He also oversaw the first experimental vineyard established at Oakville by the U.S. Department of Agriculture.

The Lewelling and Hansen families were linked in 1943 when Ray Lewelling (son of Harvey) married Vera Hansen (daughter of Hans). The photographs on the following pages were made available through the courtesy of Vera Hansen Lewelling. Most have never been published.

Most housewives did not need to shop in town a century ago, traveling salesmen came calling with their wares. J. Rutledge sold paints, oils, brushes, glass and painted house and carriage signs. He also sold space to Geo. Beach, local Realtor as is indicated by the advertisement behind the wagon wheels.

Lewelling's Chinese servants, "Tan" being the one on the right, the other not identified. Many Chinese disliked being photographed because it was feared the film might capture their spirit. The Chinese made up as much as 80% of the field and winery work force in the valley about the time this photograph was taken.

Even the vines were young when Lewelling took this photograph of the new Beringer winery in the early 1880s. A century of tree growth has all but obscured this particular view.

WINERY MYSTERY SOLVED. *For years historians have been searching in the Napa Valley for the old Peterson winery, built in 1885 at Vineland station, south of St. Helena. Lewelling photographed the structure the year it was completed.*

Taken less than a year after it was constructed in 1885, this symbol of the popular television soap-opera, "Falcon Crest" was once home to San Francisco banker Tiburcio Parrott. Some of Napa Valley's first varietal wine of the Cabernet Sauvignon grape made Parrott's wine world famous a decade before the 1900s began.

Fritz Beringer had not have moved into his fancy new home at the Beringer winery when Lewelling took this photograph. Construction had begun in 1883 and fire did serious damage to the interior less than two years later.

In the early 1900s teams of men such as shown in these two photographs were seen as heroes in Napa Valley. They restored the phylloxera-ravaged vineyards with disease resistant vines. The resistant root stock was imported from France and in the field, grafted to cuttings of vines like the Cabernet Sauvignon or Zinfandel. A good grafter was one who worked rapidly and had a success rate of 95% or better with grafts.

Hans Hansen took this photograph of his field grafters about to go to work. The snapshot is far better composed and of greater clarity than the previous two which have Hansen in both (the man in the suit) and were taken by a neighbor. Most of Hansen's snapshots have been lost.

Most wineries carried out their annual fermentation outside, not inside the winery, usually under a shed roof. The fermentation tanks here at the John Wheeler winery, at Zinfandel lane and Highway 29 are clearly visible. Wheeler was sure Prohibition meant the end of wine production so he demolished his winery in September 1923.

Not far from the presentday Robert Mondavi winery stood this vast complex known as the H. W. Crabb wine cellar. Crabb grew hundreds of varieties of grapes and knew more about them than any other person in the state. His wines ranked among the to five in the valley. His "To-Kalon" label virtually disappeared after the winery burned May 28, 1939.

be carved into a wall of stone half the height of the winery, would provide the most attractive tunnels in all of California!*

McIntyre designed the winery so that it faced the east and he left room for twelve windows and two large doors. The building was to be 51 feet high. The stone for the massive walls could not be cut from the nearly perfect seam of rock to be used for the tunnels, rather it came from a nearby hillside "not a mile away, and is easily worked and splendidly adapted to building purposes. It can be cut and molded into any shape with an axe when first taken-out, but hardens with age," noted the *Register* in April.

Alfred A. Tubbs, a founder in San Francisco of the Tubbs Cordage Company did something quite different from Estee—he refused to get off the train at Napa and rode it to the very end, Calistoga. Here in 1882 he began his first purchases of land, the John Hoover farm of 200 acres and the J. M. Wright farm of 122 acres. His mansion was built immediately, the winery could wait. His home reportedly cost $40,000 to build, that was much more than most wealthy newcomers spent on their winery .

Tubbs' interest up valley may have stemmed from his friendship with the men who had founded the Napa Valley Wine Company in the 1870s: Krug, the Beringers and M. G. Ritchie. Tubbs was named president of the wine organization the year after he arrived in the valley even though he was not making wine and had no grapes for sale.

Tubbs, of course, had to have the best winery architect in California and took himself to Rutherford in July 1886 to see Hamden W. McIntyre. One month later, the work began and then was halted within weeks. The Star of August 20 explained:

> The excavation made for the Tubbs wine cellar is not satisfactory, as the rock at each side slacks and falls to the floor. This will be overcome, however, by constructing a wall of stone or brick against the crumbling rock.

The carpenters worked overtime to have the Tubbs wooden winery ready a month later for the *first crush* that fall of 1886. And either Tubbs purchased many tons of grapes or his first harvest was magnificent for he produced 125,000 gallons of wine. The wooden structure also served for wine production the following year and it was not until '88 that the stone building was completed. He gave the name "Hillcrest" to his winery, because of the view, and the style of architecture was described as "castellated"— "built like a castle with turrets and battlements."*

It was not unusual for two wealthy men to combine resources for the construction of a winery and this is what Seneca Ewer and J. B. Atkinson did in Rutherford. Unless they knew each other in the Sierras panning for gold, they may not have met until the wine boom brought them together. They both came to California in '49 but Ewer settled in Butte County, ranching, practicing law and occasionally being elected to the State Assembly. Atkinson settled in San Francisco and operated a very successful wholesale commercial business. Ewer moved to St. Helena in 1870, helped found three banks, including being president of the Bank of St. Helena and gave the city its first water system.

During one of the lulls in construction of Inglenook, they talked McIntyre into designing an all stone structure near Ewer's 100 acres of grapes in Rutherford. The stone was cut at a quarry on Howell Mountain and enough was needed for a 60 by 125 foot, two-story winery. The description of its operations from the *Star* a year after it was built, deserves quoting:

> The grapes are carried direct from the wagon to the crusher, some 40 feet above, by means of an improved elevator, which takes back the empty boxes at the same time. The juice and pomace are carried from the crusher by means of long chutes running the whole length of the cellar, from which they are distributed to the various tanks by heavy galvanized iron spouts. The arrangement seems to us to be as near perfection as any we have seen.

A sampling of the previous year's Golden Chasselas wine elicited equally generous compliments.**

In the *Star*'s Christmas edition in '85 there is a column listing all of the construction for the past year in the vicinity. Among the twelve

---

*The old wooden wine cellar burned long ago, but the sturdy wine castle survives today as Chateau Montelena.

**In 1923 Georges de Latour moved his Beaulieu wine operation into the Ewer and Atkinson winery. By means of additions built afterward, the facade is entirely hidden from view, making it impossible to compare it to Far Niente or other McIntyre designed wineries .

names which included either an addition to a wine cellar or a new one, is Fritz Rosenbaum. Rosenbaum had settled just north of the Beringers (in the German neighborhood of the town where he could speak his native tongue). Very successful at importing and selling plate and window glass in San Francisco, he had begun making wine in his basement in '79, the year after he built his attractive, two-story Victorian style home. He made only 3,500 gallons the first year but by the time his name was added to that Christmas edition list, he had 13,000 gallons of wine.*

Not more than a mile or so south of Rosenbaum, William Bourn picked out a site for a gigantic winery, the largest in California or very close to it. There was something about the land just north of St. Helena that caught the eye of many investors, it may have been the proximity to Charles Krug who ranked among the top wine makers in all of California. Bourn had the riches, earned from California gold mines, to buy and build anywhere plus he had an idea for a semi-cooperative winery which might change the way the entire valley industry functioned thereafter.

Henry Pellet summed up the need for Bourn's ideas better than any statement he could have issued. Pellet, as president of the St. Helena Vinicultural Club, struck at the heart of low prices for wine and the huge San Francisco wine warehouses that controlled it when he said:

> This meeting has been called for the purpose of hearing the proposition Mr. Bourn has to offer, and the opinions of those present on the matter. The object of his cellar is to lift the wine industry out of the slough it is now in and to get out of the clutches of the San Francisco wine dealers who have us by the throat. We should erect this cellar so as to be able to hold our wines and not sell at the prices offered to us.[IV.35]

The year was 1888, the month March and the price of wine had fallen so low that the bloom was off the great wine boom in Napa and everywhere else. There was far too much wine for the market,

---

*In 1962 Michael Robbins began restoring the house and resumed wine making there under the name Spring Mountain. Thirteen years later, William and Alexandra Casey of San Francisco purchased the house, completing its renovation and added a new wine making addition for their St. Clement brand wines.

although that obvious fact was not what Pellet or anyone else in the industry wanted to hear.

What Bourn and partner Everett Wise proposed doing was building a million gallon winery on the following terms: (1) they would produce wine from anyone's grapes, on shares, and store the wine entirely separate under the owner's name; (2) the wine would be held until a buyer could be found and then and only then would he be paid; (3) or the grower could sell his grapes directly to the winery and he would be paid directly. "No Malvoisie, Mission, inferior grapes or grapes in bad condition, will be received for wine making."

The intention was to build a great inventory of superior Napa Valley wines, well aged, and available to buyers from the East. The quality would be strictly controlled. It was expected that the prices paid for the wine would be far above that offered by the great San Francisco wine emporiums which paid no attention to local identity. Once in the city all wine was "California" though it was stored by grape variety.

There was one other aspect of the proposed new winery which did not meet with blanket approval—Bourn proposed that he would put in $25,000 cash but wanted each grower who intended to use the facility to subsidize it by contributing 1,500 tons of grapes—repayable in three years. The wine would cost .02¢ per gallon to store each year and there were other fine points that seemed to get lost in all the debate. R. E. Wood did not favor it nor B. Ehlers who thought a 5% subsidy should be levied to raise the funds, as 1,500 tons for a small grower was a lot, but for a large vineyardist like Bourn (who had 600 acres in grapes) it was nothing.

Two weeks after this first meeting, an agreement was reached for the construction of the Bourn & Wise winery. Hamden W. McIntyre came up from Rutherford to offer his advice. San Francisco architects Percy & Hamilton drew the actual plans for building 400 feet long by 70 feet wide with a front center section protruding 20 additional feet and 50 feet wide. The cost of the winery was so high and so staggering that many growers must have pulled back in fright—a quarter of a million dollars!

The site for the winery had been a relatively steep hillside before a sharp cut was made into the soil, providing a level spot for construction. The soil removed thereby was carefully spread down to the main road and then terraced—a year later the change was hardly noticeable.

The walls were built of stone from a nearby quarry and the mortar used was the newly available Portland cement. Portland cement was used for the entire flooring on the first level and the second floor as well with iron bars embedded to give additional strength. Columns reinforced with iron were used for support and it was only on the third floor that the traditional heavy timbers were finally utilized. All three floors were used for aging and storage, the crushing of the grapes took place in what was the attic.

"Greystone" as the winery soon came to be affectionately called, also was the first winery in California to be operated by electricity and lighted by electric bulbs. The boiler and engine to produce this new kind of power was located under the 20 x 50 foot projecting wing from the central portion.

There were grand plans for "thirteen" wine tunnels to be dug deep into the hillside behind the winery. The first, 80 feet in depth, was completed by the fall of 1889. It was 16 feet wide and 12 feet high, big enough for a horse and wagon to drive through, which may have been in the minds of Bourn and Wise as a means of moving wine.

Unlike Gustave Niebaum, the names of the builders of this giant wine depot were not long associated with the winery. Everett Wise sold his interest to his partner within two years of its opening and moved to Healdsburg. In 1894 Bourn sold the Greystone to Charles Carpy and though the family had a home south of town, he seldom could be found there. San Francisco was more to his liking.

Bourn really did not relate well to the wine men of St. Helena. He may have owned six hundred acres of vineyards, but he rarely even walked through his vineyards—it was just an investment. He did not attend viticultural meetings. He may have made a slight miscalculation as well, when he told the first growers' meeting to consider his winery project: "The object is to get the wine business out of the hands of the Jews."

It was true that many men of Jewish background were the owners of the great wine marts in San Francisco, which ultimately purchased most of the wine made in the state. There were companies like Lachman & Jacobi, S. Lachman & Co., B. Dreyfus & Co. (of which Emmanuel Goldstein was one conspicuous member), C. Schilling, Kohler and Van Bergen and Alfred Greenbaum & Co. Gustave Niebaum was once asked if he were Jewish since he sold most of his wine through Greenbaum & Co., and his closest friends were Jewish. He often said "yes," although he was Finnish Lutheran.

The great wine glut which spread over California in the late 1880s had nothing to do with Jewish wine merchants. There was simply too much wine being produced for the market and the market needed expanding through good advertising.

Ernest Dickman, associated with the Edge Hill winery, knew exactly what was wrong and told his colleagues one day that the "wine business could be resurrected and placed on a paying basis through the means of 'printer's ink.'" His idea was to rent warehouses in major eastern cities, fill them with fine wine and then make a "strong bid for the public patronage—both retail and wholesale—by means of advertising on a large scale."[IV.36]

Charles Wetmore claimed restaurants marked up the price too high on wine and this drove away customers. Wine could certainly be sold for the same price as tea or coffee, and still make a profit for everyone concerned.

Adolphe Grossman told his neighbors again what none wanted to hear in a letter to the editor of the *Register* just before the 1888 fall crush began. There was just too much wine being produced and the market reacted as it would with any other product, by declining sharply.[IV.37]

Viewed from a statewide perspective the situation was not nearly so bleak. The Pacific Bank of San Francisco, which monitored the growth of the industry more than any other commercial institution, was pleased to point out that about $75,000,000 had been invested in vines and wineries during the decade. Across California's landscape, 5,000 individuals now owned vineyards and wine production which was nearing 20,000,000 gallons annually, could be expected to climb another ten million within a few years.

"From year to year in the future not only the quantity but the quality of our wine will improve, till California is as justly celebrated in the new world as France is in the old," boasted the *Pacific Bank Handbook of 1888* which included the above statistics.

Arpad Haraszthy had some of the same enthusiasm for the future of the industry when he told the Sixth Annual Viticultural Convention in San Francisco in March:

> At this period, after eight years of existence, the Board of Com-
> missioners believe that there are planted not less than one hundred

of these plantings have revolutionized public opinion in favor of California wines, and new markets conquered that the most sanguine among you scarce hoped for.[IV.38 (Italics added.)]

After Haraszthy's dire warnings of a few years earlier on over planting, such positive remarks were like a healing ointment on an open wound. There was a brighter side, after all.

Ironically, the vintners of Napa Valley had been doing everything right for several years without realizing it and as the decade closed, it all paid off with unbelievable results. *It was in the year 1889 that Napa Valley moved up dramatically to become the premier wine region of the United States.* The French wine industry, at the Paris World's Fair was really responsible for putting the royal crown on this achievement by awarding to local wine makers more wine medals than any other region in California or other state.

There were broad hints much earlier that Charles Krug's repeated calls for wine quality not wine quantity might be paying off. For example, *Harper's* of March 9, carried an exceptionally long article on California wine. Three and a half pages of the publication, which was nearly newspaper size, gave the most intimate look at California wine ever presented by an eastern publication—it was a milestone achievement.

Author Edward Roberts reserved for the Napa Valley his highest superlatives:

> The two best known valleys—those having a soil and climate adapted for the production of the choicest grapes from the Medoc, Bordeaux, and Rhine Valley districts—are Sonoma and Napa.
>
> I cannot imagine a more sheltered pretty nook than the upper Napa Valley.
>
> It is a little world in itself. . . .
>
> Several of the Napa growers own estates that have no counterpart in America.

He mentioned particularly, Inglenook, the Beringers, Charles Krug, Tiburcio Parrot and Estee.

Napa Valley was treated so exceptionally by Roberts because they treated him with great care. He was wined and dined and carriaged from one end of the valley to the other. It appears no other region took this interest in the wine writer. Roberts was candid enough to admit it in this unusual paragraph:

There is little to choose between Sonoma and Napa valleys. Both are picturesque, shut in by low hills, and in either are many vineyards where one may initiate himself into the mysteries of winemaking. In selecting Napa Valley we were influenced to some extent by the introductory letters given us in San Francisco. Having them, we knew that the largest vineyards would be open to our inspection.

To be fair to Sonoma Valley, which tended to rest on its laurels earned in part from Agoston Haraszthy, growers and wine men there were fighting what seemed a losing battle with the phylloxera. The completion of a second railroad through the valley, from Vallejo to Santa Rosa, also had caused many vineyards to be uprooted as one scheme after another emerged to sell "country property" to investors in San Francisco.

Buoyed by so many compliments it was little wonder that the Napa Valley united as never before to send wine to the World's Fair in Paris in '89. France had never allowed American or California wines to compete in one of its international competitions, although it had somewhat condescendingly given a few certificates previously to American wines. This time, however, the French felt some need to be more friendly to their American cousins since American rootstock, resistant to the phylloxera, had just proven the savior of their great winescape.

George Husmann had accepted the responsibility of gathering the California wine to be sent to Paris. In a letter to the *Register* of October 25 he quite brusquely described his task:

> I was treated more like a beggar asking alms, than the agent of a Department [U.S. Dept. of Agriculture] trying its best to advance the interest of the wine growers of the State. From Sonoma County, which is so fond of calling itself the cradle of the wine industry of the State, I could get but five or six exhibits and not one from the southern part of the State, although I spent several weeks there trying to wake them up. Nearly all of the exhibits came from Napa county, and a few from the dealers in San Francisco . . .

Of thirty-four medals or awards given California entries for wine, brandy or champagne, Napa Valley collected twenty of them! That was nearly three-quarters of the entire coveted collection. Migliavacca in Napa City won the only Gold for the Valley; Wetmore and Adrian Chauche of Livermore each won Golds as well as the Board of State Viticultural Commissioners.

and Adrian Chauche of Livermore each won Golds as well as the Board of State Viticultural Commissioners.

Silver medals were won by Beringers, Greenbaum & Co., S.F. (for Inglenook), Henry Hagen of Cedar Knolls, Napa Valley Wine Co. and the Weinberger winery (now operated by Mrs. John Weinberger).

Bronze medals went to Chris Adamson, Rutherford; Brun & Chaix of Oakville; Charles Krug (of course); John Matthews, Napa and V. Courtois of St. Helena.

Honorable Mentions from the French in 1889 were barely rated below the Golds—just winning some type of recognition was reward enough. California wines collected five in this category, four going to Napa Valley: Edge Hill Winery, St. Helena; Ewer and Atkinson, Rutherford; Adolphe Grossman of Napa and last but by no means least, the sometimes barber Jacob Schram.

Eight awards were given to California brandies: Henry Hagan of Napa won a Silver medal; Napa Valley Wine Company, Silver; H. W. Crabb, Oakville, Bronze; Edge Hill winery, St. Helena, Bronze; Nouveau Clos, St. Helena, Honorable Mention and Krug picked up his second award with an Honorable Mention for Brandy. Krug and Edge Hill were the only double winners for Napa Valley.

It took most of the following winter for valley residents to calm the euphoria which followed the Paris wine competition. Everyone wanted to believe what the *Merchant* claimed on October 22, but which few dared to utter:

> In fair competition with the whole world, the wines of California have carried off twenty-seven medals [*] of which four were gold, eleven were silver and twelve bronze, besides honorable mention in seven cases. . . . It means that France, our greatest rival, has declared to the world that the products of California's vintages rank with those of her own in point of excellence.

The *San Francisco Chronicle* did not straddle the fence as did the *Merchant* in its enthusiasm for the "California" wine awards. Napa was clearly the big winner. On the 6th of October it carried a long story on the Napa Valley, calling the lower portion the "California Medoc" and announced a major change was taking place:

> Napa vineyards are well known on the Pacific coast, but until

---

*This is for wine only and does not include champagne or brandy.

within the past few years the district nomenclature of wines were comparatively unknown to Eastern people, the generic term of 'California wine' being the title under which the productions of the State, no matter from what county they originated, were introduced. Today Napa wines stand high in public favor. Vineyardists such as Morris M. Estee, Jacob Schram, Captain G. Niebaum, H. W. Crabb, and others have in many ways attracted attention to the superior productions of the valley.

The adjectives did not stop there, especially for Judge Stanly's wines of the Carneros. He rated several paragraphs of highly complimentary observations.

There was a cause and effect set in motion by all the publicity which is difficult to trace. For example, Frona Eunice Wait, San Francisco's first woman journalist, published that fall her book *Wines and Vines of California*. It was the first book written for the wine consumer and she devoted the most lengthy chapter to Napa, calling it "The Banner Wine-Making County." Had she planned it that way before Paris? It hardly seems she could rewrite any portion of the text but she may have changed the title of the chapter!

Letters soon arrived from eastern publications inquiring as to what time of year was the best to visit the Napa Valley. One even came from London, England where Charles Oldham, a member of the wine importing firm of Grierson, Oldham & Co., inquired about accommodations during a planned tour of the wine country. When news of this trip leaked out, the *Merchant* front paged the story. At last the English were coming to California to taste and purchase local wines, or at least that was the hoped for result.

After months of sampling wines, brandies and champagne, and being treated with even more kind attention in the Napa Valley than had been Edward Roberts, Oldham announced he would be purchasing Inglenook wines, among several he found to his satisfaction in the state. If the Paris competition brought Oldham to Napa Valley, all the effort by Husmann and others was paid off handsomely.

The year 1889 was certainly the capstone to the valley's efforts to reach the front rank of wine producing regions in the state, and no doubt the honor could be extended to cover the United States, as well. There simply was no other region which received so much attention thereafter.

This momentum, in retrospect had been building for quite some time. For example, at the Sixth Annual Viticultural Convention held in San Francisco in March 1888, Napa Valley won 22 medals in the dry wine category; Alameda County was second with 17 awards, followed by Santa Clara with 4 and only 1 each for Sonoma and Santa Cruz. Sweet wines produced in the county garnered another 4 awards, with San Joaquin and Fresno counties each winning 2.

One of those awards was won by the Goodman brothers for wine made at their Eshcol winery: "First Place" for an 1886 "Cabernet Sauvignon." This may be the first award ever given in California for a clearly marked Cabernet Sauvignon.

The Cabernet Sauvignon was the darling variety of the Bordeaux Claret wines and one Wetmore and Krug and others were championing at each and every viticultural discussion. It certainly had been imported and planted by French immigrants in Santa Clara County in the early 1850s, but none would have then considered using the name of the grape on the wine they produced. That would have been an unheard of departure from centuries of European tradition.

It almost certainly was a retired English army captain who introduced the concept that wine made almost exclusively of the Cabernet Sauvignon grape could be produced and consumed in California. James Drummond, descendant of a Scottish banking family, settled in nearby Glen Ellen, Sonoma Valley, in 1878. He knew fine wine, having had it served in the household where he grew up and from travels through France's wine regions. Drummond planted the grape immediately, along with several hundred varieties, and in 1884 at the State Viticultural Convention offered it for tasting. Wetmore observed:

> It [Cabernet Sauvignon] is only experimentally known here at present. The sample of wine made by Mr. Drummond in 1882 was more admired at the last Viticultural Convention than any other on exhibition—notwithstanding its youth.[IV.39]

It may be that Drummond's curiosity and willingness to break with tradition (he married a divorced woman and was ostracized by the family, an explanation in part for settling in California) led to the first varietal wine of the Cabernet Sauvignon. Almost certainly this helped trigger the movement in the 1880s to experiment with the production of all kinds of wines without following the tried and true standards in France where blending was the only correct procedure, all else was heresy.

Less than six months after the Paris event, the *San Francisco Examiner* published a special fourteen page section on the wine and raisin industry of California. An entire page is devoted to describing publisher Hearst's Madrone winery in Sonoma Valley, but then Inglenook was similarly honored plus generous treatment for Crabb's To Kalon wines and the Napa Valley Nurseries of Leonard Coates.

Although Napa County had a diversified agricultural economy, vine planting now moved into portions of Napa's landscape reserved for other industries. For example, in the Napa Redwoods, surrounding Mt. Veeder, the summer resort industry ran into serious difficulties. There was not enough local help to plant vines and carry trunks of weary San Francisco travelers.

Napa County had always leaned toward the summer resort as a primary means of maintaining its economy, in part because there were still so many residents who opposed the consumption of alcoholic beverages. There were bubbling springs of mineral waters everywhere and the mild, sometimes hot, summer sun attracted thousands of laborers and their families from in and around San Francisco which was blanketed with fog from June on.

Calistoga had been the first portion of the valley to be developed for summer vacationers. The so-called "White Sulphur Springs" west of St. Helena were much appreciated by consumptive patients and vacationers from as early as the mid-1860s.

The "Mt. Veeder Resort" began operations in the late 1870s and though the trip to its lofty and always sunny cabins was arduous compared to other resting places, it was the favorite for men, women and children with strong legs. The landscape here often seemed nearly perpendicular.

Mt. Veeder, located twelve miles northwest of Napa City on the Sonoma County boundary rose to 2,677 feet and considering that travelers at Napa began from an elevation of only 60 feet, this was an ascent of some moderate proportions. The name, incidentally, was that of the Rev. Peter Veeder, a Presbyterian minister in Napa before the Civil War who appears to have received nearly divine inspiration for his sermons by frequent climbs up these slopes.

In the winter, this western portion of the Napa County received copious amounts of rainfall, so much so that the California Redwood tree was indigenous to the region. In the *Register* of July 11, 1879 may be found one of the early descriptions of a modest somewhat loosely defined valley referred to generally thereafter as "The Redwoods." If Mt. Veeder was the focus of a story in the local press, this name was interchangeable.

Because of the superbly clean air, views stretching clear to San Francisco and mountain hiking, visitors found the Mt. Veeder resort more attractive often than similar places on the valley floor. Indeed, nearly all of the first settlers in the Redwoods quickly converted homes to self-styled resorts during the summer months.

Hudemann's Resort preceded the one on Mt. Veeder by some years and was at first the summer retreat for anyone in the Bay Area of German nationality. Herman Hudemann had purchased the largest naturally cleared landscape in the Redwoods in the 1860s and by '73 had a ten acre vineyard. His vines were used primarily for making home wines to be consumed by his guests. He built a stone winery 30 x 20 feet though no documentation exists as to the precise year.*[IV.40]

Hudemann is not the pioneer wine maker of the Redwoods. Stalham Wing made wine from grapes grown on his farm in the shadows of Mt. Veeder as early as 1864. At the Napa County Fair of that year, he was one of only five wine exhibitors. Except for the references to his fruit growing and wine making in the *California Farmer* of October 4, 1864 nothing else is known of his agriculture or viticultural pursuits.

By the mid-1880s, small wine cellars were being constructed on many of the small farms and more trees felled to make land available for vineyards. John Hein could produce 20,000 gallons in his stone winery; Dr. M. B. Pond (the county physician and leading exponent of a state asylum high on Mt. Veeder for tubercular patients) had a 16,000 gallon winery; A. S. Roney probably used most of his small production of 1,000 gallons for summer visitors to his resort; the same may have been true of F. Mara with 800 gallons and Peter and John Gartman with 2,600 gallons.

In 1886 J. H. Fisher began construction of a more commercial winery on the southwestern slopes of Mt. Veeder. It measured 52 feet

---

*The winery still survives, though long unused for that purpose on the site of the Christian Brothers, Mont La Salle winery. This is now under long-term lease to Donald Hess of Switzerland and his Hess Collection winery.

across the front and 32 feet deep, recessed into the hillside. Because of the location, hauling wine by horse and wagon was difficult and Fisher kept his production to about 20,000 gallons.*

Another wine maker who brought significant attention to the Napa Redwoods in this period was Dr. J. A. Bauer, who owned the old Stalham Wing farm. Bauer claimed to have found a remedy for the phylloxera vine disease by using quicksilver. He may have found cinnabar on his own property and had it reduced to quicksilver in ovens at one of several mines just west of Oakville.

For a brief period, San Francisco newspapers carried stories on the Bauer quicksilver cure for the phylloxera including an endorsement by Prof. F. W. Morse of the University of California. A few months after Bauer cabled the French government seeking a $60,000 prize for eliminating the vine pest, Prof. Morse withdrew his premature announcement noting that Bauer's vineyards were now succumbing to the disease. While Bauer and the University suffered some embarrassment, the Napa Redwoods had emerged from obscurity for a large number of Bay Area newspaper readers.

Bauer's wine production was also small and along with Ernest Streich's newly opened Castle Rock winery, probably gave the Redwoods a total of barely 50,000 gallons of wine yearly. Wine production was held down by poor roads and steep terrain and when the creeks were high, which could be frequently during the winter months of high rainfall, wine makers were almost isolated from the Napa Valley and outside markets.

There were many Napa Valley wine makers who kept one eye on the expanding hillside vineyards around Mt. Veeder because of a quiet but enduring argument about the quality of hillside grapes as compared to the valley floor. Ernest Streich had chosen what appeared at first to be a nearly inaccessible place for his Castle Rock vines, as did John Brandlin another German immigrant farmer. Taking their cue from Jacob Schram and Charles Krug's new interest in Howell Mountain, these men were convinced the best wines would eventually come from vineyards with a view.

This debate was argued rather frequently in the press, although somewhat indirectly. For example, when Edward Roberts wrote his long story on "California Wine-Making" for *Harper*'s in 1889, he was

*This is now ~he site of the Mayacamas Vineyards winery~ owned by Robert Travers. An addition was added in the 1950s almost equal the size of the original.

merely repeating what he had obviously heard in the Napa Valley;

> In the lowlands—the level portions of the valley—there is more
> moisture and a ranker growth than on the hillsides. From this fact
> has arisen the absorbing question as to which soil produces the
> best wine grapes. On several of the properties both the uplands and
> lowlands are being tested. Experiments now made seem to conclu-
> sively prove that the best wine—that having the richest flavor—is
> made from the hill grapes.

Thomas Hardy of Australia made the same point in an 1885
visit:

> I find a very marked difference in the wines made from grapes
> grown on the hillsides and those of the plains, and the principal
> men also recognize it and are now planting largely on the hillsides.[IV.41]

The debate of hillside versus valley grape quality quietly disappeared as the decade of the '90s progressed and the phylloxera vine
disease laid waste to mile after mile of vineyard. There would soon
not be enough grapes to keep every winery in operation. The *Star* of
September 28, 1900 claimed:

> Wine making is now fairly under way and while the scenes of
> activity about the cellars are not as marked as ten or fifteen years
> ago there will still be considerable wine made,
> At Beringer Brothers most of the grapes purchased come from the
> vicinity of Calistoga. . . . At Greystone about fifty tons of grapes are
> being crushed every day now, two crushers being in operation most
> of the time. The grapes for this cellar come mostly from the vicinity
> of Calistoga and also from Howell mountain. . . .
> At James Moffitt's place [Krug's] Bismarck Bruck is making fine
> progress with the work. Only the grapes of the home place are being
> made up and the yield will be in the neighborhood of 20,000
> gallons. It seems strange to an old-timer to see so little wine made
> at this immense cellar where in years gone by there was an output
> of several hundred thousand gallons.

The farmers of the Carneros and vintners had suffered this same
fate much earlier than those just described by the St. Helena
newspaper. The disease had crept in so inconspicuously that few
growers realized what was happening. There was no great debate
such as occurred later at the county viticultural organizations.

The "Carneros" was a general term applied to the region in the
1880s, but it went as well by such names as the "Fly district" or "Las

Amigas" for the school and road which bisected a portion of the low rolling landscape.

E. C. Priber claimed in his *Report* in '93 to the State Viticultural Commission that the disease had crossed into Napa County at the James Duhig farm in the Carneros, and it was "here that the phylloxera made its first appearance in Napa County." He estimated this happened ten to twelve years previously.

Exactly twelve years earlier indeed, T. B. McClure of the Carneros had reported to a meeting of the Napa Grape Growers in early September 1881:

> Inspected a number of vineyards in the Huichica creek and the Sonoma districts; found the pest present in every one to an extent greater than was supposed. The whole Winter vineyard was attacked in spots.[IV.42]

Given this eyewitness testimony the vine pest had to have been in Napa County considerably earlier, in the late 1870s.

The "Winter vineyard" was that founded in 1855 by William Winter of Indiana and co-author of the Gold Rush book *Route Across the Rocky Mountains* . . . Winter had constructed the first winery in the Carneros region in '71.

Considering what must have been the depressing state of the Winter vineyards, it seems rather surprising that a gifted and talented New York and San Francisco journalist would purchase the Winter ranch in '81. James Simonton acquired his 1,115 acres in January, and within months began the most ambitious project ever attempted in California to find an eastern American grape root totally resistant to the phylloxera and adaptable to California.

Simonton did not so much as plunge a single shovel blade into the earth himself in this phylloxera quest—he was a rich enough man that he could afford to have it all done for him. For the *San Francisco Call* or *San Francisco Bulletin* newspapers which he partially owned, he saw the prospect of making the "search for a phylloxera cure" a great journalistic scoop. The *Bulletin* gave more space to coverage of the disease than any other Bay Area newspaper.

Simonton was very aware, certainly, of the viticultural boom then underway in California. He had lived and worked in Paris, traveled widely in France and saw the growing consumption of wine in America as another sign that America was growing up. He had been told by his doctors that he had to resign his position in New York as General Manager of the Associated Press or his fragile health would collapse completely. The Napa Valley was the answer, quite obviously.

Fate or fortune stepped in to assist Simonton in his goal when one of the most illustrious men in American viticulture chanced to visit California and the Napa Valley in 1881. The man was George Husmann, professor of Viticulture at the University of Missouri.

Husmann was German born but had come to the United States at the age of eight years, in 1836, with his parents. Well educated privately by a school teaching father he followed the crowds westward to California with the discovery of gold. When a sister and brother-in-law died in Hermann, Missouri, he returned immediately to their farm and assumed management of it. He was a farmer by instinct, and turned with a passion to fruit growing and the native vines.

Husmann also had a natural flair for writing and began corresponding with any American grape grower who would exchange ideas with him about viticulture. Out of this letter writing came in 1868 his first book *Grapes and Wine*. Two years later he formed the Bluffton Wine Company, of Bluffton, Missouri and soon had 1,500 acres of vines under cultivation. With his partners in that enterprise he shortly founded a publication called the *Grape Culturist*" There was no other periodical like it in the country and his contributors ranged from Nicholas Longworth of Ohio (father of American champagne) to Orange Judd, Charles Downing and Norman Coleman.*

Husmann suffered through several financial reverses in those years, losing his Bluffton company and finally accepting the position of Superintendent for the Department of Pomology and Forestry at the University of Missouri in 1878. He began teaching a class in viticulture, only the second such class on a university level in the country. (The first was begun in 1876 at the University of California, Berkeley, by Eugene Hilgard.)

Husmann was an organizer of the first rank, wherever he went he talked friends or delegates to conventions into forming new

---

*Many years after Husmann died, his Napa City home was finally demolished by a relative, circa the 1930s. All of his correspondence, manuscripts, etc., were carried out to the backyard and burned.

societies relating to horticulture or agricultural pursuits. The Mississippi Valley Horticultural Society, later renamed the American Horticultural Society came out of a meeting in 1879 at Rochester, New York. He also found time to write the same year, the first edition of what soon became the most popular text in the country on wine grapes, *American Grape Growing and Wine Making*.

When California founded the Board of State Viticultural Commissioners in 1880 and news began to spread across the country of a wine boom in the state of huge proportions, to replace the failing French wine industry, Husmann could restrain his enormous curiosity no longer. He took the train for the Pacific Coast and apparently completely by chance met in the Napa Valley, James Simonton.

Simonton and Husmann were fated to meet. Both relished publicity. Simonton had gotten himself ejected as a journalist from the United States Congress—perhaps his earliest notoriety. Husmann saw in the phylloxera a *cause celibre* which would earn him national attention beyond the vine and wine industry. He never stopped verbalizing or writing about his ideas until the day he died, some twenty years hence.

Simonton hired Husmann to take over his Carneros estate, renamed "Talcoa Vineyards" (an Indian word meaning "laughing land"). Hundreds of acres were planted to vines with experimental plots for nearly every native American vine species growing east of the Rocky Mountains. Charles Wetmore told the State Viticultural Commissioners in 1882:

> The most important plantation of American vines that has been attempted thus far, is that of Mr. Jas. W. Simonton, in Napa County. Several hundred acres are planted and being planted, in resistant stocks, both for direct production and future grafting. Among the stocks in this vineyard are twenty-five thousand seedling *Riparias*, and thirty thousand seedling *Californicas*. The state will watch the progress of the vineyard with great interest.
>
> Being under the management of Professor George Husmann recently of the University of Missouri, we have in effect in this a well-organized experimental vineyard for testing resistant stocks, amply supported by private means, and ably conducted for the demonstration of one branch of viticulture.[IV.43]

Whenever Husmann had something new to impart on the phylloxera he would write long letters to the *Bulletin* which, of course, printed it all! On September 28 that year, Husmann reported the conclusions of Hermann Jaeger in Missouri that a local grape called Vitis Rupestris proved very satisfactory as a resistant rootstock or any of the Riparia classification of grapes.

Had James Simonton not died most unexpectedly on the evening of November 1, 1882, the Carneros would have been made famous for proving what type of eastern American grapevine, resistant to the phylloxera, was most adaptable to California climate and soil conditions. Simonton had made no provision to carry on the work after his death. A daughter, Matilda, married to a Frenchman named Adolphe Flamant, arrived within three months to run the estate and then she died. The death in 1889 of her brother Frank, executor of James' estate, soon embroiled the heirs in a vicious quarrel which involved New York and Napa lawyers for many years.

Husmann left Talcoa two years later convinced, however, that any grapes of the Riparia classification (Elvira, Missouri Riesling, Taylor, Uhland, Amber, Pearl, Marion, etc.) would work well in Napa County in the vine disease battle. That he would eventually be proved wrong does not detract from the noble experiment carried out on the ranch.

There were at least two dozen vineyardists in the Carneros in the early 80s, besides the Simonton ranch, but the total acreage was under five hundred. The vintners, in addition to Husmann at Talcoa, included: T. B. McClure, 13,000 gallon winery; Charles Robinson, 30,000 gallons; and Judge John A. Stanly, 200,000 gallons.

Stanly had begun experimenting with resistant roots the year after Husmann began his work and by the end of the decade was a believer in Riparias. He told a surveyor for the Viticultural Commissioners Report on phylloxera in 1893, "The only vine I think absolutely resistant is Riparia. I would never plant anything else."

Whatever the truth of his observation his wines ranked second to no other vintner in the Napa Valley or county for quality. His Carneros wines frequently brought higher prices when sold to large distributors like Gundlach-Bundschu of Sonoma. At the 1888 wine competition in San Francisco sponsored by the Viticultural Commissioners, he won three First Place awards (for Port, Tannat and Valdepenas) and a Second Place for Zinfandel—that accounted for 4 of 22 awards won by Napa Valley.

Authorities like H. W. Crabb told an interviewer in 1895 that

Stanly had "the best vineyards in Napa County."[IV.44] He was inter-
viewed and lauded extensively in a *San Francisco Chronicle* article on
October, 1889 headlined "Lower Napa Valley. Its Prospects for Wine
Making. The California Medoc." Said Stanly:

> I consider that the lower end of Napa Valley is the most suitable
> locality for grapes that will yield red wine. My reasons for this
> statement are that the district is within the range where sea air
> permeates the atmosphere. From this sea air the vines extract
> properties which increases the tannin in the fruit. The soft pall of
> mist which hangs over the lower end of the valley in the winter
> mornings serves to shield the vines from frost and at the same time
> affords nourishment to the plants.
>
> The saline properties existing in the sea air is also valuable and
> imparts that peculiar flavor to the fruit and wine which is so
> noticeable a feature in wines grown in the Medoc district of France.

Whether his observations were precisely accurate did not matter,
again the fact that a major news journal, *in San Francisco*, carried the
quote gave it reliability.

By an odd coincidence, it may have been the same person who
inspired both Judge Stanly and James Simonton to pioneer the
planting of resistant rootstock in Napa Valley. That person was a
Frenchwoman named the Duchese de Fitz-James of St. Benezet,
France, although it should be mentioned that she was of Swedish
birth, being the daughter of the Swedish ambassador in Paris.

In 1881 at the International Phylloxera Congress held at Bordeaux the Duchese became an ardent and outspoken advocate of
resistant rootstock from America for fighting the disease. She boldly
rejected searching for a remedy in various chemical agents. Her
faction at the International Congress won over the majority of the
delegates and gave France its only real solution to the disease.

Simonton may have read about the Duchese while traveling in
France or would have known of her by name from his years in that
country as a foreign journalist. The conclusions of the Congress—so
meaningful to what Stanly and Simonton faced in the Napa Valley
that very same year—would hardly have escaped their notice.

There is also the slightest possibility that California's first
woman to build a winery, Josephine Tychson took some small
measure of inspiration from the Duchese's actions. In the 1880s
women in the wine industry were just beginning to emerge from

kitchens and closets where they might sip wine discreetly, but never in public. When Josephine's husband took his own life very unexpectedly, she proceeded with their plans to build a winery not far from John Weinberger and Charles Krug.

Napa Valley's first winery built by a woman had barely progressed far enough in the fall of 1886 to allow the work of crushing grapes and wine making to proceed. The *Star* first reported the construction August 27, and a week later noted that wine making had begun. Nels Larsen was in charge of the new facility which had a capacity of 30,000 gallons. Five years later she had vineyards covering sixty-five acres and 110 tons of her own grapes. She grew Zinfandel, Rieslings and "Burgundy" grapes, the latter often covering varieties not identified.

The Tychson winery which took shape in 1886 was exactly 50 x 50 feet square, entirely of wood, two stories and built in an excavation into the hillside just north of St. Helena.*

Mrs. Tychson's closest neighbor was Mrs. John Weinberger, also a widow after her husband's murder some years earlier. Josephine Tychson loved horses and fast speed when driving her carriage into town although if she picked up Mrs. Weinberger, she was politely asked to rein in the spirited horses. If her two children accompanied her, John and Annette, they were given a brief directive to hold on and off the three of them went, chickens flying, dust swirling and the Chinese standing quietly nearby, bemused.

Unlike her neighbor, Josephine did not bother to send her wine to the World's Fair in Paris in 1889. There is no record of Tychson wine being entered in any wine competition, though records for "entrants" do not exist for most wine events. Mrs. Weinberger won a Silver medal for her wine and considerable praise—the only woman in the famous Paris competition from California to be so honored.

Hannah Weinberger took over a much larger winery after her husband's death than Josephine Tychson operated and was much more active in the wine making processes. Whenever a publication,

---

*The original Tychson winery was demolished in 1899 and replaced with stone, renamed many years later "Freemark Abbey." In 1967 after years of neglect three partners: Charles Carpy, William Jaeger and Frank Wood resumed wine production.

such as *Resources of California* for June 1885, carried a story on the Napa Valley, Hannah received strong compliments:

> We next come to Weinberger's Winery, Mrs. J. C. Weinberger, proprietor. The vineyard consists of 100 acres, eighty acres of which are yielding handsome returns. The cellars are well arranged and supplied with all the wine-making apparatus necessary for a first-class winery. During 1884, there were 90,000 gallons of all kinds of wines made here. The residence is located, like the cellar, on the slope of the hill, thus commanding a fine view of St. Helena and the valley.

When Frona Eunice Wait visited the valley in early 1889, gathering material for her book published that same year called *Wines and Vines of California*, she must have purposefully over-looked women such as Hannah Weinberger. She is mentioned once— by name only. Wait's wine compliments are all reserved for men.

Wines and Vines of California as the first book written for the wine consumer, rather startlingly was the work of a woman who also laid claim to being the first of her sex to become a newspaper reporter in San Francisco. The book was so successful that William Randolph Hearst asked her to oversee the special section on California wine making for the *San Francisco Examiner* in April 1890.

Wait, again, in the *Examiner* special on wine devoted full pages to Inglenook or Hearst's new purchase in Sonoma Valley Madrone Vineyards. Niebaum's reputation for white-glove inspections at the winery, the selling of his wine only in bottles and his magnificent wine castle earned him considerable notoriety. Anyone who was "good-copy" attracted Hearst's attention but Wait may have been a little too quick to bow to commercial pressures, thus ignoring the pioneering work of women in the industry.

Kate Field was another woman who was doing much to help publicize and sell California wine, including the wines of the Napa Valley. Born in St. Louis to parents who traveled about the country acting in stage dramas, Field took to the stage naturally. She did not pursue acting, but turned to public lecturing—a widely popular form of entertainment. In June 1888, the Board of Viticultural Commissioners, which included Charles Krug, hired Field to undertake a national lecture tour on the subject of wine. The Board realized something had to be done to counter the popularity of Temperance lecturers like Carrie Nation who drew large crowds with fire and brimstone speeches.

As the decade of the 1880s closed, one of the most significant changes to come about in California wine making was the emergence of women in the industry. They proved they could carry out all of the tasks men had heretofore directed. In Fresno, Marie Austin pointedly hired Chinese laborers to pack her huge supply of raisins for shipping all over the United States. In an interview in the *San Francisco Merchant* in March 1884, she argued:

> With natural moisture at eight feet below the surface, excessive watering or irrigating is injurious to grapes in the San Joaquin Valley." Austin realized that the "saccharine" or sugar content of the grape was directly affected by water at the wrong moment in the growing cycle. She obviously was as well informed as her male counterparts, perhaps more so!

In central Sonoma Valley, three wine widows were attracting almost as much attention. Kate Warfield, Eliza Hood and Ellen Stuart all continued to make wine after their husbands died and won medals in many county and state fairs. At the State Fair in 1883, brandy made by Warfield won the Gold Medal, much to the chagrin of many male entrants. A loud outcry from the losers forced the judges to repeat the blind tasting and Kate Warfield was awarded the top prize again. The notoriety this event elicited resulted in Warfield becoming a national figure in the wine industry.

It was in the selling of wine, through advertising or promotion, that women seemed to excel and this was an ingredient of short supply in Napa Valley or lacking in much of the state. Wealthy men had rushed in to plant vast vineyards and build huge and beautiful wine cellars on hilltops or central valley locations with wide, sweeping vistas. For some peculiar reason they largely ignored the publicizing of their product. Kate Field and Frona E. Wait were accomplishing more to win new wine consumers with the pen and spoken word than had been achieved in a decade of direct selling.

Most Napa Valley vintners, much to their credit, understood the growing need for this kind of assistance. It had been a hectic decade of growth and involvement in testing grape varieties, new wine making equipment, unpredictable labor supplies, and even pondering the proper construction of wineries.

Few who entered the wine industry as outright newcomers had

vast majority of eastern wine drinkers would refuse to even sample what California produced, feeling it was far too inferior to the great wines of France and other European countries.

There is the perception too that the wine industry needed change, the acceptance of more modern means of wine making for example. Women added a major contribution here for they were not traditionalists, carrying no long held beliefs about wine production because none had been passed on to them by recently departed husbands or family.

In the Napa Valley changes were relatively easy to implement. Most of the winery owners were newcomers. In nearby Sonoma County, for example, where many more foreign immigrants, such as Italians, had settled, old world methods survived far longer. Anyone asking an old Italian vintner to help fund Kate Field's work would have been met with a strong *no capisce* even if he did understand the English language.

V. Napa Valley Becomes America's Premier Wine Region: the 1890s

early in the spring of the year 1891, officials in the White House in Washington, D.C. announced a tour of western United States by train for President Benjamin Harrison. This was not to be a whistle-stopping tour to win votes. Harrison was only in his third year in office. Rather, the President wanted to see the country, its people and what it produced—from manufactured goods to agricultural products. That included wine, of course. Or did it?

In California the presidential train ride was to begin in San Diego and traverse the entire length of the state. The vast array of activities packed into each day suggested rather dramatically how starved Americans on the West Coast were for a share of the presidency. The office was so venerated by this date that the holder was nothing less than royalty.

Napa Valley residents had high hopes the President might actually spend some time in their lovely countryside. After all, it was Morris Estee who had nominated Harrison for President at the

Republican convention. Surely the President would return the favor by staying a night at Hedgeside, the home and winery of Estee on the outskirts of Napa City.

The grand highlight of the President's visit to San Francisco was to be a banquet in the magnificent Garden Court of the Palace Hotel. Several hundred could be seated for dinner, but this would not begin to accommodate all who felt they deserved to be favored with an invitation.

It quickly became apparent a great many reputations were going to be tarnished by being left off the guest list. This was the case as well, with many of the presidential luncheons and sightseeing tours. Even California's governor, Henry Markham, was slighted until he finally returned to Sacramento in a huff.

What the Banquet Committee did to California and Napa Valley wine was even worse.

An elaborately printed dinner card or menu for the evening, with enough courses to produce possible indigestion, *did not include one locally produced wine*. The wines and Champagne to be served the President of the United States while visiting the heart of the California wine country, were all from France!

Charles Wetmore was so furious that had dueling been *de rigueur* he may have challenged General W. L. Barnes to a duel. Barnes was the presidential aide who oversaw the details of various parties and banquets, including the wines used. Wetmore, since serving as the Chief Executive Officer of the Viticultural Commissioners, still acted as a quasi-spokesman for the entire wine industry.

This slight, if it could not be called an oversight, touched Wetmore's pride for another special reason. The *Examiner* had asked him to write a story on viticulture for the special pre-presidential visit edition, of April 26. The entire top half of page 14 carried the industry and Wetmore's proud boasts in a highly informative and modestly biased report:

Twenty Million Gallons of Wine Produced Annually. One Hundred Twenty Thousand Acres Cultivated in Raisin and Table Grapes. Fifty Thousand People Engaged Directly in the Rural Work.

Pure wines, good enough for the President, are prominent features in the wonderful development of American industry on the Pacific coast,

He added:

> It will probably occur to the President at the coming banquet to
> have his glass filled with a California wine, when he responds to
> California's welcome. Try it, Mr. President. We assure you that you
> will survive the ordeal and that you will say you have tasted worse
> things than California wine.

When Wetmore discovered the "oversight," he quickly collected a case of the best wines available, including his own, and sent
them to Gen. Barnes for sampling. This was several days before the
arrival of the President. Not one word of the controversial matter had
leaked out to the press or public. The situation could easily have been
rectified with little further damage.

Barnes refused to open even one bottle and abruptly returned
the case—at Wetmore's expense. He may have done this on the
advice of his other committee members, some with suspiciously
sounding French names like Alfred Bouvier, or Marcus D. Boruck.

The story was finally picked up by the *Examiner* the day Harrison
reached San Francisco. Within twenty-four hours many of the other
dailies, the *Alta, Call, Bulletin, Chronicle* carried this slight to the
California industry. Harrison, only mildly disturbed by the incident,
asked Barnes to have a new menu printed to include some of the local
vintages .

The new dinner card added insult to injury in a way only a
piqued presidential aide might do. The original card had been
handsomely engraved, the type of keepsake people put into attic
trunks and passed on to grandchildren. The second card had the
appearances of a beginning calligrapher, which may explain why
none survive.

The banquet lived up to all that was expected of the marvelous
Garden Court of the Palace, the finest hotel on the West Coast. The
first course was served promptly at 9 p.m., "Eastern Oysters on Half
Shell, " followed by a consomme soup. Hors d'oeuvres included
stuffed olives, caviar and anchovy salad. The accompanying wines
so hastily added were simply "Hock-California" (a sweet Riesling)
and "Sherry-California. " There had to be some grumbling that no
brands were mentioned but at least it was California wine.

"Sauterne-California" was served with the "Sacramento Salmon.

Four meat courses were offered next, "Chicken à la Louis, "
"Filet of Beef à la Richelieau, " "Lamb Chops aux Petits Por" and

"Tripe with Truffles." (The French influence could hardly be missed.) "Claret-California" was the accompanying wine.

How there could have been room for another meat course is uncertain, but "Roast Young Turkey" followed with the only beverage which might help the beleaguered dinner guests who overindulged, Champagne. At this point any California vintner present should have stalked out of the Garden Court. All of the Champagnes were from France and were listed by brand.

Champagne was also used to accompany the "California Asparagus" now being served, plus a selection of four desserts and the usual fresh fruits, cheese and coffee.

Most San Francisco newspapers were kind enough to list all of the California wine brands served at the banquet and five of the nine were from Napa Valley: Hock from the Napa Valley Wine Co., Riesling from Inglenook, Jacob Schram's best white wine called "Schramsberger," Estee's best Sauterne from Hedgeside and the finest Claret (Cabernet Sauvignon) of the Napa Valley Wine Company.

(Alameda County contributed three wines: Wetmore's Haut Sauterne and his Margaux Souvenir Claret, plus Julius P. Smith's "Olivina" Sauterne. John Doyle's "Las Palmas" Claret of Cupertino, Santa Clara County was served and finally Arpad Haraszthy's "Eclipse" Champagne.)

Why Gen. Barnes refused to list the California wine brands after honoring the French Champagne, could only be taken as a personal affront. A reporter for the Associated Press found it all so intriguing that he sent the details out over the national news wire.

Harrison and Barnes accomplished something for California wine that was lost sight of in the immediate feuding. Only a large expenditure of funds could have garnered so much publicity in the Eastern press as did this slighting of Inglenook's Riesling or Schram's hilltop wine. The presidential banquet turned into a publicity bonanza for California wine, though some would have considered it highly negative.

Harrison, incidentally, did not visit the Napa Valley on this trip. He may have lost a few votes which was critical in the next election for it was won by Grover Cleveland.

President Harrison's reelection difficulties actually could be traced to the growing Prohibition movement in the United States. His aides, including Barnes, certainly did not want the President to give any offense to the tens of thousands who increasingly pushed for the complete abolition of the production of wine, whiskey and beer.

The *Pacific Wine and Spirit Review* claimed in June 1893 that even "Napa City has voted in the Prohibitionists and gone dry," but the story was not quite right. The Prohibitionists had succeeded in getting a ballot measure in Napa outlawing the sale of such beverages and came very close to winning. In one Eastern voting district of the city, those opposed won by only 30 votes, 496 to 466.

Nationally, the Prohibition Party was stirring up emotions with growing energy. In June 1892 Gen. John Bidwell of California was nominated for president at its convention. That fall the party fell far short of expectations, Bidwell winning only 264,133 votes compared to over 5½ million for the victor, Grover Cleveland.

Hiring Kate Field some six years previously by the State Viticultural Commissioners was a partial response to the threat posed by the Prohibition movement. Someone had to counter the rapidly growing press coverage of the Anti-Saloon League and Prohibition Party by pointing out alcoholism was not due to the presence of such stimulants but to the economic plight of so many working men and their families.

For those who researched the origin of such things, the birth of the Prohibition movement in the United States could be traced to the founding of the women's suffrage movement in Seneca Falls, New York by Elizabeth Stanton and Lucretia Mott in 1869. Voting rights as well as improved conditions in the home for women were tied to curbing the abuse of alcohol. The Prohibition Party actually came into existence the same year, on the coattails of the abolition of slavery movement.

Garrit Smith, twice an Abolition Party candidate for President of the United States, needed a new cause once the Negro was freed. He found this purpose in alcoholism:

> Our involuntary slaves are set free, but our millions of voluntary slaves still clang to their chains. The lot of the literal slave, of him whom others have enslaved, is indeed a hard one; nevertheless it is a paradise compared with the lot of him who has enslaved himself—especially of him who has enslaved himself to alcohol."[v.1]

However, it was a young woman from Kansas named Carrie Nation who caught the attention of the press for the Prohibitionists.

She and several other brave female companions, walked into local saloons with axes and began breaking up the place. Glass flew in all directions and so did the male inhabitants once they realized she was driven by a strong conscience.

The WCTU or Women's Christian Temperance Movement and the highly political Anti-Saloon League were founded in the same years.

Another indication of the strength of the movement is clearly visible in the General Assembly of the Presbyterian Church in 1887. Meeting at Philadelphia, the membership voted to adopt "unfermented" grape juice for use in the Holy Sacrament of Communion.

Benjamin Harrison returned to California and to the Napa Valley less than six months after losing the election to Cleveland. Hunting attracted him to the valley, not its scenic views or any product of its vineyards. Still, just to be favored with a visit by so distinguished a gentleman was a high compliment.

"No less than fifteen hundred people were at the depot Monday morning to witness the arrival of Gen. Benj. Harrison," began a story in the *Napa Daily Journal* of March 27, 1894. "The public schools were dismissed, the College, likewise, and even the children of Shurtleff district, out near the Asylum, were excused from their lessons and, headed by their teacher, tramped into town to catch a glimpse of the only living ex-president."

If Harrison visited the Hedgeside manor of Morris Estee, it was not reported in the local newspaper. He did spend three days at the Napa Soda Springs and journeyed to the marshes of Suisun for a day of hunting geese.*

The visit in its entirety was so uneventful that few, if any citizens even thought to write about it in personal diaries or letters. Certainly some local wine makers must have assumed he would mend his political fences after the Palace Hotel incident.

This was not the style of the taciturn Harrison who probably had long since forgotten any of the details. There is no record of his visiting a local winery or drinking a glass of wine.

---

*There was another reason for Harrison visiting Napa Soda Springs. According to an obituary of owner J. P. Jackson, in the *Napa Daily Journal* of September 27, 1900, the two men had been law partners.

The ex-president's poor social manners regarding wine only contributed to a deepening mood of uncertainty in the valley. There was far too much wine in storage. All the excitement engendered by the Paris World's Fair had abated, although magazine writers were still sending inquiries about Napa wines and still seeking instructions on whom to visit and where to stay.

To have the father of Napa Valley viticulture die suddenly, though perhaps not unexpectedly, was a further serious blow. Charles Krug died at 5:30 a.m. on Monday morning, November 1, 1892. The season's grape crush was barely completed. It was not the way to start a new month.

"Mr. Krug has lived to see the ups and downs of the wine industry and of life generally," reported the weekly *Star* four days later. "His pathway has not always been strewn with flowers, but has oft times been rugged and covered with thorns. Adverses in business frequently visited him, but were met bravely and battled manfully. He has always taken an active part in the furtherance of the wine industry."

Krug's obituary covered two full columns. He had been born 67 years previously on March 1, 1825 near Kassel, Germany. His parents were moderately wealthy for at the age of fourteen he was sent to a "Latin School," or high school. He attended the University of Marburg, completing two years. In the summer of 1847 he traveled to Philadelphia where there was a large community of German immigrants. August Glaser invited him to teach at the experimental "Free Thinker's School," although precisely what courses he was to instruct were not mentioned.

Charles Krug had a mind of his own at a very early age. To leave his family in Germany and come to the United States is a clear indication of this fact. His association with Glaser fuels such an assumption as does his return to Germany to participate in an attempt to set up a German Republic. In September 1848 he was arrested and sent to prison.

He was freed after only a few months, supposedly by a more sympathetic political party, but his father's modest wealth may really have been the contributing factor. His father may have sent him to California, to get him out of Germany, contradicting any assumptions that Krug was attracted by the Gold Rush. Young Krug arrived in San Francisco in 1852. He never claimed later in life to have dug or panned for gold. He did take up editing the first German language newspaper in the city, the *Staats Zeitung*.

This, too, was short employment. Krug liked to be constantly on the move, seeking new challenges. San Francisco was filled with men of many nationalities and diverse political backgrounds. This is what attracted him to a Hungarian named Agoston Haraszthy. That fateful meeting provided direction for the remainder of his life.

Haraszthy had taken part in a revolution in his own country and been driven into exile. Now, his abiding interest, like most immigrants seeking to establish themselves in a new land, was making money. He saw great possibilities in grapes and wine. He convinced Krug of the same fact, though they both made a fateful error in choosing Crystal Springs as the place in which to inaugurate this venture. They quickly discovered that the cool summer fogs which pour over the hills to the west, can and usually do prevent grapes from ripening properly.*

When Haraszthy found employment with the San Francisco Mint, Krug joined him. The year after Haraszthy acquired the old Buena Vista vineyards and wine cellar in Sonoma (1857), Krug pulled up his San Mateo vines and planted a vineyard nearby. To spend one warm September in the tiny village north of San Francisco was enough to convince anyone that this country was the natural home of the grape.

There was one basic difference separating the two men. Haraszthy had a way of making money, or finding all that he needed to finance his ventures. Krug did not and it was almost enough to destroy a beautiful friendship. While Haraszthy was buying up hundreds of acres of land for his fiefdom, Krug borrowed a small apple cider press and traveled to the Napa Valley to make wine.

Lady Fortune then stepped in to provide a way out of Krug's financial dilemma. At the Bale Mill just north of St. Helena, he put his cider press to work pressing grapes for Louis Bruch and met Caroline Bale, one of the daughters of the late Dr. Edward T. Bale (he died in 1849). The thirty-five year old Krug may have been more than ready to settle down, which would have been motive to marry Caroline. Charles and Caroline were married the day after Christmas, 1860, settling on the generous landed inheritance from her father.

---

*Haraszthy at times, had little viticulture savvy. He tried grape culture in Wisconsin, then in San Diego with disastrous results too.

Krug promptly sold his Sonoma vineyard and rarely thereafter mentioned his connection to Sonoma Valley. It is likely the close friendship with Haraszthy ended.

The major highlights of Krug's later life give evidence of his remarkable success. He was one of the architects of the Board of State Viticultural Commissioners, and helped organize the St. Helena Vinicultural Club becoming its first president.

The German immigrant from Kassel translated many German viticultural documents for use by his neighbors. He was on the committee which saw to the publication in 1877 of *Grapes and Grape Vines of California*. The lush watercolor illustrated book was of immediate fancy to book collector and vine grower alike.

Along with close friends, Krug formed the Napa Valley Wine Company which established the first distribution agencies in eastern United States for valley wines. Although Kohler & Frohling began shipping wine in the 1850s to eastern dealers, the Napa Valley Wine Company appears to be the first in California to develop its own agencies for the distribution and sale of wine.

Charles Wetmore once claimed that to be a neighbor of Krug automatically increased the value of a vineyard by $100 an acre. This observation was an honor accorded no other grape grower in California—at least in print.

It is curious how many men actually took Wetmore's advice of locating near Krug. Jean Laurent did. John Weinberger, the huge new Greystone winery across the street, and also the Tychson winery—about two dozen built within a mile or two of him. Even his chief wine maker, Jacob Beringer, picked out a spot almost within calling distance of Krug. Was it the good soil or being near Krug?

If Charles Krug had one overriding dictum it was, "What is good for Napa Valley is good for me and what is good for me is good for Napa Valley."

This concept may explain in part his financial troubles. In June 1885 the *Star* surprised many readers by carrying a story on Krug's financial failure. It required nearly a full column to list all of his creditors. That fall, he crushed grapes from his wife's vineyards, claiming he was commencing "winemaking for the third and last time."

During the summer before Krug's death, he had been ill and frequently went to the German Hospital in San Francisco for treatment. In September, he suddenly lost the use of his tongue through partial paralysis. Two months later, his wife Caroline died. His world was unraveling at an ever increasing pace. The Fates, which had been his friends through so much adversity, now seemed to turn against him. He must have welcomed death twelve months later.

Few valley residents received the funeral accorded Krug. It was probably the largest ever held in the small town and certainly taxed the community's ability to cope with such an event.

It was not difficult, of course, to understand why Krug would thereafter be called the "father of Napa Valley viticulture." He was not the first to plant grapes, nor the first to make wine or even the first to build a winery. *No man in Krug's century had done so much to encourage qrape growing or quality wine production as had he.* And that included Agoston Haraszthy of nearby Sonoma, who, after all, lived in California barely a dozen and a half years. Charles Wetmore may have matched Krug's accomplishments in some respects, but he became prominent only about the year 1880 (though he would live much longer).*

Krug should have been named the first president of the Viticultural Commissioners, not Arpad Haraszthy. Haraszthy was probably given the honor out of respect to the accomplishments of his father.

---

*It is always challenging to speculate on just what causes one individual to stand out so far and above his peers, as did Krug. Being an immigrant in a strange land is usually enough to drive such persons to extra lengths for financial success. He also had to prove to his family back in Germany that he made the right decision when he left them. Often in a new country, an immigrant is forced into a sort of lesser-status and Krug would simply have not been satisfied without achieving an equal rank with his fellow growers or wine makers. He must have put a great deal of energy into learning the English language, for example.

Krug liked change in his personal life and accepted innovation in viticulture. He willingly tried new grape varieties. He married wisely but sometimes he may have had goals that were too high, as with the expansion of his winery in 1880.

No other Napa Valley name shows up so consistently in the printed record as does Krug's. As far back as 1862 he attended a wine convention in San Francisco. His name is conspicuous in the reports of every wine meeting thereafter.

Finally, Krug certainly enjoyed communicating with reporters. He did not mind seeing his name in print. He had what might now be called a healthy ego, in search of exposure. That may be one of the universal characteristics of those individuals who are well remembered decades or even a century after death.

He was exceedingly hospitable, the latchstring of his door always drawn to receive and entertain friends and his lovely home near town has been the scene of many happy gatherings,

added the local newspaper obituary. Good friends and sharing his dinner table set Krug apart from many of his contemporaries. Krug was a master at providing entertainment in his home during an era when amusement was hard to come by in this community north of San Francisco.

He may have undertaken such tasks as much for his family as for the outsiders who enjoyed his company. He and Caroline were parents to five children of which one boy, Charles, Jr., died in infancy. At Krug's funeral, daughters Linda, Anita and Lolita were present and a son Karl (possibly with a middle name of Charles for he afterward went by the latter name).

"The planting of grapes for wine making purposes has practically ceased," claimed one authority some months before Krug's death.[V.2] The emphasis in California viticulture had shifted dramatically to raisin grapes with most of those varieties being planted in the San Joaquin Valley. They could be grown in Napa Valley, and were to a small extent, but there was little interest in all the effort it took to dry, preserve and pack shriveled grapes! Wine production had leveled off at about 15,000,000 gallons statewide and there indeed, had been little growth in this area for the past four to five years. Sales did not increase even with experts like George Husmann saying of the '90 crush: "The best in quality and quantity that I have seen in this State out of nine consecutive ones since 1881."[V.3]

Discouraged, some growers began planting fruit trees between the rows of grapes. The prune was the popular favorite. Clarence Wetmore, brother of Charles and now a Viticultural Commissioner observed, "It may take one or two years to clean up the surplus wine that has accumulated during the past three years." Or it might take six or seven years, he should have said; it looked that bad.

"Something is the matter with the wine industry of this State," warned the San Francisco Chronicle with much forthrightness. "Our annual product of wine is very little, if any greater than it was six or seven years ago. . . . It is not on account of any defect in the quality of our wine."

"There is not a more unprofitable calling in the State today than vintaging and vinegrowing," added the reporter.[V.4]

One solution proposed for the market slump was to build brand identification. Napa Valley wine makers were pioneering this field for the entire state, especially Gustave Niebaum and his right-hand man, Ferdinand Haber.

Very few wineries marketed their wine under their own brand name. Isaac De Turck, some years earlier candidly told an interviewer for Hubert Howe Bancroft, "No, I have no brand for my wines. Sonoma wines, all wines produced in Sonoma County are known as Sonoma wines." What De Turck didn't say was that California vintners in the 1880s were fighting just to get their wines accepted in the marketplace, alongside the French and German. Individual identity did not matter so much.

Niebaum and Haber felt it was time to put the emphasis on "Inglenook" rather than California and go after the higher quality and more expensive side of wine retailing. To achieve the quality standard they wanted, Inglenook wines would only be sold in glass. (Napa's rapidly escalating reputation had to be a factor, as well, allowing Niebaum to put aside the word "California.")

The *Chronicle* had also offered the recent observation that until a few years ago, the "district nomenclature of wines were comparatively unknown to Eastern people, the generic term of 'California wine' being the title under which the productions of the State, no matter from what county they originated, were introduced."[V.5] This began to change suddenly because of the exceptional wines coming from Niebaum, Schram, Crabb and Estee in the Napa Valley.

In an article titled "Establish More Brands," the *Wine and Spirit Review* applauded the new direction in selling wine. The editor who wrote the story, begins: "The tendency of the principal producers and merchants during the past three or four years has been toward the establishment of distinct brands. We have encouraged it by every means possible."[V.6]

It took a long time to build a reputation, unless one had sufficient funds to spend on promotion. Niebaum sent Haber east to meet with wine buyers of private clubs and restaurants or the press. He even attempted to meet with ex-President Grover Cleveland (before he won a second term) to explore the possibility of stocking West Coast wine in the White House. There were few men like Haber in the California wine world as yet.

Haber's greatest success was with the press. It almost certainly was his effort that resulted in a full page being devoted to Inglenook in the *Examiner's* viticulture section of April 6, 1890. *The Illustrated American, San Francisco Argonaut,* and two books—Frona Wait's *Wines and Vines of California* and Daniel O'Connell's *The Inner Man* were equally generous and laudatory of Inglenook. Haber prodded the *Wine and Spirit Review* into carrying a story on the "Elegant Glasses and Tankards Owned by Mr. F. A. Haber of Inglenook Farm."[V.7] He simply never missed an opportunity at publicity for Inglenook. (He may have taken his cue from Krug. Niebaum himself shunned the press.)

Building a wine brand in Napa Valley was far easier than in other wine counties. Good things just kept happening to Napa producers. There were more world's fairs, for example, with wine competitions. It seemed crucial to win an award for one's self esteem. Now there was finally time to consider how highly you were regarded by your neighbors. A new opportunity came at the Chicago World's Fair of 1893.

Chicago wanted to celebrate its growing ascendancy in national trade and hub as a railroad center. City officials searched diligently for a theme and found it in the 400th anniversary of the discovery of America. This was to be the "Columbian World Exposition," a popular nickname for America. It was derived, of course, from Christopher Columbus.

San Francisco refused to put aside its own plans for a grand display of local merchandise at a world's fair, especially the importation of exotic Oriental furniture. This one would be held in the middle of winter to demonstrate that while much of the nation shivered in the cold, Californians basked in the warm sun. Snow rarely fell on San Francisco or on the sleeping vines of St. Helena, Yountville or Napa City.

While the planning was going on for the Chicago and San Francisco wine competitions, some vineyardists awoke to the idea that perhaps they should become wine producers. Why fight the low prices for grapes, the real money to be made seemed to be in wine. Fortune Chevalier of San Francisco knew it. He had been aware of its value for a long time since he imported French wines and dealt in so-called "native" or California wines. In the spring of 1891 he began construction of a winery high on the hillsides of Spring Mountain, west of St. Helena.

Chevalier may have had an ulterior motive for building a winery. For some years he had faced a declining supply of wines, Brandies and Champagne from France for his San Francisco store. This was due to the phylloxera in Europe. What supplies he received were not up to the old quality. One solution was to make wine himself.

Chevalier had come originally to California for the Gold Rush. He may also have wanted to establish a leaded glass window factory—his artistic specialty.

As a youth, he had apprenticed in this trade of highly creative window design, used primarily in churches or public buildings. In France this was a craft of high merit. When he began considering the idea of going to San Francisco in the early 1850s, he may have fantasized on the urgent need for his technical expertise. This supposition is borne out by the fact that he loaded several dozen windows of varying sizes on the very ship he took for California. San Francisco, he discovered much to his chagrin, was a shanty town by and large. He put aside window design and began selling and importing liquors.

The success of wineries founded by French immigrants contradicts in part, the concerns for the overproduction of wine in the 1890s. Chevalier sold every barrel of wine he produced. The quality was excellent no doubt, and he had the retail outlets in San Francisco. Krug had maintained all along that there was no surplus of fine wine, only of mediocre or poor quality wine.

There were other men of wealth willing to gamble on Napa's wine future. George Schonewald, manager of the elegant new Hotel del Monte in Monterey, had owned vineyards in western St. Helena for years. He had built a stone wine cellar in 1885 but only made wine in the structure one year. He spent little time in St. Helena until the year 1890 when he built his very elegant mansion on Hudson Street which he called "Esmeralda." (A later owner renamed it "Spottswoode.")* Schonewald knew Napa's wines first hand—the hotel featured Estee and Schram wine on the dinner menu. Curiously, he built a full stone basement under his house for wine making, resuming that occupation in 1891.

---

*The old house was renovated in the late 1970s by Mary Webber Novak. A wine label with the name "Spottswoode" was introduced in 1982.

Schonewald attracted some special attention to his viticulture work when he imported vines from France which were all bench grafted to the Rupestris St. George rootstock. Some of his neighbors may have quietly laughed behind his back. That grapevine was not the first choice for being phylloxera resistant. He may have responded by asking which vine had really proven it could handle that terrible insect? No one had an answer.

Lillie Hitchcock Coit, a San Francisco socialite with a somewhat eccentric reputation, had a small winery built in 1892. Her father, Dr. C. M. Hitchcock, had settled in the hills behind the Bale Mill more than a decade earlier, for his health, so Coit was no stranger here. She did manage to send a collection of dried grapes to the Paris Fair so she actually could share in some of the great honors bestowed on the valley in '89.

Lillie gave the name "Larkmead" to her home. The Southern Pacific even named a nearby trainstop Larkmead. The area was filled with larks which awakened even the heaviest sleeper on spring mornings. Mrs. Coit had the financial means from both her father and husband to indulge her whims and fancies; she did so by going to places shunned by proper ladies. She had concepts for feminine decorum far ahead of her time and would have made a good suffragette except that she had no interest in social causes.

Not far away, St. Helena cooper, S. P. Connors had erected a small wooden winery nearly a decade earlier which he generally referred to it by the name "Larkmead." It was perhaps the *Star* which first laid the name on Connor's wine cellar, not the man himself. The newspaper had to identify the location in some way. In September 1885 the journal stated: "The Larkmead cellar presents a very busy appearance," and a few weeks later: "The Larkmead Cellar of S. P. Connor is worked to its utmost." This was its second year of operation.*

Larkmead winery went through a series of successive ownerships and/or operators. It was rather small, all of wood and not highly attractive. Kohler & Van Bergen, the San Francisco wine house, leased it one year, so did V. Courtois. Finally in '93 a Swiss family named Salmina fell in love with the location and settled in. They did

---

*In 1958 Hanns Kornell moved his Champagne cellars to this location and the winery has since been honored with his name.

not have the funds to buy the winery, but they were willing to bide their time.

The Salmina family had been in the valley for at least thirty years prior to leasing Larkmead. Frank Salmina had begun wine making in 1867 on a ranch just south of where Horace Chase established his Stagg's Leap home much, much later. He was still producing wine when Chase dug into the hillside for his first wine storage tunnel. John Battista Salmina worked for his cousin Frank in the 1870s before purchasing the William Tell Hotel in St. Helena.

Battista, who never used his first name, had a strong thrifty side to his character and invested half of every dollar he earned in real estate, primarily in vineyards. He was particularly fond of Conn Valley and there had St. Helena stone mason J. C. Mixon build a stone winery for him in '95. He owned vineyards in several locations near St. Helena and when the Larkmead winery was made available for lease, he jumped at the opportunity to centralize his future wine making. Fortunately, too, a young nephew named Felix Salmina agreed to manage the winery.

Felix was still a teenager when he arrived in the Napa Valley in the 1880s. He had a talent for constructing buildings plus a knowledge of wine making, though his stronger interest seemingly was in the latter subject.

Neither Felix nor his uncle left a written account explaining why they chose to enter the wine business in such an inauspicious year. Being immigrants with perhaps a meager reading knowledge of the English language at that time, they may not have been aware of the severe economic recession sweeping the country in 1893.

There was another possible explanation for immigrants like the Salminas turning to wine making during a downturn cycle in the industry. These individuals did not have a high yardstick for what was termed "success." If they eked out a small profit and everyone in the family ate well, that was enough reward. There was little or no opportunity to buy land in Switzerland (or France or Germany, etc.) for younger sons. To own a hundred acres, with a barn and a winery, was to own a kingdom.

Battista Salmina had prudently waited for an opportunity to invest when land values declined. In the mid-90s he knew the time was right and convinced his nephew to go counter to the trend of those abandoning the vineyard business. That was the secret of great financial wisdom—if you believed wine still had a future in America.

Antone Nichelini, another Swiss immigrant may have sat in on some of Battista's economic lecturing at the William Tell Hotel. There were not many Swiss natives in the entire valley, but being lovers of music and dancing, all gathered frequently to converse in their native language, share food, beer, sometimes wine, and news of Switzerland. Nichelini already had a vineyard on the steep slopes of Sage Canyon, east of Rutherford but he did not make wine commercially. Something or someone nudged him into that decision.

The Nichelini winery took shape in the spring of 1896. It was built in modest proportions. Stone was used for the first level, the other stories being constructed of wood. It adhered to the side of a canyon wall almost as if glued into place. Antone must have felt right at home.

If the truth be known, Nichelini really did not need Salmina's advice. The success of small wineries in Napa Valley depended on finding an untapped market for their wines. Nichelini only had to transport his puncheons of wine seven or eight miles his ready market, the dozens of magnesite miners who, considering the work, may have had an unslackable thirst.

"The Chiles Valley magnesite mines have undergone more than the usual amount of annual development during the past year," recorded the *Star* of December 28, 1894. "These are the only lodes of this material now being worked on this coast." Magnesite was a hard form of carbon of magnesia, "so hard is it, that a sharp edge will cut glass," added the writer, although there was no precise explanation of its use.

Horace Blanchard Chase purchased land on the east side of the valley and built a summer home he labelled "Stag's Leap." He was the son of a wealthy Chicago businessman and dabbled in several investments, including vineyards. He had a home in San Francisco and travelled frequently, often to Europe. Wine making, which was on his mind too, was just a step or two above being a hobby.

There is no record of the name Stag's Leap being applied to the region before Chase arrived. The first mention in a valley newspaper came in a story in the *Register* of May 19, 1893:

The person who leaves the train at Yountville and inquires the way to 'Stag's Leap,' has no trouble in gaining the desired information. The road rises gradually to the eastward, leaving Napa Valley behind. Here are vineyards and cozy homes, and here 2 miles from the station is 'stag's Leap,' the delightful summer residence of Mr. and Mrs. Horace Chase.

After several paragraphs of florid description of the gardens and grounds, the reporter added:

Rising abruptly behind the house are towering hills from which the inspiration 'Stag's Leap' was derived. They stand in majestic grandeur and as sentinels seem to give the place a certain individuality.

To credit Horace Chase with the first use of "Stag's Leap" may be incorrect. Just down the road lived one W. K. Stagg! He had lived in the area for some years, an ambitious farmer with hundreds of fruit trees, acres of corn, vegetables, berries, thirty acres of grain but no vines.

Wine was far down Chase's list of priorities at Stag's Leap for he built his elegant, two story stone house, with imposing tower, four years before the winery. The house was finished inside with polished woods—the grand staircase and floor to ceiling fireplace were breathtaking for the first time visitors.

"Mr. Chase has just completed a tunnel 150 feet long, which will be utilized as a wine cellar, and 40,000 gallons can be stored therein," stated the *Register* of May 5, 1893. The tunnel length was slightly exaggerated, but it does establish wine production nonetheless. A more complete stone cellar in front of the tunnel was completed the following year.*

Wine makers of Scottish origin were a rarity in all of Napa Valley. Scotlanders did not even show up in the nose count made of nationalities in the city of Napa in 1892. An inquiring reporter for the Christmas edition of the *Register* counted nearly 400 German immigrants, 276 Irish, 149 Swiss, 128 English, 89 Italian and 43 French. There were two Scottish brothers named Rennie in St. Helena who may have wished they had not chosen the valley for their home—bad luck seemed to plague them.

---

*Chase made wine here barely a dozen years before encountering severe financial losses. He lost the farm and no wine was made on site until 1972 when Carl Doumani reopened the wine tunnel.

Well educated with university degrees, William Rennie had first immigrated to Australia and was on his way home for a visit when his brother James talked him into taking a look at the wine potential of Napa Valley.[V.8] The year was 1887, and William decided to postpone returning to Scotland. Taking his accumulated earnings, he invested them with his brother in the Martin Furstenfeld ranch just north of Inglenook. The closeness to Niebaum's lovely estate may have been of some influence— like being next to Krug, the land value had to be higher.

There were producing grapevines on the ranch, so the following year William and James made their first wine in an outbuilding. Two years later, in August 1890, their three-story stone wine cellar was completed just in time for the fall crush. For several years they barely managed to produce 50,000 gallons annually, though they claimed to have introduced the first hydraulic press operated by a gasoline engine in Napa Valley. James liked to brag, somewhat in the old Scottish tradition, that he extracted more free juice from pressing the pomace than any other winery in the valley.[V.9]

Although the Rennie brothers had room for at least 80,000 gallons of wine, the winery was almost half empty when E. C. Priber rode up in his buckboard seeking phylloxera damage information. They told Priber one-third of their vines were infested, some of which could produce only one more year. From 60 acres they harvested only 80 tons of grapes. The infection was likely well established when they purchased from Furstenfeld. Had he advised them of the vine louse? They were innocents from abroad who perhaps should not even have built the winery.*

Within a short time the brothers were faced with financial difficulties. William reluctantly accepted management of the Greystone winery only two years later. In one of those strange examples of tragedy following tragedy, William's wife of barely ten years died the same month he accepted the position at Greystone. In November, 1900, the interior of the Rennie winery was gutted by a raging fire.

It is truly remarkable that any winery was established in the Napa Valley during the early years of the 1890s, especially after the

---

*There was no wine making from 1900 until 1979 when the Komes family refurbished the building, calling their new wine "Flora Springs."

year 1893. A growing restlessness with the national economy had sown seeds of deep discontent with banking institutions and investing in stocks. In early May, a sell-off began in the stock market which turned to panic. Over fifteen thousand businesses failed to survive the year, and 642 banks had to close their doors.

Not one of Napa Valley's banks suffered such a fate which is some testimony to the stability of the economy in spite of the phylloxera and the tricky wine market. In San Francisco, the Pacific Bank, the leader in agricultural loans, did fail. A large loan to the California Fruit and Raisin Growers Association, which had defaulted, was given as one of the reasons for the failure.[V.10]

It is no surprise then that many Napa grape growers reacted with anger whenever the subject of the spread of the phylloxera was mentioned in the newspapers. That kind of publicity was certain to hurt land values or the price of vineyards if one wanted to sell. There were too many problems for the grower—the producer got all the credit, the vineyardist little or none. The wine maker made money; the grape grower barely survived. It is certain that many growers hid their phylloxera damage from public scrutiny.

When E. C. Priber's Report on phylloxera damage was published in 1893, Napa grape farmers became so infuriated they were ready to do battle, at least with fisticuffs. The Board of Viticultural Commissioners was suppose to be on their side—publishing such damaging statistics was not considered pro-vineyardist. Several of them made this point in a long article in the Register of January 24 of that year. The report was so "filled with errors" as to make it useless, they claimed.

Priber's Report showed a decline from 18,229 to 16,651 acres of grapes in only two years. Of 577 vineyards in the county, 244 showed marked evidence of the disease. The Report gives a detailed analysis of each grower, by name and location, in the county. Anyone reading closely came to the certain conclusion that production was dropping precipitously. The Rennie brothers' harvest of only 80 tons from 60 acres was a good example.

This may explain why Salminas, Chase, Schonewald and many others were willing to enter into wine production at so peculiar a time in history: declining vine production meant declining stocks of wine and inevitable higher prices—in the future!

George Husmann came to the defense of the Priber vine collection of facts. (A. Warren Robinson did the actual survey; Priber may have written it.) In the *Register* of January 27, he stated: "I venture to predict that there will be but little left of all the vines in Napa Valley, except those on resistant root, within two years." That was a sobering prediction, especially since Priber-Warren found only 2,000 acres of so-called resistant stock.

The disease had reached three miles north of St. Helena and, "It can be but a question of a short time until the Calistoga vineyards suffer as those of the lower valley," added the *Register* of January 24. Candidly, the writer added: "It is difficult to secure correct information on such points, vineyardists are loathe to give such information, as well as to give information as to stocks of wine on hand."

Henry W. Crabb had his own theories about the future of the valley if the disease was not stopped. He, too, foresaw the only surviving vineyards being those on resistant rootstock, but he was equally concerned about the dangers of overproduction: "Vines cannot, for any great length of time, remain healthy and vigorous with the annual overproduction of from six to twelve tons of fruit per acre.[V.11]

This seemed to directly contradict the findings of the Priber *Report*, but in actuality it was not. Crabb was describing the long-standing tendency to let a healthy vine produce as many grapes as nature allowed. He believed the phylloxera would not have been the dire scourge of the valley had the vines been better treated. They were so weakened by allowing 10 to 15 ton crops per acre that they succumbed almost overnight.

There was one more bit of sand to rub into the open wound of viticulture in the valley, indeed in all of California. The *Report* to the governor of California by the Viticultural Commissioners (released in 1894) estimated France's wine production at "thirteen hundred million gallons." This was double the figure of just a few years previously. Through careful management of vineyards (Crabb's point) and the widespread introduction of resistant rootstock, France's vineyards were rebounding. If they regained their old markets in the United States, the future was going to be bleak for California.

For the Italian immigrant families flocking to the valley and replacing the Chinese laborers, all of this was the proverbial "blessing in disguise. There were many vineyard owners who simply abandoned their farms, leased or sold them to the Italian farmhand and returned to San Francisco. By doing all the work, an Italian family could cut production costs and survive on the meager income. Many also began immediately planting European vines on their own roots, between rows of dying vines.

Italian immigrants began arriving in the Napa Valley in the early 1880s.

"A large number of Italians find employment in the vineyards in town and vicinity," noted the *Star* back in April 1880. The newspapers in the small wine communities in California generally ignored their names, somewhat the same as they had done with the Chinese.

In the *History of Napa and Lake Counties* published in 1881, twelve pages were devoted to a listing of every vine grower in Napa County. There was not one Italian name listed unless it be the "Baretta Bros." of St. Helena. Some names like "Sciaroni" were actually Swiss-Italian. (The telltale letter "i," for example, on many Italian surnames is missing from any name in the twelve pages.)

There were about 4,600 Italian immigrants in all of California at the beginning of the decade. Most were residents of the Gold Rush counties or San Francisco. In Napa, Italian woodcutters sometimes advertised wood for sale. Many cut wood and shipped it to market in San Francisco.

With the growing numbers of Italians came a corresponding decrease in the Chinese employed in Napa Valley. By the turn of the century, most had disappeared from the vineyards and certainly from any wine cellar activities. Those that remained were the faithful household employees.

The Chinese contributed to their own displacement by demanding higher wages just as the Italians arrived. Most Chinese were unaware of this new emigration of workers. They knew that because of the Chinese Exclusion Act (and the extension of 1894 authored by Thomas Geary) their numbers were decreasing. The law of supply and demand should have resulted in naturally higher salaries.

The *Star* recorded in the late 1880s that the strike of Chinese for more pay had "led to the employment of more white labor than usual" and the *Calistogian* added that they wanted $20 a month salary, up $5 from the usual fee. By the fall grape harvest of 1889, the situation was crystallizing rapidly: "There seems to be a growing disposition to substitute white labor for Chinese. . . . Although early in the season to estimate, we think there will be quite a decrease in the number of Chinese employed in this section this year," added the St. Helena editor.[V.12]

There was yet another reason for the Italian worker pushing the Chinese out of Napa Valley. It had to do with the major change in the height of grapevines.

Agoston Haraszthy was the early proponent of the concept that the vine trunk should be kept low, so that the canes grew close to the ground or lay upon it. His theory was that this hastened ripening. In Europe and his native Hungary, that may have been a necessity in cool summers but not in the hot September weather of California. Krug was among those early advocates of higher heads to the vine trunk so that the canes, with the grapes, would be about waist high.

As Edward Roberts described in *Harper's* of March 9, 1889, "gathering the grapes is laborious work, the picker being obliged either literally to kneel or to bend his back to a painful degree." White workers refused such work or complained so much vine owners would not hire them. When the Board of Viticultural Commissioners advocated the change in the height, most replanting to phylloxera resistant vines immediately followed this advice.

The Chinese were missed by most valley residents who had come to depend on them for household help, gardening and even the caring of small children. Many children grew up not with a white or black mammy, but a stern Chinese male who complained constantly that his employer's sons and daughters were poorly disciplined.

For more than thirty years, since the building of the railroads, the Chinese had been a customary part of small town California life and on rural farms. They certainly made life easier for the average family, freeing them of so many domestic chores from preparation of meals to chopping wood. They hauled tons of rock out of vineyards and piled them neatly along the roads, creating mile after mile of stone fences.

It is questionable how many stone wineries were actually built by the Chinese. In the 1880s when most of Napa Valley's stone wine cellars were constructed, the Italian stone masons deftly cut the soft stone from hillside quarries—with the help of some Chinese. (This is well documented, including through the use of photographs.) There is little evidence, on the other hand, of Chinese exclusively pursuing such tasks. Certainly, the slow, arduous task of creating tunnels out of solid rock must be the work of the Chinese. This was done with hammer and chisel, a million tiny cuts into the stone that took infinite patience.

The most significant contribution of the Chinese may have come in the enhanced quality of life through sharing their special culture. A Chinese funeral, for example, was an occasion not to be missed by any Napa resident. When Lea Hau was killed by a falling eucalyptus tree on the Niebaum farm in January 1894, his funeral offered a real break in the routine of St. Helena residents.

> After a long performance at Chinatown, in which mourners and members of the Chinese Masonic order took part, the body was conveyed to the cemetery in due form. First came the express wagon filled with roast pig, roast chicken, rice, burning punk, etc., then the hearse, flanked by six Chinamen on each side. The hearse was followed by some fifty Chinamen, all wearing a band of red and white.
>
> A Chinese band was the next feature, making a hideous noise. Judging by the sound, we were made to believe they were playing 'The Last Chord.' There were about ten vehicles, another Chinese band making up the end of the procession.[V.13]

When all the formal rituals were completed, the food was gathered and carted back to Chinatown where the invited guests enjoyed a feast. This was not an ordinary funeral. Hau was a man of some wealth and stature.

Unfortunately, the Chinese contribution to the wine industry of Napa Valley and California was quickly forgotten. In a booklet published by the California Wine Association later in the decade, describing in detail its wineries in Napa Valley and elsewhere, this historical misstatement was included:

> Grape growing in the Napa Valley dates from the earlier sixties, while Livermore Valley, and Santa Clara County, the last of the principal producing sections, was not brought into prominence until much later. The story of the growth of the industry in nearly all of these districts is much alike. In all there was a hardy mixed population—American, French, Germans, Italians; in all every attainable variety of wine was tested . . .

No mention of the Chinese except as they might have been included in the phrase "hardy mixed population." The Italians were quickly accorded unusual honors, in part because so many were moving into winery ownership themselves. The statement on Santa Clara County also displayed a sad ignorance of viticulture and wine making history.

It was not long before the initials "C.W.A." were included in almost daily conversation in Napa Valley. Some of the words used to describe its activities were of the four-letter variety. Others believed the *California Wine Association* offered the first real hope in stabilizing not only wine prices but wine quality. The controversy over the establishment of this organization, however, brought dissension among local vintners that was unprecedented. The wounds created would take a long time to heal.

Four Napa Valley wineries were part of the original makeup of the C.W.A., formally inaugurated in August 1894: The Greystone winery (now owned by Charles Carpy), the Uncle Sam winery, C. Carpy Sons winery-Napa and the Napa Valley Wine Company.

In San Francisco, the large wine warehouse of Kohler and Van Bergen, Kohler and Frohling, B. Dreyfus & Co., S. Lachman & Co. and Arpad Haraszthy added what was the real muscle of the huge association. (Haraszthy withdrew in less than one year's time.)

An Englishman named Percy T. Morgan was the most energetic individual behind the project, although it was the money of banker Isaias Hellman and Benjamin Dreyfus that guaranteed its operation. Hellman and Dreyfus had been involved in forming the vast Cucamonga Vineyard project as well as other investments. The key individual with the most knowledge of wine was Henry Lachman and he was given complete authority for buying grapes, blending wine and other technical aspects. Actually, the combination of individuals resulted in a pool of unusual talent for the wine industry.*

There was no question that the C.W.A. viewed Napa Valley as the centerpiece of its quality table wine operations. In the aforementioned booklet published in January 1896, the first page is devoted to "Where Our Wineries Are." Greystone was the focus:

> Whoever visits the Napa Valley and reaches the town of St. Helena in the heart of the Napa Valley Wine District, must inevitably have his attention called to 'Greystone,' our magnificent stone cellar which is a landmark for miles around, and which, for centuries to come, will be an enduring monument to its builders and owners.

---

*This also included a youthful Almond R. Morrow, who after Prohibition became the first president of the Wine Institute, San Francisco.

These comments and some of which followed, may not have pleased the city of Napa: "After the first classification at 'Greystone,' the wines not retained in the lower vaults are removed every year to the City of Napa. In this noted wine *entrepot* we have two large warehouses on both sides of the Napa River, formerly the property of C. Carpy & Co., and the Napa Valley Wine Company." It may have mollified Napans somewhat to be called the "noted wine entrepot," but still the "first classification" of wine was to age in Greystone.

The C.W.A. booklet also gave considerable space to the great San Francisco wine cellars. In the city's naturally air-conditioned climate from May to October, there was no better place to store and age wine. S. Lachman at 453 Brannan Street had a storage capacity of two million gallons; the Dreyfus brick cellar was one block away, holding over one million gallons; around the corner at Third and Townsend was the Kohler & Van Bergen cellar, holding two million gallons; and at Second and Folsom was the headquarters for C.W.A., in the Kohler and Frohling wine vaults of three million gallons.

In the city of San Francisco alone, the California Wine Association could store eight million gallons—nearly half of the production for one year in California.

This control of the wine assets of the state still did not suit the higher vision of Morgan and others. They began buying or leasing wineries as fast as the ink would dry on one contract and they could begin negotiating another. It was rumored they would soon purchase Brun & Chaix winery at Oakville, lease the Chevalier winery and wine cellars in every major producing region in the state.

Even the *Star* was convinced the C.W.A. was the salvation of the wine industry. An editorial on June 29 asserted:

> It seems the height of folly to oppose a scheme which comes to us offering such terms at this opportune time and our producers should, we believe, stand in and make the formation of the syndicate possible.

By September the wine industry was faced with a serious quarrel. Charles Wetmore abandoned the C.W.A. concept, claiming the growers were being cheated by their rating system of "inferior, ordinary, superior and fine." Judge Stanly was vehemently opposed to the C.W.A. as were Jean Chaix, R. W. Lemme, John Swett and Pietro Rossi.

The result was a new group called the "California Winemakers Corporation" which offered 15 cents a gallon for all wine then available. That was only a five cent increase over what C.W.A. offered. Wine would be graded by local inspectors of acceptability to the corporation—not unknown or unqualified employees based in San Francisco. If a battle map had been drawn it would have shown that neighbors on either side of a road were in opposing camps. It was a sad and disgraceful situation after the long history of cooperation which was the trademark of Napa Valley vintners.

A cooling off period was needed now. A few timid voices even suggested that the fault really lay with the Viticultural Commission itself. Indeed, the syndicate concept had evolved out of the June 1 Board meeting.

Often the origins of a controversy, like that now dividing Napa residents, becomes so clouded or obscured it is not addressed subsequently. That may have been the case here as wine dealers, wine producers and growers developed a jealousy over the spreading fame of Napa Valley wines. The C.W.A.'s emphasis on Napa Valley wine (and later documented in the 1896 booklet) reflected the growing perception that wine from the valley was very special. Judges from Dublin to Chicago and San Francisco to Atlanta said so in the 1890s at World's Fair after World's Fair.

In August 1892, Dublin, Ireland hosted a Distillers and Brewers Exhibition, inviting such beverages, plus wines, from all over the world. Fifteen awards were made to California, Napa taking half. The nearest competitor was the San Joaquin Valley producers combined; they received four medals. Henry Crabb, Jacob Schram, the Beringer Brothers, Inglenook, Giuseppe Migliavacca and the Napa Valley Wine Company won the medals, the latter company winning two.

The San Francisco *Chronicle* reporting the awards on October 7, quoted Judge H. E. Hudson as saying he believed California had obtained world class rank with its wines, many of which surprised him very much for their exceptional quality. The judges could not believe an 1882 Brandy sent by George West & Sons of Stockton was Californian, for it bore a striking resemblance to French cognacs.

Next came Chicago, the big one for California. As an American World's Fair with international judges, Chicago was an important and growing wine market.

Titled the "World's Columbian Exposition," it opened May 1, 1893 to much fanfare and then sudden foreboding as to the wine competition. This was to be the first time California wines competed in an open American judging.

Napa had its detractors and they would be waiting impatiently to have the last laugh if Napa Valley wines did not repeat the Paris awards of six years previously, or those at Dublin. French wine snobs in the United States were still convinced the native wines did not rate on any equal basis with Bordeaux's finest.

The sense that all was not well in Chicago began with the furor over the method of judging. The Fair Board appointed John Boyd Thatcher to oversee the competition; he found this new prestige so heady he proved extremely difficult to work with, even for the jurors themselves. A. E. Dubois of Florida was one who later described the unusual circumstances he and others faced:

> Owing to the late date the jurors were summoned to Chicago, the lack of a suitable place for the storage of California wines, and also, to all appearances, as shown by the dryness of the cork, to the bottles having been kept standing too long, many samples were found out of condition, especially white wines and Burgundies.[V.14]

John T. Doyle, president of the Viticultural Commissions later wrote, "Whatever result of good may have attended these efforts in other departments, it is certain that so far as viticulture is concerned, they were a dismal failure."[V.15]

"The difficulty began at the beginning," added Doyle. There were two spaces for California's exhibits, either in the Horticultural Building or the California State Building. It turned out four or five private firms had contracted for most of the space, leaving little for the California wine presentation. "For want of the necessary information it was impossible to even suggest any remedy to this absurd state of things."

California wines were to be made available at the restaurants at the fair, but the caterer refused to carry more than a few brands. It appeared nothing could change the situation. Then Doyle discovered that Thatcher had appointed only one wine juror for each classification of wine! And he placed all American entries into one group, with no comparisons possible with the French entries.

The State Viticultural Commissioners hastily talked Charles F. Oldham, of the London Firm of Grierson, Oldham & Co., into sampling and reporting on all of the California entries. The views of one of the most prestigious wine firms in England would be some compensation for the missed opportunity for a clear-cut international wine event.

Oldham's succinct observations were widely quoted thereafter in the press and reproduced in detail in the Viticultural Commission's *Treatise on Wine Production*, published in 1894.

Oldham may have had some difficulty standing up after the impromptu marathon sampling of 370 wines covering all categories. He knew the international wine community was looking over his shoulder for he covered wine purity, how long each sample had been in the bottle and/or in wooden barrels, the proper classification of the wine and even if the proper bottle was used (Claret in the French-style Claret bottle, etc.). A judge this fastidious would help blunt any criticism of his findings.

The tasting was undertaken with all labels removed or poured into glasses so that Oldham saw no brands. His wife and Dr. H. W. Wiley of the U.S. Department of Agriculture did the pouring.

Once back in England, Oldham summed up his California wine experience for Ridley's Wine & Spirit Trade Circular, the issue of February 12, 1894:

> That California, with its manifold advantages in all these respects, is rapidly taking its place as one of the principal wine-producing countries of the world is undoubted, and it is not surprising to those who know the facts of the case. The sooner these facts become more widely known the more quickly will California wines attain, more especially in this country, the high place in public estimation to which their excellent qualities assuredly entitle them.

Because of changes in the awards categories, it is difficult to ascertain how many Napa medals were won but twenty-four is a good count, about double the medals won by any other wine county in California or the United States. Among the Napa winners were: Brun & Chaix, C. Carpy & Co., Crabb, Ewer & Atkinson, Beringer, Estee, Louis Zierngibl, Napa Valley Wine Company, Otto Norman, Migliavacca, Parrott and Schram.

There was very little time for self-congratulations before all of these producers and many more were scurrying about their cellars for wine to submit to the San Francisco Midwinter Fair. Since this was a California event, all of the mistakes made in Chicago would be avoided.

The concept behind this fair or exposition was to demonstrate to Easterners how lovely were the winter months on the western shores of the United States, especially in California. The Fair opened January 27, 1894 in Golden Gate Park. The Viticultural Palace, a striking building of 75 x 50 feet with a dome over its center was not christened by the clink of wine glasses until April 7. This proves the best laid plans often go awry. Since the Midwinter Fair only ran to July 1, visitors had to drink up fast.

The Viticultural Palace was the only minor problem as far as the wine industry was concerned. The Executive Committee functioned smoothly and included such Napa names as Parrott, Repsold, Priber, Carpy and Frederick Beringer. (Again, Napa had more representatives than any other county.)

Of 216 wine entries, in all categories, representing California, only 39 received awards. The jury was most parsimonious in granting recognition for wine quality. Only five awards were given, for example, in the Sweet Wine category which attracted 36 entries.

This time there was no overwhelming victory for Napa wine, although it still won the unofficial honors for most medals—nine. The Napa Valley winners were: Brun & Chaix, Schram, Beringer, Crabb, Parrott, Ewer & Atkinson and several new names—A. Grimm, Henry Hagen and Kortum & Fuelscher.

There was a marked cooling in enthusiasm in the valley for such wine events, by those passed over again. Judge Stanly (whose wines often sold for the highest prices in the valley) was not a winner, nor George Schonewald, Inglenook, Chevalier, Edge Hill. There was still Atlanta.

Atlanta, Georgia wanted to awaken America to its existence: Like Chicago, it was the trading hub of a vast territory encompassing southeastern United States. As had happened in the Chicago wine competition, there were major problems which seriously diminished the value of a wine medal.

About two dozen California wineries entered the 1895 Atlanta wine competition, nine from Napa Valley. Fourteen came away with medals, some of them significant. Henry Crabb and Tiburcio Parrott each won the Diploma of Honor and Gold medal. Inglenook picked up a Silver medal and Parrott a second, a Bronze for his Burgundy wine. The showing for Napa vintners was disappointing.

The lack of enthusiasm for Atlanta may be traced in part to the greater wine interest in an exposition scheduled the same year in Bordeaux, France. The French officials were not as excited about California's entries as in 1889. In fact most came prepared to dislike every foreign wine submitted. They were even candid enough to admit to such a prejudice in the journal *Le Nouvelliste:*

> All of us had been spoiled, as it were, by the wines of our own countries, and having palates accustomed to these, attended this tasting with disagreeable impressions on our minds and such feelings were certainly unfavorable to foreign wines. Nevertheless, in the long series of red and white wines, of different proprietors, and years and of different vintages, which were shown us, we found many wines which resembled our best hill products of the wines of Burgundy.[V.16]

The French publication warned that California wine was likely to become a "formidable rival" although admitting that "incontestably, Bordeaux wines are better than those of California." California's vast landscape and potential for wine production frightened many Frenchmen. Statistics in the story document the growth in value of California wine in only three years of from twelve and a half million francs to nearly seventeen million francs.

No top awards were accorded California or American wine entries. A Silver medal went to the Cupertino Wine Company and a similar award for Inglenook Brandy. Bronze awards were picked up by Charles Carpy and Henry Crabb. An Honorable Mention went to Beringer, Crabb and the Napa Valley Wine Company. Fifteen other awards were spread thinly among the state's wine producers including Brandy production.

Bordeaux finally deflated the Napa wine balloon enough to bring everyone back down to the ground. Napa could still boast of more wine awards in the 1890s than anyone else; its reputation was secure. What happened or did not happen in Bordeaux was of little consequence anyway. There was little press coverage of the event.

Despite all of the wine accolades heaped upon Napa Valley's wine men and women in recent years, the rupture caused by the creation of the California Wine Association refused to go away. In mid-decade, the St. Helena Winegrower's Union finally gave full vent to its collective anger by passing a resolution urging the abolition of the Board of State Viticultural Commissioners. It was a horrifying concept to all long associated with the Board and what it had accomplished. Charles Krug in particular would have turned over in his grave.

Governor James H. Budd signed the Legislature's bill disbanding the Board in the spring of 1895. The *Wine & Spirit Review* captioned its obituary: "A Case of Prohibition Rejoicing." The journal singled out the *Star* for some of its most barbed criticism in an issue of April 6:

> And now, just a word to journals of the St. Helena Star calibre: Their prejudices against the Commission aided the fight against it. How does the St. Helena Star relish the situation which places the vine growers of the Napa Valley as helplessly in the hands of Boards of Supervisors as are the saloon men?

Without the Board to fight off local option, or Prohibition, who was going to take on Napa government when it tried to impose a halt to wine making? That was the question posed. As speculative as that sounded it was within the realm of possibility. Quite a few Napa County voters were willing to wipe out the economic base of the region. That political undercurrent had existed since pre-Gold Rush days.

Then there was the University of California, Berkeley and its Professor Eugene Hilgard, in charge of viticulture instruction. Wetmore and the old Viticultural Commission disliked the professor, a little more with each passing year. The reasons were not put into print, for posterity, but the editor of the *Wine & Spirit Review* certainly recorded each encounter and added his own complaints.

Winfield Scott was the editor who often took aim in editorials at Hilgard and as much at the University. He could see no sense at all in funding a viticultural department which had only half a dozen students. When he discovered two women were enrolled part-time in the classes, he exploded with sarcasm and invective. Women had no place in such a course, the entire department ought to be abolished.

There may be some explanation too, in all of this feuding and fussing for the treatment Robert Louis Stevenson received in Napa Valley on his death. He died in far off Samoa in the late afternoon of December 8, 1894. By then among the best known authors in the western world, Stevenson was the toast of New York and every large city he visited. In Napa Valley, had he returned to the site of his book *The Silverado Squatters*, he would have been ignored and shunned. *This was the first book written on the valley other than local histories.*

Scottish born Stevenson began his small narrative on Napa in a quiet and most unassuming tone, hardly one which might be suspected of later giving offense:

> The scene of this little book is on a high mountain. There are, indeed, many higher, there are many of a nobler outline. It is no place of pilgrimage for the summary globe-trotter; but to one who lives upon its sides, Mount Saint Helena becomes a centre of interest. It is the Mont Blanc of one section of the California Coast Range, none of its near neighbors rising to one-half of its altitude. It looks down on much green, intricate country.

When those words or the author's notes for them, were penned in the summer of 1880 in Napa Valley, Stevenson was totally unknown. There is no record of his name in any Napa County newspaper in that year. Even after the book was published, it contributed little to his fame here or elsewhere. Rather, it was *Treasure Island* and most especially *The Strange Case of Dr. Jekyll and Mr. Hyde* which caught the public's fancy.

Silverado Squatters was first serialized (in a shortened form) in *Century Illustrated* in November and December 1883, but not one word was printed in Napa Valley mentioning this fact. When the book was published a month later in Boston, nothing was noted in the columns of the *Star*, *Calistogian*, *Journal* or the *Register* about the publication. Since Stevenson had visited the pressroom of the *Star* in the summer of '80, someone there should have recalled the event.

When Stevenson died, the St. Helena newspaper did record on December 21:

> Robert Louis Stevenson, the novelist died at his home in Apia, Samoa, December 8th of apoplexy. In 1880 he came to Napa County for his health and lived for several months on Mt. St. Helena where he wrote the 'Silverado Squatters' founding the story on the old Silverado mines in that locality.

The *Calistogian* again ignored Stevenson as did the *Register*, although the *Journal* carried a two sentence obituary.

(Why there was no local pride taken in the author's residence is puzzling. His book called attention to the valley, as did many booklets and pamphlets being published at that time. Immigration was something very much sought after. One chapter is devoted to Napa Valley wine. Stevenson describes keeping his local wine stored in the cool shaft of the old mine and Jacob Schram in particular received some praise for his wine.)

Stevenson's wonderful childhood adventure, *Treasure Island* had its genesis, in part at least, during that summer of 1880, when he, his new wife Fanny and her young son Lloyd lived on the side of Mt. St. Helena. The abandoned mine shafts, piles of slag, old lanterns, boots, rattlesnakes and the ghosts of departed miners—all hovered about providing inspiration. Stevenson used this background to make up stories on the spot for young Lloyd who, along with his mother, suffered from diphtheria that summer.

Treasure Island was actually published before Stevenson's book on Napa Valley, in the summer of '83. It, too, did not draw any particular public interest at first, although serialization in an English youth magazine resulted in an unexpected influx of letters. It was the book *The Strange Case of Dr. Jekyll and Mr. Hyde* which made him a celebrity. When he returned to the United States in 1887, New York reporters vied for interviews.

Chapter Four of the *Silverado Squatters*, entitled "Napa Wine" should have endeared the author to local wine makers. Stevenson indicates he was very aware of the phylloxera invasion of France's vineland. He must have read newspaper accounts in San Francisco of the prospect that California wine would replace that of French for he wrote:

> And at the same time, we look timidly forward, with a spark of hope, to where the new lands, already weary of producing gold, begin to green with vineyards. A nice point in human history falls to be decided by Californian and Australian wine.

This chapter, only a few sentences further on, offers some indication of why Stevenson was pointedly ignored in spite of his contribution to its wine notoriety. The Scotsman did not find California wine particularly to his liking, all the kind words about Schram to the contrary:

> Meanwhile the wine is merely good wine; the best that I have tasted better than Beaujolais, and not unlike.

He followed this with a description of counterfeit wine labels he was shown in San Francisco. Labels for mythical wine chateaux which led Stevenson to conclude:

> They were all castles in Spain! But that sure enough is the reason why California wine is not drunk in the [eastern] States.

His reasoning, based on one experience, was so illogical as to likely infuriate most Napa vintners. Only a fraction of California wine was sold in bottles requiring a label; most of it was dispensed in bulk, directly from barrels or puncheons. Eastern dealers sometimes used such labels, but then the wine was not necessarily identified in any way with the state.

There is much else in *Silverado Squatters* that is very unflattering. His introduction to the city of Vallejo and a night spent in a rundown inn, is filled with not so subtle barbs. His attitude changed only a little when he reached Calistoga. Among other comments is this: "... here probably, is the office of the local paper (for the place has a paper—they all have papers)." A newspaper was some pretense at civility! The editor of the *Calistogian* must have found annoyance at that jibe. Stevenson may have been reacting to the fact that California newspaper editors did not buy or publish his writings.

Stevenson's main characters in the book are even less flattering. The Hansons, who lived in the old Silverado Hotel, near the toll road, are depicted as moronic. So were most of the boarders including the local school teacher. His entire chapter called "The Hunter's Family" literally drips with disdain. This may have been a popular literary position to take for English writers.

The Jewish shop owner, who hauled him up to the abandoned mine near the Toll House, was treated no better. Therein may lie an even greater source of displeasure with Silverado Squatters locally. Stevenson depicted the Jewish shopkeeper in extremely derogatory phrases. Perhaps, in the context of the time, he merely followed common parlance instead of what should have been originality. Stevenson does state at one point in this regard:

> Take them for all in all, few people have done my heart more good, they seemed so thoroughly entitled to happiness, and to enjoy it in so large a measure, and so free from afterthought; almost they persuaded me to be a Jew.

He called his Jewish merchant "Kilmer," but he referred almost certainly to one Morris Friedberg.

Unknown to Stevenson, the Friedbergs were highly respected in Calistoga. Morris had opened one of the first stores in the village when Brannan arrived along with the railroad. When his oldest son Charles married Henrietta Feder in San Francisco in March 1885, the *Calistogian* gave one full column to a description of the nuptials. That was unusual coverage for a small weekly.

The Friedberg wedding reception in Calistoga was hearty, friendly and large with over 80 guests (which must have been most of the town). This, too, was duly reported at some length. "Kilmer" and his family did not have the reputation Stevenson attributes to them or the newspaper coverage would not have been so extensive and of a far different tone! There was plenty of anti-Jewish prejudice present in California.

Robert Louis Stevenson was ill, quite ill, during his summer sojourn on Mt. St. Helena. His financial situation was critical until his father sent him a cable granting an annual stipend on which to live and write. His remarks about the Napa Valley reflect the tragedy of his situation.

His not so subtle criticisms of the people of the valley and its lack of sophistication may also be his journalistic or literary style. To the residents living there, what he wrote was highly unflattering. Within that context, it is no wonder he was a nonperson in Napa Valley by the time he died—at least in the columns of the small local newspapers.*

Henry W. Crabb's death on March 2, 1899 was as critical a loss to the valley wine industry and California, as Krug's demise. He was not so public a figure as Krug, but he literally picked up where Hungarian Agoston Haraszthy left off in the 1860s with vine experimentation (Haraszthy abandoned California in '69 for Central America and was never heard from again). Crabb planted far more varieties in carefully controlled plots than did Haraszthy, and he willingly shared his knowledge with any vineyardist who would listen to him.

---

*Stevenson's most frequently quoted phrase from his book is "the wine is bottled poetry." Unfortunately, the final qualifying phrase "these still lie undiscovered" has been overlooked, which means he never arrived at that conclusion at all.

When Frona Eunice Wait wrote her book *Wines and Vines of California* she gave an entire page to Crabb's fine wine, adding: "As a successful wine-maker Mr. Crabb is without peer in the State." At the Sixth Annual Viticultural Convention in San Francisco the previous year, 1888, he overwhelmed everyone and probably himself, by walking off with seven First Place awards. No one else matched him. If his wines had not proven Wait correct prior to the book's publication, his successes in the next decade certainly would.

At the Paris competition of '89 Crabb only won a Bronze medal, a major letdown almost certainly. He was a winner at Chicago, received two Gold medals at the San Francisco Midwinter Fair, and in Atlanta his To Kalon wine was given one of the seven Golds awarded. He won a Silver medal (the highest accorded) at the Bordeaux tasting in 1895. No name probably appeared more consistently on these awards list than Henry W. Crabb.

Crabb was seemingly in good shape financially up until his death, but that may not have quite been the case. For some unknown reason, he mortgaged his vineyards for $41,000 to the Goodman Bank in Napa, just four months before his death. When his estate could not repay the loan, the bank and the sheriff sold his holdings at public auction. On June 15, 1899 an officer in the bank, E. S. Churchill, made the highest bid and took over To Kalon. What had Crabb done with all that money? There was no answer to that question.

(Less than half a dozen years later, twenty acres of the Crabb ranch were deeded to the University of California for an experimental vineyard site. Crabb's work was to be carried on long after his death, a fitting memorial to the Napa Valley wine pioneer.*)

The near crisis state of the wine industry at times in Napa Valley never seemed to affect Napa City nearly as much as elsewhere. Agriculture tended to be more diverse in the lower end of the valley, and then there was the pressure of local Prohibitionists. Newspaper editors had to steer a difficult course between all of these factions.

An attempt to demonstrate this greater diversity in farming may have been one of the motivations for a summer long "Visit to the

---

*Crabb's original winery burned in a fierce blaze on the morning of May 28, 1939. It was never rebuilt. In 1965 Robert Mondavi purchased much of the former To Kalon estate and built his winery and planted his vineyards into the same soil.

Farms" column in the *Register* beginning June 7, 1895. There was something other than grapes and wine being produced in Napa County, that point was made very clear.

"Visit to the Farms" did offer yet another overview as to how pervasive viticulture was in the valley. The column proved to be a milestone piece of wine journalism demonstrating that wine making as well, was indulged in at even very small farms.

"Southwest of Town," or the Carneros district was the headline used the next week for the column. James Duhig had four acres of vines in which the phylloxera was first identified, his neighbor, U. H. Anderson, a "small family vineyard."

This rather trivial accounting of viticulture is not so important as was what it demonstrated about the spread of the phylloxera disease. The Priber *Report* of only two years earlier, credited Duhig with *forty* acres in vines. Could there have been some mistake? Further on in the column Charles Robinson is credited with "35 or 40 acres" of vines, Priber recorded him growing 60 acres! Viticulture in the Carneros would soon die out if the vine death rate continued unchecked.

Judge John Stanly's farm had the only significant Carneros vineyard to survive the phylloxera. It was also the only farm with more acres in vines in '95 than reported to Priber (200 acres now versus 125 earlier). Stanly had championed the resistant vine and was thoroughly convinced the Riparia class of resistant roots from eastern United States would prove sound for the valley.

Stanly's high standing as a wine producer put heavy pressure on him to continue growing grapes, phylloxera or not. The *Daily Journal* in June '93 described his wine cellar in these terms: "The wine cellar, spacious, cool and of almost even temperature the year round, first attracts. Great casks filled with the choicest vintage on every hand; in the sub-cellar, by the light of candles that the Judge remarked 'only makes darkness more visible,' we trod our way. Many thousands of gallons of rare clarets are aging in these vaults."

Gustave Niebaum purchased Stanly wine. So did Gundlach, Bundschu. Stanly had enough market savvy to hold his prices down and knew he also had something special, as this quote from the *Star* of March 9, 1900 demonstrates:

From the Stanly ranch, below town, 18,000 gallons of wine is being shipped to Capt. Niebaum, Rutherford, and 18,000 gallons more is

going to Gundlach, Bundschu & Co. San Francisco. This wine is
the choicest claret, vintage of '98, and sells in these wholesale
quantities at twenty-five cents per gallon.

It is from grapes that ripen about one month later than those
grown up valley, and their quality is greatly improved by the salt air
in which they mature. The Stanly ranch carries 300 acres of
phylloxera proof vineyard. Also 100 acres of orchard . . .

Vines had disappeared completely from another Carneros
landmark and that was the historic Thompson ranch. It also deserved
to be honored as the birthplace of the valley's *viticulture industry*. The
Register republished some of the background to the ranch for all the
newcomers in the area:

The Thompson ranch, now owned by Chas. A. Allen, is a veritable
landmark in California, being over forty years old. It was purchased
by Wm. N. Thompson from Gen. M. G. Vallejo, who had laid out
a townsite a mile square on the place, and some of the stakes are
still standing, relics of the past. Subsequently Mr. Thompson
purchased about 300 acres more, making a total of 650 acres.

Mr. Simpson Thompson, a brother of William, came to California with the intention of putting up a gas works, but gave up the
project. He then came to the Soscol place and took charge of it. This
was about 1852. Upon his arrival on the property, Mr. Thompson
lived for some weeks under the spreading branches of an immense
oak, making his own bread and doing his own washing. The tree
has been carefully preserved, and is surrounded with a rustic
arbor.[V.17]

Simpson, besides planting every type of fruit tree he could find,
planted grapevines and began supplying cuttings for the earliest
vineyards in Napa Valley and Sonoma, immediately after the Gold
Rush.

The *Register's* "Visit to the Farms" column covered much of
Napa Valley up to and including St. Helena, but one area not
touched was Wild Horse Valley in the very southeastern region. Even
E. C. Priber (or Robinson) skipped the widely scattered vineyards in
this hilly region. The principal road into Wild Horse Valley was so
steep and had so many switchbacks that even horse and buggy travel
was discouraged.

Wild Horse Valley lay high in the hills directly east of Napa City,
partly in Napa County and a good portion in Solano County. The
name could be traced back to the 1860s when an escaped stallion

from a local ranch finally found a mate of similar instincts and founded an obstreperous herd that angered the local populace by jumping over farm fences.

Joseph Vorbe and his brother Ephrem loved the story so much they purchased a good chunk of the valley about 1880. Within a year they had vineyards. Ephrem was cashier for the Swiss-American Bank of San Francisco (the title then carried responsibilities similar to the president in later years). He could have known wealthy Napa Valley investors like Niebaum, Estee or Benson and certainly would have known the Goodman brothers who founded the Goodman Bank of Napa.

The Vorbe vineyard may have reached sixty acres in size before phylloxera set in. The '93 study on the subject mentions "J. Vopt, Napa," which surely is a misspelling and should be Joseph Vorbe. The information provided fits: "Total 60 acres; all in bearing, soil loam, vineyard mountain; exposure west and south; crop 100 tons; cooperage, 50,000 gallons of which 10,000 is oak and 40,000 is redwood . This vineyard is on the extreme ridge of hills dividing Napa from Wooden Valley."

It was nearly impossible for any other grower up there to have a vineyard of that size, the configuration of the hills and water drainage precluded such a large acreage except on hillsides facing Napa Valley. The Vorbes made wine and may have leased their tunnel-cellar at times. The *Register* of December 23, 1883 apologized for "omitting the name of Pierre Fournier, of Wild Horse Valley, near Napa, who made 1,000 gallons." The name was not mentioned thereafter.

There were other small vineyards, Antonio Furtado had 11 acres in vines in the years around the turn of the century. The Sequiras had a similar acreage, but the only pre-Prohibition winery is believed to be that of Vorbe. On the southern end of Wild Horse Valley, F. W. Behrens had 8 acres in grapes.

One late arrival in Wild Horse Valley who did have a strong interest in wine medals was Constance Malandrino. The Swiss immigrant was superintendent of the large Uncle Sam winery for Charles Carpy and subsequently the C.W.A.

Malandrino purchased the Behrens ranch in October 1897 and immediately began expanding the vineyards. There were fine grass covered hillsides to plant to vines, although some were steep. He did not build a winery. It would have been illogical to do so when all of his grapes could be crushed at no expense in the Uncle Sam winery. Malandrino did not keep his own wine separate and thus could not win medals for Wild Horse Valley, but he had much to do with the many medals won by the California Wine Association after 1900. Unfortunately, the C.W.A. did not acknowledge the work of individuals like Malandrino.

Wild Horse Valley was one of the least known regions in all of Napa County until a drought in the 1890s turned the attention of the city of Vallejo to its water storage potential.

Vallejo, a dozen miles south of Napa City and built along the shoreline of the San Francisco Bay had prospered in recent years from the establishment of drydocks for the United States Navy. When the town wells began to go dry, city officials feared the navy might close up and move its ship repair facilities. There was a frantic search launched for a dam site to catch and hold water from the heavy winter rains.

When it became known the hills comprising Wild Horse Valley received unusually heavy rain during winter storms, and the land was largely in Solano County, city supervisors knew their collective prayers had been answered. In 1894 Lake Frey, named for one of the Supervisors, was completed and the water crisis over. All of this frantic activity was recorded carefully in Napa newspapers, and Wild Horse Valley would henceforth be included in the geographic description of the county.

"It is a long, steep grade that leads upward, at least one who travels it for the first time will think so," observed the *Star* when it began a story on Spring Mountain, west of St. Helena. No wonder Priber *et al* missed these growers as well, in his phylloxera study. The story in a December 5, 1890 issue continued:

> On the way we pass the extensive and well kept vineyard of the Beringer Bros., cared for by tenants who reside in one of the two houses located on the hillside.*
>
> Then on and on till the beautiful home of W. R. Lemme is reached away on the summit. Nature has done much here, and the hand of man has assisted in making this one of the many ideal mountain homes to be found among the hills bordering Napa

---

*This is now the site of the Streblow winery at 2849 Spring Mt. Road.

Valley. . . . Yes, there is a vineyard near at hand, and a wine cellar of goodly dimensions.

Lemme's other neighbors, besides Tiburcio Parrott, were barely mentioned in the story, in part because so few were wine makers or major grape growers. This particular story was not so much a visit to farms as it was a visit to the wealthy farms of Spring Mountain.

Lemme's wine cellar had been built in 1876, making it third in age on the west side of the valley to Jacob Schram. It was 40 x 75 feet, the first floor of mixed rock and concrete. Until he built his own road across the face of the high hills, Lemme had to drive down to St. Helena and then take the main Spring Mountain Road back to visit his neighbors.*

A third Spring Mountain winery was mentioned briefly in the 1890 story, that of Otto Hirschler. He owned land straddling the Sonoma-Napa County boundary and appropriately called his wine cellar the "Summit Winery." It was 64 x 64 feet of stone and three stories high. That was a good sized winery in the 1890s. (His vineyard was missed, too, in the Priber *Report*. His vineyards or those of his neighbors must have been good sized to support or fill so large a winery.)

Carl Conradi of Oakland never told a newspaper reporter why he chose Spring Mountain for a vineyard site in 1890. His location like Lemme's, required the building of a new road to reach it. He was in the cigar and tobacco shop business. Since it was popular then for businessmen to smoke cigars, his was a very profitable enterprise. Priber did include a brief explanation in his *Report* on why Conradi and others chose the high hills, the reasoning was not new:

> This vineyard is on Spring Mountain which is a favored locality, as phylloxera has not yet made its appearance, and frost did no damage in the spring of 1892.

Conradi must have spent some time on horseback riding through the hills looking for a special place above the frost line.

---

*Lemme's winery, called La Perla, ceased operations with Prohibition. San Francisco wine importer Jerome Draper purchased it in 1944 but died before he could restore the cellar. His son still hopes to reopen the original winery at some future date.

There is no record of when the first vines went into the ground at the Conradi farm or when he planted with resistant rootstock. He certainly must have used the Rupestris St. George, for his production was so good by 1904 that stone was cut from a nearby hillside and wine making initiated. The name "Conradi" was cut into the stone over the door but no date, as was customary at the time.*

The advantage of mountain-planted vineyards in mitigating frost damage was somewhat of an unwelcome recurring theme in this decade. There were three major periods of frost, some of the cold so severe it wiped out the grape crop in portions of the valley. The first of these frosts came on March 31, 1892. At a meeting of the Winegrowers Union eight days later in St. Helena, George Husmann was one of the few to report "his vineyard in Chiles Valley had escaped with but little damage."[V.18]

In mid-April, 1895 the frost was so widespread that it was described as the worst cold weather for the vine in northern California since the year 1880. The adjective used in the newspapers was "calamitous frost." The following spring was no better with Sonoma County growers around Geyserville finally adopting a technique used for a decade and a half in Napa Valley:

> Claus Meyer, a well-known vineyardist of Geyserville, has experimented upon means of averting frost until he had found something which has proven most efficacious. During the cold nights recently, between the hours of 3 and 7, he built large straw fires and wherever the smoke hovered the frost failed to appear and he has, thereby, saved his whole crop of grapes. Other growers should follow his example.[V19]

The Healdsburg *Tribune* which reported this story required one and a quarter columns to list all of the damage done by the frost. It was peculiar that the lessons learned by Groezinger at Yountville in the late 1870s and widely adopted in the valley thereafter, did not spread to northern Sonoma County. Even in Napa, many new

---

*Renamed the Keenan winery in 1977 when it was restored by San Francisco insurance man Robert Keenan, the founding year of the winery eluded research for some time. Fortunately, St. Helena nurseryman David Whiting saved the original "Day Book" of the winery when he left the property in the late 1940s. This document verifies the 1904 founding date plus provides much other early history.

residents seemed to know nothing about the bitter experiences or lessons like this learned by long-time growers.

This concept of frost damage being easily prevented by smoke was practiced in Europe for centuries. In the year 1882, when frost damage was widespread in California, the *Star* had recorded "that smoke does actually protect the vines against frost, was demonstrated during its recent visitation, when on one occasion, the temperature fell to 28 degrees, and those who smoked thoroughly suffered but slightly."[V.20] The same report noted that for several mornings, "the valley was completely smudged."

Jacob Beringer boasted proudly the previous year that he had discovered the frost barely nipped his vines where he had trained them to grow high on the stake, not low as was the common practice. He also was convinced that his tonnage increased by using six foot stakes in his vineyard with subsequently high vine trunks.

Arguments over high and low staking never seemed to reach any conclusions. It was this way with so many other aspects of the industry.

Manuring of vineyards drew nearly as much heated discussion. In Europe, it was absolutely necessary to rejuvenate the aged-old vineyards with fertilizer. Was it needed in California? William Scheffler of Edge Hill spread both bone meal and gypsum on his vines, but Henry Pellet thought simple barnyard manure would do.

Jacob Schram complained at one meeting of growers about insects boring into his wooden casks. They dug deeply enough for the casks to leak. A solution proposed was to soak the barrels in hot water liberally diluted with alum, then apply linseed oil as a coating when the barrels were dry. The worms that collected in huge numbers on the native oaks were voracious consumers of grape leaves many farmers discovered. The only remedy for this complaint seemed to be frequent cultivation of the soil, to kill the worm when in the chrysalis stage.

None of these problems were so threatening in the mid-1890s as that other insect or parasite which required a microscope to examine, the "phylloxera vastatrix." The word "calamity," too, was most appropriate to describe what was happening in the Napa Valley. Nothing before had caused so much suffering and grief among vineyardists as did this seemingly unstoppable disease. When one so-called resistant vine after another failed, the finale seemed very clear. Vine culture was just about over in Napa Valley.

One of the last publications of the Viticultural Commissioners, its *Report for 1893-94*, devoted half of its space to the most advanced view on the phylloxera—from a translated text by French scientist Valery Mayet. He began:

> To write on a subject after so many other authors, and to summarize and recapitulate the mountains of books, treatises, memoirs, notes and pamphlets concerning it, offers many difficulties. Such is the situation, however, of whomever desires to-day to write upon the phylloxera.
> . . . With the phylloxera, the abundance of material becomes almost an obstacle. It is true that some researches were made in the past decade; but during this short period what floods of ink, what outbursts of impracticable ideas, what foolish plans have been devoted to securing the prize of 30,000 francs offered for a remedy.

Mayet wrote that Dr. Henry Schimer of Philadelphia identified in 1867 both the wingless and the winged form of the insect associated with the grapevine. He did not know it lived on the roots of the vine and had been surviving there comfortably for perhaps thousands of years. Each eastern American grape simply tolerated the pest over its lifetime. This was not the case in Europe after it arrived quietly and unwelcome. It was supposed the American vine pest had travelled to Europe sometime in the 1860s, first to England.

The *California Farmer* for July 31, 1857 offered a possible solution to the phylloxera's first oceanic voyage. Someone who signed a letter "R. Buchanan" reported that:

> Mrs. S. J. Kellogg of Cincinnati, who resided for many years in France, has lately received an order from Bordeaux for cuttings and roots of our American varieties, and Col. Marshall P. Wilder, of Boston, has been commissioned by the government of Belgium, to send over all our best selections of grape vines, and also samples of our wines.

Kellogg and Wilder may be the two Americans most responsible for exporting the disease to Europe. If Mrs. Kellogg complied with the request for "roots," there is little question the phylloxera arrived in France's Bordeaux region in the late 1850s.

(Why the American disease was not transported to Europe at least a century earlier is puzzling. French Huguenots founded "New Bordeaux" in what later became South Carolina, in 1764. They cultivated the local grape and brought French vines with them. The

French grapes succumbed quickly to the high humidity and probably the phylloxera. Certainly homesick Huguenots who returned to France, would have taken samples of American vines back to their home village. The disease should have arrived sometime between 1764 and the 1850s.)

The French concept of replanting vineyards on "resistant rootstock" was quickly accepted in California. Charles Krug had been one of the first growers in Napa Valley to begin wholesale replanting of his vineyards. In the latter years of the 1880s, he adopted or initiated the "avenue system" of replanting. In the first row of a vineyard, he had his workmen plant a Riparia root between each dying vine. (The vines were planted seven feet apart.) He skipped the second row but repeated the procedure in the third row, the fifth, the seventh, etc. The diseased rows were removed when production ceased or was close to it.

The Riparia vine was the favorite of German immigrant Julius Dresel of Sonoma, who may have been the first in California to plant resistants. The year was 1878. The vine originated in the woods of Missouri, Kansas, Iowa, Indiana and even portions of Texas. Its grapes were commonly known as Solonis, Clinton, Taylor, Elvira and Franklin.

This knowledge of the various eastern vines came from France, too. Translated documents like Gustave Foex's *Practical Manual of Viticulture Reconstitution of Southern Vineyards* being one source. (It was republished in the *First Annual Report*, 1882, of the Viticultural Commissioners of California.)

Judge Stanly in the Carneros, Husmann at the Simonton farm and Henry Hagen had been early advocates of the Riparia root as the answer to the phylloxera. Professor Husmann's favorite was the Lenoir. He could not stop talking about it whenever the subject came up. The Lenoir did graft well when European vines were added to the vineyard, a strong point in its favor. Its adaptability to California was uncertain.

When the University of California at Berkeley began researching resistant vines, Prof. Arthur Hayne ran into some problems with the Lenoir. The vine appeared to be a hybrid of the American species of vines known as *æstivalis*. This meant it was not of the Riparia classification. The *æstivalis* had been rejected by the French because it did not adapt to the European countryside; this was true also in

California. (In wet years, the Lenoir would survive well in California, or if planted near a water source.)[V.21]

The Priber Report to the Viticultural Commissioners demonstrated clearly that the Lenoir vine was not going to work in California. Wetmore reported a year later:

> The Riparia is still the favorite variety, and in fact, hardly any other is planted, simply for the reason that our knowledge of the other resistant varieties is very limited.[V.22]

In another twelve months, the disease had been confirmed in Contra Costa County and then was found in Livermore Valley. In Healdsburg, a writer using the pseudonym "Vitis" wrote somewhat sarcastically of the fear no one wished to utter:

> A report has lately gone the rounds of the press, that the Riparia vines in Napa county are dying out on hillside locations. Local growers here have been much exercised over the statement, fearing that resistant vines were not doing all that is claimed of them.

This article appeared in the December 5, 1895 issue of the Healdsburg Tribune. Was Vitis right? That was now the most asked question in Napa Valley, Sonoma and elsewhere.

The University of California at Berkeley, much to its discredit, found a good high, strong fence and straddled it. Prof. Hayne wrote a letter to the Star, published January 3, 1896 stating there was some merit to Husmann's charges claiming the cuttings were often handled improperly and the plows were not penetrating the soil deeply enough. He spent a portion of the letter politely deflecting Husmann's barbs that he, Hayne, had not been born when Husmann was already tromping the vineyards of America. Hayne admitted the Missourian was right but that his knowledge of resistant roots appeared shortsighted.

Another crisis was about to erupt over California's vinescape, especially in the Napa Valley as viticulturists realized all their Riparia planting had been for naught. The University quickly put Hayne to work writing a booklet with the latest information on resistants. Published the following year, Resistant Vines now came down clearly on the side of the Rupestris St. George as right for California!

Hayne delicately explained how the error of the Riparia came about:

After some years of experiment it was found that the Vitis Riparia was the best all-round group for the majority of European soils. This is shown from the fact that today, out of 2,500,000,000 of vines grafted on resistant stocks in the Old World, probably 1,700,000,000 are grafted on Riparias. (page 17).

Hayne began the next paragraph: "While the Riparia is beyond a doubt the best species for the average European vineyard land, it by no means follows that the same is true of California." That now startling revelation had probably come to light only months earlier.

Professor Hayne cautiously worked his way through about twenty pages of explanation before he stated categorically on page 29:

As already said, it is thought that in the majority of California soils the Rupestris will have to be relied on rather than the Riparia as is the case in Europe.

For anyone with the presence of mind to go back to Foex's *Practical Manual* ..., he would find Riparia defined as the "river-bank grape of the Americas." The Rupestris originated in the same states as the Riparia but chose as its home, open countryside, particularly the gravelly sides of ravines.* It liked sunshine, the Riparias home tended to be in shady areas of the landscape.

Hayne points out in his booklet that there are hundreds of Rupestris types or varieties. The University had studied many of them and came to the conclusion that the Rupestris St. George suckered less than the others, grew more erect (easier to harvest) and grew better in a variety of soils and climates.

Despite the credit the University took for turning to the Rupestris St. George, much of the success which followed belonged to a Napa Valley grower. George Schonewald had opened a winery in the stone basement of his grand home west of town. He, too, had the Riparia and by the mid-point of the decade had lost most of his vines. Five years later his neighbor Henry Tucker told the *Star* it was Schonewald who had proven to California growers the Rupestris was the final answer:

---

*Husmann in a letter to the *San Francisco Merchant* of January 2, 1885 claims Hermann Jaeger of Neosho, Missouri was the first or one of the first to ship the native Rupestris to France. Jaeger found the vine growing wild in "Indian territory" and Arkansas.

He [Tucker] thinks Mr. Schoenwald is entitled to great credit for expending large sums of money in importing Rupestris St. George cuttings from France and experimenting with them as he established beyond doubt, the fact of the adaptability to the soil and climate of Napa Valley.[V.23]

There was a bit of a question in the unfolding story at this point. Hayne's booklet was published in 1897. An "Introduction" was actually dated "December, 1896." Schonewald ordered his vines apparently in the summer or fall of 1897—perhaps being influenced to a greater or lesser degree by the University's endorsement. Who deserved the most credit at this point?

It is not an exaggeration to claim that many growers had become distrustful of the University by '97 and paid little attention to its recommendations. Whether this distrust was merited was not the point, the bad press in recent years had derailed the creditability of the University. A reputable grower whose name was not associated with the controversy might be the only person to influence large segments of the industry.

Schonewald had his first Rupestris St. George roots in the ground in the spring of '98. The grafted vines grew so fast that his field crew cut the vines back severely after only the second year to prevent overcropping at such an early stage. That kind of news made newspaper headlines and was read carefully wherever it was republished. By the early spring of 1901, the *Star* (and many newspapers which copied its vineyard stories) could report:

There is greater activity in vine planting this season than for many years. Rupestris St. George is undoubtedly the favorite variety and vineyardists are basing great hopes of success on the French stock which is doing so well wherever tried. The young vineyards of George Schonewald and Beringer Brothers in and near St. Helena are pointed to as offering sufficient encouragement for renewed efforts and not only in Napa County but in other dry wine sections.[V.24]

The acceptance of the Rupestris as the answer to the phylloxera came without any serious challenge! For years afterward, some growers stuck doggedly to the Riparia and even the Lenoir but the evidence was clear; the Rupestris had won the final showdown. A French immigrant named Georges de Latour, who settled not far from Inglenook in 1900, quickly arranged for millions of bench grafted

Rupestris St. George to be shipped to him for sale throughout Northern California. The *Wine and Spirit Review* would even refer to him a decade hence, as the "savior" of California's vine land, quickly forgetting the honors it had bestowed on Schonewald. Of course, a great many people deserved some recognition including Arthur Hayne, that youthful professor who often seemed to know as much or more than the old-timers in the industry.

There is an intriguing explanation for the ready and rapid acceptance of the Rupestris rootstock. Napa Valley's wine industry was nearly wiped out by the year 1900. Everything that had been prophesied about the demise of France's wine vats twenty years before, now was coming true for the region stretching from the Carneros to Calistoga. Something had to be done.

The worst year of the phylloxera panic was not easy to pinpoint. The *Star* of August 28, 1908 noted in retrospect:

> The acreage in bearing vines in Napa County this year is larger than at any time since the phylloxera wrought such havoc in this valley, ten or twelve years ago . . . (1896 to 1898).

Historian Tom Gregory in his 1912 *History of Solano and Napa Counties* turned to George Husmann, Jr. for a chapter on viticulture. Husmann reported only "2,000" acres of grapes as growing in the county in 1901! His source was no doubt the *Reports* of the State Board of Equalization, which did cite such figures for 1897 and '98 respectively. But by 1901-02 there was a fullfledged replanting in progress with 3,500 producing acres in the latter year and another 1,500 acres not bearing.

Olives and olive oil were another way to earn money when the vines were succumbing to disease so the planting of olive orchards spread rapidly in Napa Valley during this time period. Adolphe Flamant had done much pioneering work in this regard on his portion of the Simonton ranch in the Carneros. He even published a booklet in the late 1880s on how to grow the olive. Olive growing became a boom industry as more and more Italian immigrants settled in the valley. Olives and the oil made from them were indispensable food products for Italian families.

At a Farmer's Institute held in Napa City in November 1896, Prof. Arthur Hayne came up from Berkeley to impart his knowledge on the olive tree. Hayne claimed the market for olives could not be supplied in California, in part because so many growers did not process the olives properly. They were largely inedible.

Napa Valley olives when ripe, were soaked in a weak solution of lye and two percent potash. Four to six hours later, this was drained and the olives washed in fresh water to remove the bitter taste. Insufficient washing left an after taste, and this was one reason the olives did not sell well. Hayne told the farmers that olive trees would fruit in two years but "never twice on the same spot of the tree."

Tourists were an increasing part of the economy of Napa Valley, by the final years of the decade. San Francisco had added fifty thousand new residents and considerable wealth to the city's banks. Vacationing was becoming popular and the favorite spots were small communities along rivers or high hilltops where the redwood tree grew. The more ambitious vacationers made it clear to Yosemite Valley.

Napa Valley drew its share of visitors too, for it had the more famous mineral springs resorts. Aetena Springs in Pope Valley was a bit far to travel except for those who planned to stay several weeks. Calistoga's hot springs were making a strong comeback as were White Sulphur Springs at St. Helena, Napa Soda Springs near Napa City, Samuels Springs in Berryessa Valley and others scattered about the county.

The fad at this time was to drink as much of the local mineral water as possible. Each resort advertised the mineral content of the water in San Francisco newspapers or booklets available free for the asking. It was simply amazing how many minerals could be found by a good chemist in such waters! Wine certainly had its competitors. The clinking sound of bottles of mineral water gently touching was part of any trip home on the railroad and ferries in those days.*

All of those tinkling bottles of Napa mineral water had an effect not anticipated by valley wine makers. Those thousands of tourists also tasted an occasional glass of wine—introduced to the product for the first time in their lives. Wine sales began to pick up, not only in the Napa Valley but all over California.

The explanation for the increasing sales in wine were many. Large numbers of Italian immigrants certainly helped, though many of these families preferred to buy fresh grapes and make their own

*The founding in March 1897 of the publication *American Wine and Mineral Water News* (New York) offers additional evidence of the prosperity of this young industry. The publication was widely read in California, attractively made up and 30 to 40 pages in length.

wine in the basement or back shed. However the wine was made, it helped the grape farmer.

The booming national economy was the real explanation behind growing consumption of wine. American wheat farmers were selling $1.09 a bushel wheat to European countries where the crop had suffered from adverse weather conditions. The discovery of gold in the Yukon territories excited investors in stocks—they all agreed this was the "big one."

America's conflict with Spain over Cuba, and the eventual declaration of war on April 25, 1899, put the country's economy on a wartime basis. With a large army being raised, unemployment practically disappeared and wages increased substantially. The *Wine and Spirit Review* of October 31, 1899 announced in a lead story "Wave of Prosperity is Here" and opened: "The situation in the wine business has not had such satisfactory features in many years." By "features" Winifield Scott meant good prices.

George Husmann writing in the 1898 *Yearbook* of the Department of Agriculture (U.S.) admitted that the huge wine production of '97 had at first frightened the industry—a record 27,000,000 gallons of dry wine plus 7,000,000 gallons of sweet wine. Thus with the extremely short wine crop the following year, and the national economy booming, the future for wine suddenly was very exciting. He also admitted the Rupestris St. George seemed to be the final happy solution to the phylloxera disease.

Grapes were selling now for $25 to $35 a ton. Wine sold for 20 to 35 cents a gallon, depending upon its age. Ironically, unless a Napa Valley winery was filled to the rafters with unsold wine, the local industry could share only minimally in all of the prosperity. The phylloxera had nearly eliminated the local grape as a source for wine. Fortunately, the northern portions of Sonoma County had hardly been touched by the disease as had many other portions of California. Wine grapes were in abundance, just not Napa Valley wine grapes.

While the local grower might suffer, the wine maker who could import grapes from outside the county (was large enough to fund the added expense!) did quite well. The California Wine Association moved and shuffled grapes around the wine country like pawns on a chess board. The Greystone winery, centerpiece in the C.W.A.'s fine wine holdings, worked several shifts each harvest, in part to impress visiting journalists. And they were impressed. The Wine and Spirit Review described it as the finest winery in the state or anywhere, in an October 1897 feature story.

It was likely that the Greystone winery was visited in April 1896 by the richest man in America, Cornelius Vanderbilt. Charles Crocker of the Southern Pacific Railroad put his special personal train at the disposal of Vanderbilt. He and a large contingent journeyed leisurely from Vallejo to Calistoga, stopping the train to alight in vineyards whenever the urge prevailed.[V.25]

The *San Francisco Call* had sent a writer to the valley about a year earlier to gather material. The emphasis, however, was not on wine. In fact it was barely mentioned. The natural beauty of the valley, the scenic attractions were highlighted.[V.26]It did not matter that wine was overlooked; it was wine that drew the attention of so many people to the valley in the first place.

Tourism was an underlying reason for the increasing consumption of wine in California, and to a lesser degree nationally. Tourism resulted from the increasing wealth of the middle class and even of the working class in San Francisco. Wages were now high enough so that relatively poor families could afford a vacation, or sometimes a holiday weekend at Aetena Springs, Johannisberg resort or the smaller hotels of Calistoga. Well, perhaps Aetena Springs was outside the limits of their pocketbook but not a new phenomena springing up in all rural counties—farm vacation cabins.

Hundreds of farmers discovered they could renovate a small outbuilding and rent it by the week to vacationers. If they provided meals, that added more income. Many farm families moved out of their main house during the summer months and rented it. Anyone lucky enough to be near a creek or a steep hillside (for climbing) rented with greater ease. Vacations were in, in California!

There were other clear and sharp indications of this new wealth. Frona E. Wait's book *Wines and Vines of California* (1889) was written for the average reader of the *San Francisco Examiner*, not the upper classes. Daniel O'Connell's book *The Inner Man* (1891) did aim a bit higher but dining out was a pleasure widely indulged in, as was the search for unusual foods and then the wine to go with it.

Ben C. Truman's book *See How It Sparkles* in 1896 was written specifically to answer the growing demand for information about the sparkling wine called Champagne. In the previous decade, only

Arpad Haraszthy had mastered the secrets of Champagne making in California but by mid-point in the 1890s, he had a great deal of competition. Paul Masson of Santa Clara Valley, a French immigrant specialized in Champagne. Wetmore began making it, so too the Italian Swiss Colony, Korbels and half a dozen others.

Champagne had been known as the beverage of royalty, and of the wealthy class. The working class now wanted to try it, spurred on just a bit by a popular dance hall tune of the day called "Champagne Charlie." The tune was easy to remember, the words even more so:

Champagne Charlie is my name, Champagne Charlie is my name. Good for any game at night my boys, good for any game at night my boys. Champagne Charlie is my name, Champagne Charlie is my name. Good for any game at night, boys, who'll join me in a spree.

No one was producing Champagne in the Napa Valley, but this was of little consequence. The future was all that mattered, and with a new century about to begin, times had never been better. There was a solution for the vine disease phylloxera, even though a great many vineyardists did not know it yet. Napa Valley's wine reputation ranked higher than any other producing county or region in California or elsewhere in the country. Many local residents were not really aware of this fact and could not have grasped what it meant anyway.

Some of those who could not comprehend the changes taking place were Italians. It did not matter, Italian was spoken more than any other foreign language in the valley. The large San Francisco wine dealers were quick to cater to this new class of vintners. It did not take an enlarging glass to see their role in the industry a few years hence.

Charles Krug's winery, the oldest in the valley, was now the property of James Moffitt, of San Francisco. An order of the superior court in Napa had permitted its sale for a mere $35,880 to satisfy creditors. Another wealthy San Franciscan, Alfred Tubbs, did not survive the decade to see the wonders of the next century. He died in his apartments in the Palace Hotel in late December '96. Judge John Stanly lived to the year 1899, then died too, before the New Year began.

There simply was no way to paraphrase what had transpired during the decade, except to state that Napa Valley had grown and matured (to liken its aging to a human being), matured so rapidly it was well into middle age by the time the decade ended. It did this none too gracefully at times, for example, when neighbors barely spoke over the formation of the C.W.A. and when it helped bring about the demise of the Board of State Viticultural Commissioners.

On this latter subject, except for that San Francisco wine journal, there was remarkably little criticism in the state press. It may be that many people agreed with an observation made in a Sacramento newspaper some years before:

> Valleys and mountains comprise the topography of Napa county, expressed in general terms. To be more explicit: a range of the Mayacamas Mountains forms the western boundary line of the county, at the base of which, and extending the whole length of the county, lies Napa valley, the queen of all the valleys in the county, as well as of the whole State.[V.27]

VI. Recovery and Confrontation With Prohibition, 1900-1920

 f the French immigrant influence in Napa Valley wine making had been somewhat minimal prior to January 1900, all of that changed dramatically with the arrival of Georges de Latour. Like his predecessors, he had difficulty with the English language, but he had the foresight that California wine could and would one day match that of his native land. He might take a half century to prove his point.

What de Latour accomplished can only be compared to the work of Charles Krug. Krug was the father of the Napa Valley wine industry but de Latour not only nursed it back to health with imported phylloxera resistant vines, he made wine quality his primary goal. Niebaum, Stanly and Krug would have toasted his endeavors had they all been his contemporaries.

De Latour was surrounded in controversy almost from the day he arrived. His pockets and wallet were so empty that he ended up being sued frequently for back wages or failure to pay his bills. These stories were buried deep inside the local newspapers. His work with resistant vines and Cabernet Sauvignon wine made the front pages.

Unfortunately there is no evidence that de Latour made any wine before the year 1904 (in a rented cellar), and the first "Beaulieu winery" did not come into existence for another five years or until 1907.

De Latour was a native of the Bordeaux region of France. That in and of itself was enough to guarantee qualifying as an "expert" on fine wine. He had been trained as a chemist in a Catholic university, which gave him a status in California few other wine makers possessed. Most of his peers were men who had grown up in wine making families but had little technical training other than what was passed from one generation to another.

When de Latour arrived in California he did not locate an old winery and buy or lease it. For fifteen years he gathered up unwanted and unused argols, scrapped from inside wine tanks. This he processed at San Jose, Healdsburg and finally at Rutherford, into cream of tartar for home baking. He was rather well known to Napa vintners by the time he purchased four acres of land, house and barn in May 1900 from Charles P. Thompson of Rutherford.

There is a persistent question regarding this purchase which suggests much about the background of de Latour. There were many more French immigrants living in San Jose and between Healdsburg and Cloverdale than in the entire county of Napa. San Jose could have been the unofficial French capital of California in the nineteenth century. Why did de Latour settle in Napa Valley?

The answer may be that de Latour wanted to be near to one of the most prominent wine brands in the state, Inglenook. Or it may be that his perception was that the soil at Rutherford, next to Inglenook, provided what he wanted for his future wine production. He knew the Zinfandel and Mission, the most widely planted vines, would grow anywhere but the right soil for the varieties of his homeland was another matter.

Wine making and even viticulture were not subjects of prime interest during most of that first decade to the former Bordeaux resident. Even collecting argols from his neighbors for cream of tartar was a minor pastime. Georges de Latour soon discovered he could pay his bills by importing bench-grafted phylloxera resistant vines of the finest European varieties. He did so not in the tens of thousands but in the millions. De Latour helped replant and rebuild the grape industry of most of California, 1900 to 1920.

Napa County had less than five thousand acres in wine grapes when de Latour arrived. A train ride up the west side of the valley and a wagon ride back down the east side demonstrated how sick the vineyards really were. Many growers had tried so called resistant roots, only to find they were not adapted to California's climate or soils.

George Schonewald had received rave press notices for his work with the Rupestris St. George, and this may have been one more reason for de Latour settling in Napa rather than closer to his French-speaking friends. Schonewald did not care to provide his neighbors with the St. George root—most of which had to come from France. De Latour probably arranged with friends in France for the vines—all in one or two letters.

By October 1907 the *Wine and Spirit Review of San Francisco* was pleased to observe:

Since the destruction by phylloxera of the vineyards in California, the farmers have been looking for a vine with which to restore their vineyards permanently. Many experiments have been made, but few have been successful. The *Wine and Spirit Review,* having at heart the interest of the public, has constantly watched the progress made in California, and now is in a position to conscientiously recommend to vineyardists the vines imported from France by G. de Latour, of Rutherford... The fact that the California Wine Association and the Italian Swiss-Colony buy their vines only from him is sufficient proof of the excellent quality of his goods.

De Latour appointed agents for his vines in many towns throughout Northern California, and the *Star* of March 5, 1909 reported he had 450,000 vines ready for planting. (By 1915 the *Spirit Review* referred to de Latour's vineyard as "famous," the adjective derived from all the notoriety attendant on his success with the Rupestris St. George.)

De Latour had begun his own experimentation with French grafted rootstock as early as April 1901, according to the *Star.* In January the following year he leased the Harris winery to store wine that he had purchased the previous several months. In September 1904 he rented the Thomann cellar and began making wine for the first time in the valley.

There is the possibility that de Latour began buying bulk wine the same year he arrived in the valley, 1900, and afterward regarded the year as the birth of his winery named Beaulieu. This all may be related to a heated controversy involving the local priest, Father Blake, recommending wine for altar use.

San Francisco's Examiner newspaper eagerly sought out stories which touched on sensitive issues and sacrosanct institutions, like the Catholic church. Only months before de Latour purchased land in Rutherford, the *Examiner* carried an expose story detailing how Father Blake in St. Helena recommended certain local wineries to priests in other states. It was inferred that he or the church received some type of compensation.

The *Star* carried all of the details including Blake's explanation that he did live, after all, in the heart of fine wine country and inquiry letters from fellow priests did arrive in his mailbox. He vehemently denied any wrongdoing and declared he would henceforth make no such recommendations.

Georges de Latour must have seen another ready opportunity and seized on it, eventually obtaining letters from the San Francisco archdiocese stating he produced wine according to the strict canonical law. In another twenty years this business would expand phenomenally, but in those early years the profits were small.

Since ready cash was a major problem facing de Latour, he contracted the sale of all of his grapes as soon as they came into production to the California Wine Association. They were crushed at the Greystone winery north of St. Helena. This included the grapes planted or harvested on 125 acres he purchased in 1903 from Joseph A. Donohue.

For this and other reasons, de Latour had no need to open a winery on his home farm until 1907. This was Beaulieu.

An Italian immigrant named Joseph Ponti confirmed years later that this was true for he started to work for de Latou on the morning of February 4, 1907:

> He came down to the vineyard, and we talked. I talk French, I still do, as much as I do my own language.... He says, "You look like an intelligent boy, I want you to learn the wine business. Would you care to do that?"
>
> At that time there was no winery, it was just the beginning. They had an old barn there, it was two story, up above they used to keep the hay, and down below the horses. So he had made some partitions there, and he had about, oh I would say two dozen barrels of wine. That's all he had.[VI.1]

The renewal of Napa County's vineyards, helped so much by de Latour, brought a resurgence in winery construction during the early years of the century. The Salminas at Larkmead hired builder Wilbur Harrison of St. Helena to oversee a new all-stone wine cellar. What he came up with would reach to 33 feet in height, be 66 x 66 feet square and the timberwork was so massive, a freight train could have been parked inside.*

The actual work on the winery began in March 1906 with the pouring of a five foot thick concrete floor. Why this huge slab of concrete was needed is not explained in newspaper stories except that 16 tanks of 160,000 gallons capacity each were built in place as soon as the concrete dried.

Huge redwood beams were used for the second floor, in part because 50 tanks of 1,250 gallons each were to be housed there, plus all of the fermenting equipment.

Larkmead was a monument to the man who drew the plans and oversaw the construction. Like Hamden W. McIntyre who drew so many designs for wine cellars after Inglenook, Harrison soon became the local expert on winery architecture. His father had built row-house Victorians and business buildings in Oakland and Berkeley, now Harrison literally galloped from bungalow to fruit dryer, to wine cellar. He must have arrived at each site calling out directions and left in as much of a hurry yelling orders to those left behind.

Some of the individuals who hired Harrison were not easy to please and made his task all the more difficult. Bautista Salmina had Harrison build the stone walls around the old Larkmead winery so that work could go on inside uninterrupted. Consequently before one stone was in place, the door frame was raised, Salmina climbed up a ladder and poured champagne over it. When Harrison's workmen finished the 33 foot high stone walls, and the roof was in place, the walls of the old wooden Larkmead winery were gently taken apart, piece by piece. Not a drop of wine had been spilled.

Up on Spring Mountain Road, the Hart family ordered a stone bridge 75 feet long built between the main road and the hillside, spanning a usually dry creek. Halfway into the project, the winter rains arrived early and took out the half finished bridge. Harrison

---

*Today this is the site of the Hanns Kornel Champagne Cellars. Kornel acquired the historic property in 1958.

replaced all the materials, at his expense and began all over again. He built it so solidly that even a major disaster could not dislodge it. (The bridge is still the main entrance to Chateau Chevalier winery.)[IV.2]

In exactly the same year as the new Larkmead winery was being built, a half dozen miles closer to St. Helena Antonio Forni completed his stone winery. He even copied the Salminas by insisting the old wooden cellar inside and its wine, not be nudged an inch. When the new stone walls were complete, the old building could be disassembled.

Forni, like the Salminas, had been a hotel owner in St. Helena and with the declining availability of grapes due to the phylloxera, decided the time was right for entering the wine business. He leased the Tychson winery from a nearly bankrupt Josephine Tychson in 1895. Her financial problems were largely due to the phylloxera and the death of her vines.

Four years after his lease began, Forni began construction of a stone wine cellar that would take seven years to complete. At times it must have been difficult for the stone masons or carpenters to know which direction to build. First, Forni ordered stone walls to surround the old 50 x 50 foot, two story redwood Tychson wine cellar. These were slightly more generous, 55 x 73 feet. Then he had a stone addition built on the St. Helena side. Finally, he ordered a stone wall to run 143 feet on each side and 92 feet front and back. The front would reach almost to the St. Helena-Calistoga highway.

When Forni's cellar was completed in 1906, he had workmen install bronze plaques on either side of the front door, one read "1895" and the other "1906." They would confuse visitors and owners for decades afterward, everyone assuming the first winery on the site dated to '95. Since Tychsons had made wine in the first cellar for the previous nine years that should have been considered when making a decision on the real founding year. Forni, after all, did make wine in the Tychson cellar, as well. He would have been wise to use "1886" as the first of the two dates.

Charles Forni, a nephew of Anton, helped in the construction of the winery. He delighted in recalling the story years later of the Tychson building being left intact inside until the final stone was in place. Uncle Anton fretted and fussed as if the builders might harm his precious wine merely by making too much noise.[VI.3]

Anton Forni made a fortune from his wine produced in his "Lombarda winery," although he would not live long to enjoy the fruits of his labors. Forni had Italian cousins working in the marble quarries of Vermont and while on a visit there discovered they and hundreds of other Italian immigrants had no steady source of dinner wine. This may have been his motivation in the first place to go into wine making. For years Lombarda wines went monthly by the rail carload to Barre, Vermont. Anton died just as the annual crush began in August 1908 in St. Helena.

Ironically, not far from the Vermont marble quarries a death occurred the year after Forni's which should have been noted with considerable solemnity in the valley. Unfortunately, not one word of the death of Hamden W. McIntyre was carried in a local newspaper. He had been born at Randolph, Vermont and after working many years for Niebaum and then Leland Stanford in Tehemna County, he returned home to take over the family business, including the local phone exchange.

McIntyre's obituary, covering a full newspaper column in his hometown, mentions his employ at Inglenook and for Stanford but there is not one word on all of the architectural plans he drew for so many wineries in Napa Valley, Sonoma County, at Livermore, Vina Vista and other distant points. McIntyre probably did more than any other single individual to begin winery touring by the general public for at first they came to view these new architectural wonders, the wine was secondary.

McIntyre might not have recognized the local Napa wine industry in 1909, so much had happened to change it in only twenty years. Electricity was one of the changes in fashion. It had the capability to turn night into day, or almost, and that was a dream come true during the late work of the crushing season.

Most Napa residents probably saw their first glowing electric light bulb at the circus. As early as September 1880 the *Petaluma Courier*, for example, reported the Cole Circus exhibited the "first introduction of the wonderful electric light." Electricity was produced by a gasoline engine of thirty horsepower. Actually, similar generators producing electricity were used in local vineyards to shock grapevines—the hope being that the phylloxera might succumb. Needless to say, the concept had failed.

The Napa Gas and Electric Company had provided Napa City with electric street lights for some years before electricity generated from mountain streams became commonly available in 1900. The old gasoline engines often sputtered and ran erratically, illuminating the town brightly some nights, or hardly at all on others. In St. Helena water power electricity arrived in June 1909. Two years later the *Star* was able to report:

> A great step forward in cellar equipment has been taken during the past year by the installation of electric motors and electric lights.

The electric motor alone meant a half dozen laborers could be laid off for much of the movement of wine from tank to tank or to puncheon, was accomplished by hand pumps.

The first winery in Napa Valley, incidentally, to be lighted by electricity was probably Greystone, this was from a gasoline engine installed in April 1888. In 1903, however, John Benson had a water driven generator installed in the basement at Far Niente winery to light up his cellar. Whether he had the water year round, however, is questionable.

Electric pumps were crucial in the experiments to cool freshly crushed grape must so that it would ferment at temperatures considerably below that outside. "Stuck" wine was an on-going discouraging problem, particularly when hot weather settled in for protracted stays. The picked grapes were often left to sit overnight, but even that might not help cool them sufficiently.

By encircling wine fermenters with copper tubes and pumping cold water through the pipes, the fermentation temperature could be lowered substantially and even controlled. The University of California at Berkeley described how to make such a machine in its *Bulletin #174* issued in April 1906. Few wine cellar owners could afford the cost of such innovation.

High cost was the reason so few winery owners bottled their wine, as well. Hand blown bottles were expensive, and even Gustave Niebaum quickly abandoned his advertised intention to "Bottle Only in Glass" as too costly. Hamden McIntyre probably was in on this decision before he left Inglenook.

Wine quality simply could not be maintained as long as most of the wine produced at the winery left its origins in barrels. The railroad also discouraged glass case shipments by charging a rate three times that charged for bulk.

In 1903 a scientist named Michael J. Owens solved some of this problem by inventing an automatic bottle making machine. The key was a wood or metal mold into which hot glass could be blown and the shape maintained. By 1910, 33,000 bottles a day were being produced and the numbers expanded yearly. Two Italian immigrants at the Italian Swiss Colony winery, Pietro Rossi and Andrea Sbarboro took up where Niebaum left off and marketed much of their wine in the East in glass. The *Wine and Spirit Review* shortly editorialized:

> One of the most satisfactory features of the situation as regards California wines is the steady and marked gain that is being made by our best wines in glass, under a genuine label and marketed by responsible business houses.[IV.4]

These "responsible business houses" were also watching ever more closely what went into those bottles. It was not enough to produce average wine anymore—to compete with European wine the quality standard was rising and rapidly. If California wines were to maintain their sales lead even in San Francisco, it was not enough to be local or native, those loyalties were quietly abandoned.

Wine quality could be improved significantly by adding pure yeast, suggested the Board of State Viticultural Commissioners in their annual Report in 1888: "The best for the purpose is the compressed yeast, sold in small cakes throughout California although any well-washed yeast will do." Professor A. P. Haynes, along with his phylloxera experimentation also suggested using pure yeast as early as 1896. A decade later Professor Frederic Bioletti issued a University circular describing the process in detail.

All of this was theoretical until put into commercial practice. The University convinced the California Wine Association to experiment with yeast in tanks of 5000 gallons each at their Geyserville plant. Over a million gallons of wine was produced with the new yeasts, plus controlled temperatures and several other factors. The industry as a whole paid little attention to the results.

The problem was communication or a lacking thereof. Most wine makers did not subscribe to a wine journal and the many immigrant vintners could not read English, although speaking it did come more easily. Of greater concern was the wide abyss separating the industry, especially the common small wine producers from the University. There was little or no working relationship.

When Rudolph Jordan took up the pure yeast cause at the Streich winery in the Napa Redwoods, some of the old attitudes began to change. Jordan had owned the old Hudemann ranch and small winery. He sold it in 1900 to Theodore Gier of Oakland (a German immigrant who found so many neighbors spoke German that English was the second language).

Jordan was invited by the Streichs to experiment with complete freedom in their wine tanks with pure yeast. He kept copious notes and wrote about his success in a pamphlet published in 1911 called *Quality in Dry Wines through Adequate Fermentations*. He wrote about the need to upgrade wine quality and his work for a May 1912 issue of the *Wine and Spirit Review*. This was the first application of pure yeast in a small family owned winery in California, and it took place in the Napa Redwoods northwest of Napa City.

Whether more than a half dozen local individuals like de Latour, Julius Beringer or Felix Salmina paid any attention cannot be determined. The wine industry was maturing and had the time now, had to take the time to look at quality rather than fretting over vine planting or winery architecture. The results would show up at various international wine competitions. One was being planned in San Francisco in 1915 for the opening of the Panama Canal. It was to be a world-class world's fair and wine event.

Had Mother Nature not interceded dramatically right in the midst of all these changes, the wine industry of California might have won recognition from even its most disparaging critics in this pre-Prohibition era. It was moving in the right direction.

An earthquake centered almost under San Francisco on the morning of April 18, 1906 succeeded indirectly in destroying two-thirds of the wine supplies of the state. Refilling this wine lake was the only concern for some time thereafter.

San Francisco on the morning of April 18, was the wine storage center for much of the state. There were as many as two hundred wineries apiece operating in Sonoma, Napa and Alameda County— all single family ventures of perhaps ten to twenty thousand gallons. This was wine made in single wall, redwood structures with no protection against the intense summer heat. Many families, especially the increasing number of Italians, made wine from the small vineyards they tended and along with the butter and eggs they sold, subsisted on the meager incomes.

The stone wine cellars such as Far Niente, Ewer, Harris and others composed only a fraction of the wine storage in Napa Valley. There was no such thing as insulation in the walls or air conditioning in these small wineries. Some cellars built into or abutting hillsides survived the heat by storing the wine in the ground floor.

San Francisco seldom worried about heat—the cooling summer fogs routinely covered the city and consequently every major winery owner had a real "wine cellar" there. If this was not possible, huge wine warehouses bought up the contents of the small rural wineries long before June 1 arrived. Dozens of cellars filled this category, wineries like Lachman and Jacobi, S. Lachman & Company, Kohler and Frohling, Gundlach Bundschu, C. Schilling & Co., Schlessinger and Bender, B. Arnold & Co., Chauche & Bon or Theodore Gier & Co. Some of these had joined to form the California Wine Association a decade earlier.

There was no clear figure on how much wine was stored in San Francisco that fateful morning. The CWA alone had about ten million gallons. Some estimates put it at 45 million gallons. If wine stored in hotel basements was included (nearly all in barrels and puncheons, often considerable) and that in grocery stories, saloons, etc., the figure easily topped 50 million.

Among the Napa wineries with San Francisco cellars were Chateau Chevalier, C. Carpy & Co., A. Finke's Widow, Gier, Grimm's Vineyard, Inglenook-through B. Arnold Co., Oakville Wine Co., Sutter Home, Dos Mesas-Cedar Knolls Vineyard and the Golden West Company of Georges de Latour.

Ironically there is little evidence of any direct damage to wine in the earthquake. Few if any wine tanks were nudged off their supports. The *San Francisco Argonaut* published pages of eye-witness descriptions in the summer of 1926 to the quake damage—everyone from policemen to journalists or individuals whose work required them to be up and about at the early hour of 5:12 a.m. There is not a single mention of red wine flowing ankle deep in the gutters.

More than fifty fires erupted, caused by the earthquake. At Third Street and Townsend, a Chinese laundry collapsed onto a basement furnace that set the rubble afire. The fire quickly spread and within an hour the entire block was burning.

This fire and each like it could have been extinguished easily with wine stored nearby. All water mains had burst. Across the street from the Chinese laundry, the CWA had 2½ million gallons of wine stored. The Hercules gasoline pump had been widely adopted by these wine cellars to move wine, and each facility had hundreds if not thousands of yards of canvas hose.

All of these wine cellars were located in an arc running from the lower Mission District (no further south than the Southern Pacific railroad station at Third and Townsend), across the financial-produce district to North Beach. The wine furthermore was kept in tanks of 5, 10, 15 or 20 thousand gallons. A hose could have been dropped into a tank, the wine run through the Hercules pump and carried blocks to fight any fire.

Why wasn't the wine used, given the extreme urgency of the situation? There is no historical response possible since none seems to be recorded! Theories or conjecture must suffice. First and foremost would be that the U.S. Army marched into downtown San Francisco three hours after the shaking began. Armed guards were placed in front of any building with alcohol. The fear was—paranoia would be a better term—that all those people losing everything they owned, would go on a drunken binge of looting and other gross misconduct.* Every saloon was closed but not before bottled beverages were systematically broken. This was done in many neighborhood markets, as well.

Still, it would seem that if a fire company pulled up to a burning building, *or block*, and two million gallons of liquid capable of putting out that fire were stored across the street, the guard might be persuaded to put down his gun!

A more likely explanation may be that since most of the wine was not in bottles with a label that noted the alcoholic contents being less than fifteen percent, it was assumed that wine sprayed on a fire would explode or burn too. The largely untrained firefighters, most appointed because of political connections, did not know that wine was frequently used at wineries to fight internal fires. Wine had put out a major fire at Korbel on the Russian River in Sonoma County ten years earlier.

For three and a half days San Francisco burned. Just under five hundred city blocks were leveled by fire all of which or most of which, could have been prevented by spraying wine on the fires. It would

---

*In fact, just the opposite occurred in part because residents were so dazed and shocked by events. All written records describe the quiet, orderly evacuation of the downtown section. Some of the apprehension on the part of city officials and army officers could be traced to propaganda of the strident Prohibitionists and their anti-alcohol crusades.

have made a poignant footnote to history since much of the wine held by the CWA had been aged for a decade and was about to be released.

Fire destroyed wine operations in Santa Rosa too, but none in Napa Valley. The Brun Chaix cellar in Oakville lost 100,000 gallons of wine, all of it knocked off supports. The French founders must not have built five foot thick floors as Harrison did for the Salminas. Or there was another explanation.

The *Napa Daily Journal* carried long accounts of damage in Napa City—the hardest hit city in the county. Many downtown buildings were severely damaged. The Migliavacca winery, all of stone was its own disaster. On the other hand, the old Mathews winery was untouched and quickly became the focus of operations for A. Repsold & Co. from San Francisco.

The 1906 earthquake affected the Napa and state wine industry in a profound way. Most of the large San Francisco wine operations were not rebuilt. The CWA moved to Point Richmond, Lachman & Jacobi to Petaluma. San Francisco was no longer the center of the California wine universe. There was henceforth no place to ship wine when the summer heat came on.

Edgar Sheehan was quoted in the *Star* of June 8 as claiming that 40 million gallons of wine had been lost. His winery and contents had survived. The increasing prices for wine meant the coming harvest would bring a bonanza for the small grower and producer alike. Buyers for some time would not cast a wary eye or breathe disdainfully of the aroma of this or that wine. The wine lake needed refilling, urgently.

Records of the State Board of Equalization for 1904 gave Napa County 7,000 acres of vineyards. The county was recovering slowly from the phylloxera and just beginning to take advantage of de Latour's importations of bench-grafted rootstock. By the spring of 1908, there were still only 9,340 acres of producing vines but with *6,200 new non-bearing vines*. Obviously, the earthquake had caused a rush back to planting. Only four years after the earthquake, Napa County was up to nearly 16,000 acres!

Percy T. Morgan of the CWA provided this review in 1910 of the previous four years:

> Planting again progressed rapidly and "all went merry as a marriage bell" until the panic of 1907. The consequent exodus of a

large number of wine-drinking Southern Europeans to their native lands, coupled with the wave of prohibition which swept over the country, caused a great curtailment in the, until then, rapidly increasing export trade, which by 1907, had reached almost 25,000,000 gallons of wine and brandy annually.[VI.5]

A "Roosevelt" panic or depression reversed itself by 1910, claimed Morgan, and a short European grape crop brought prosperity once more. Boom and bust—that cycle plagued the industry, whether caused by natural events like earthquakes or women attacking saloons with axes.

One aspect of Napa's viticulture history that set it apart from other areas was a willingness or search for self-promotion and advertising. When the grape crop was going to be too big or the wine surplus seemed about to overflow an individual or two took it upon themselves to come up with a solution.

Len D. Owens, proprietor of Aetena Springs in Pope Valley, resurrected the concept of a state vintage festival in the summer of 1909. He had help right from the start by Horatio F. Stoll, a San Francisco journalist recently hired by the California Grape Protection Association (anti-Prohibitionist) to organize and promote the new group.

The party would be held the weekend honoring California's admission to statehood, a holiday celebrated each September 9th. There would be a national costume competition, gala parade, food, wine, everything. Aetena Springs was so far out of the way, so difficult to reach, Stoll and Owens must have taken leave of their senses.

There was an ulterior motive behind Stoll's participation, and for that matter, for Owens. It was obvious Owens wanted customers at his spa. Stoll, however, had spent hours trying to organize serious opposition to the growing Prohibition movement in the United States and most especially in California. The tab for his endeavors was quietly picked up by Pietro Rossi and Andrea Sbarbaro, who felt it was crucial to bring Napa Valley vintners and growers in first—the other counties would follow suit.

A year previously, W. W. Lyman, Bismarck Bruck, Julius Beringer, E. C. Priber, Felix Salmina and others had provided the leadership necessary for a Napa-California Grape Protective Association. What appealed to them more may have been an offer by Stoll to tour Napa Valley and write a series of pieces for newspapers and magazines on what he saw. Stoll produced a half dozen of these articles, which were not short on glowing adjectives. They were meant to attract tourists—and wine consumers.

One aspect of this promotion was quite new— photography. Stoll hired photographers to travel with him about the state, shooting pictures of vineyards, spring, summer and fall. For the first time, photographs became an integral part of wine promotion. During the fall crush of 1909, Stoll also had the first motion pictures made of a winery in operation. His film, soon shown in vaudeville theaters across the country included film from each wine district of California.

Motion pictures were about a decade old by then. Nearly everyone had seen actual photos shot in San Francisco on the morning of April 18, 1906. On October 11, 1907, St. Helenans could view the first motion pictures of Grand Canyon and supposed Aztec ruins in Arizona.

Owens and Stoll's state vintage festival was dropped after its first year, but in 1912 St. Helena picked up the idea with highly successful results. For the following dozen years, routine events came to a halt in the upper Napa Valley during mid September. Actors studied parts for the annual allegory play, the wineries prepared elaborate displays for the Visitor tents or the huge parades and food of every description was fried, boiled, baked and then swallowed. Crowds came from San Francisco and other bay cities numbered in the thousands.

A much more novel idea to advertise wine was the "California Car"—a railroad car filled with products of the state with wine taking center stage. This was part of a promotion scheme to introduce eastern Americans to what grew out west. An entire train was put together with one car from each state and was called the "Western Governor's Special." The task of traveling with the train was actually rotated among the participating governors. The St Paul Press noted:

> The California car is furnished in California redwood and a grape arbor is carried out in a realistic manner. The wine exhibit is one of the best made of California products and has opened our eyes as to the extent of that industry.

Inglenook and Theodore Gier wines were among those exhibited and tasted as the train cruised across the eastern landscape.

The growing consumption of California wines in the East in large part due to an emphasis on quality by such brands as Inglenook, To Kalon or Parrott, inevitably resulted in journalists writing news stories somewhat controversial. One such story in the *New York Herald* in the fall of 1909 touched on tender nerves and bruised some wine egos.

Edward M. Tierney, of the Marlborough Hotel, was reported to have said "that American wines, through their growing excellence, are actually driving French wines from the home market. In the best cafes, hotels and restaurants patrons are now insisting upon the American grown article—in fact, they seem proud to order it. This is in striking contrast to the condition a few years ago when the average diner would not dare to order an American wine above a whisper."

Tierney added that he thought some American champagnes were "vastly superior to those brought in from abroad."

The importers of French wine and champagne took a full page in the *Herald* to denounce such prejudice. At one point the copy reads:

> Take the vines of California, investigate them, and you will find them, as a rule, green, as they ripen only during the day, and the ripening at night is retarded because of the heavy dews, which kill the grapes during the hours of night.

The writer must have thought California had climatic conditions like Kansas or Illinois, and could not have visited the state. He also stated that if the finest grape varieties from France's Bordeaux or Burgundy regions were ever transplanted to the United States, the grapes and wine would not compare at all to the country of origin. Again he apparently had no idea that most if not all of France's best grapes were growing in California and yielding equal quality wine, especially in the Napa Valley.

Underlying much of this dispute was anger by the French over the American use of the word "champagne." Champagne could only come from the Champagne district of France, what was produced elsewhere was sparkling wine, they insisted.

That might have been a legitimate argument in France where national law had *recently* forbade use of the word "champagne" outside an appellation governing the drink. In the United States the word was as commonly used as Russian rye bread, Boston baked beans or Swiss cheese.

Indeed, a federal court would rule in 1911 that American producers of bottle fermented sparkling wine were entitled to use the word "champagne" and imposed only the restriction that the geographic region accompany it, i.e., California champagne, Ohio champagne, etc. The lawyer defending A. Finke's Widow winery against this false labeling charge, did examine a witness in detail about where he had purchased his Irish stew, Boston baked beans, etc. Each time a restaurant in San Francisco was named with the judge finally halting the examination stating the lawyer's defense was clear and the point made.

Some, or a major part of the growing public trust of California and particularly Napa wines could be traced to another governmental decision made in 1906. This was the passage by Congress of a law extending the Pure Food Acts to cover wine. The *Wine and Spirit Review* claimed, "Nothing in the way of legislation could have more greatly benefited the California wine industry."

On January 1, the following year it became illegal to add fruit juice or any other liquid to wine! It had been a scandal of long-standing that some wine distributors cut or thinned their California wine with fruit juices or even water. They knew some big hearty wines, especially those of Zinfandel, could tolerate the cutting without the public knowing the difference. Wine connoisseurs might complain, and the occasional vintner from Napa Valley who visited the East Coast and sampled his own product, but by and large the modification slipped by easily.

The new law also made it illegal to "misbrand" any bottle, package or container of wine. American labels which might confuse the public as to the place of origin, were the target here. Some officials in the Department of Agriculture, who sided with the French, decided any use of a French word on a label was misleading. Had their point been accepted, no Napa Valley wines other than Zinfandel could have been sold for all relied on long familiar European words or phrases, including Port (shortened from Oporto) and Sherry (anglicized from Jerez). The Germans or Italians did not object to adoption of their wine names, just the French. The federal court decision regarding Champagne cooled quickly further attempts at change.

One minor aspect of these new laws which was not beneficial to the wine industry covered the use of sweet wines in patent medicines. Many patent medicines contained nothing that was really medicinal except a strong dose of wine, sometimes up to 20-25% of the contents. A new Sweet Wine bill passed by Congress in the same year as the San Francisco earthquake, sharply limited the amount of such wine in health beverages. The speed with which this bill went through Congress suggests the energy or power behind it was from the Prohibitionists.

In California wine production had to nearly double to keep up with demand during the first decade of the new century. This doubling was in dry table wines which went from 16 million gallons to 27 million. Sweet wine production had a three-fold increase, from 6 million gallons to 18 million but, of course, much of this was in areas other than in Napa Valley.

No small amount of this phenomenal growth could be attributed to the press attention accorded various wine displays and wine judging events at the World's Fair held every two years in this country. Promoters for these events had to work overtime to draw the large crowds needed to satisfy the sponsors and put the event financially in the black. Wine tastings, wine cafes or bistros, fountains of wine and hushed judging events of wine were good publicity.

The decade began with a World's Fair in Buffalo, then one in St. Louis (made famous by the song "Meet Me in St. Louis, Louis" and introduction of the ice cream cone), one in Portland in '05 honoring the centennial of the Lewis & Clark exploration and the Seattle-Yukon Exposition in Seattle in 1909.

Actually, the first of these events was a World's Fair in Paris in 1900. Not many Napa vintners had wines to send with W. H. Mills of the Southern Pacific Company. They underwrote some of the expenses of the California display.

France had her opportunity in Paris to strike back at America for not forbidding the use of French names. They would not permit "California Burgundy," for example, to be judged since the French claimed it could only be an imitation. Never mind that the word "California" should suggest its origins. One French judge said he would have permitted the wine had it been labelled "California wine, Burgundy type."

Henry Lachman, considered by many to be the most knowledgeable wine man in the state, saw in the French refusal an implied recognition that California wine was making them highly nervous. California wines were attaining too high a standard of excellence and the French had to put us down, he claimed.[VI.6]

Migliavacca winery of Napa was accorded a Gold medal and W. S. Keyes on Howell Mountain picked up two Golds and two Bronze awards. Newspaper accounts do not reveal the types of wine submitted but obviously no French word was used.

Residents of Buffalo, New York made a valiant attempt to host a World's Fair in 1901. It was named the Pan American Exposition and here on September 6, President William McKinley was shot. Anyone who had not heard of the Exposition previously, never forgot the day thereafter.

Charles Carpy picked up a Gold award at the Buffalo wine competition, the only Napa award but then not many vintners bothered even entering. W. S. Keyes, still heady from his fame won the year before in Paris, sent wine but came away without an award. Curiously, the wine exhibit was divided with a separate section for Southern California. This may have been due to the northern half taking so many wine medals at such events or someone took seriously at Buffalo the not infrequent discussions of dividing the state.

At St. Louis in 1904 the centennial of the Louisiana Purchase was honored. Twenty-one judges were chosen, including Europeans, for the international wine event. California wine awards outnumbered every other state or country by a huge margin. W. S. Keyes was one of the three grand prize winners, Paul Masson and Dresel & Company being the others. There was something to the Howell Mountain soil after all. Krug and Brun & Chaix had reclaimed that in the 1880s.

At Portland in 1905, fourteen foot high columns, each four feet square, were arranged with elaborate gilt mouldings and heavily corniced tops, all entwined with artificial vines. The concept was to bring back a bit of old Greece, with its early reliance of wine in the diet. Free wine samples were available and the crowds lined up each day.

California wines were nearly the only entrants in the wine competition so the judges seemingly gave everyone a Gold medal just for being there. A wine medal from Portland did not mean much in subsequent years, but some dealers blithely ignored that in their promotion.

Seattle co-honored its neighbors to the north in '09 with the Alaska Yukon Exposition, but the city had gone dry due to the

Prohibitionists and not a glass of wine could be poured. The huge Spanish Renaissance architectural style building that California sponsored, had tall columns of wine bottles immediately inside the front door—the wine exhibit could not be missed by any of the 12,000 visitors daily.

An international wine jury was also selected and this time the awards had considerable merit. To Kalon picked up five Gold medals—the fine wines mostly a holdover from Crabb's tenure. Theodore Gier won the same number of Golds, but no distinction was made as to which were from his Livermore winery or that of Napa Valley. It is curious that after so dominating wine competitions for the previous fifteen years, only two Napa wines were honored at Seattle.

The diminished presence of Napa wine brands at the Alaska Yukon Exposition had an explanation, in part traceable to the California Wine Association. It controlled significant amounts of Napa Valley wines through its operation of Greystone, Brun & Chaix, and the Napa Valley Wine Company—to mention only three of its wine cellars. The CWA won 14 Gold medals, but no place of origin (or winery name) was acknowledged by the Association. That was not its policy. Any Napa wine in those Gold medal bottles went unrecognized.

One of Napa's wine brands conspicuous by its absence at these later events was Inglenook. Niebaum had devoted less and less time to wine making after 1902 when he was named President of the Alaska Commercial Company in San Francisco. This was the source of his personal wealth, not Inglenook. In the last two years of his life, 1907-1908, he was ill and the winery practically ceased operations. It did close after his death in August of the latter year and remained without a crush for three years.

When Niebaum's will was filed for probate, San Francisco newspapers jumped on the scandal it brought to light. Niebaum followed rules of etiquette and decorum to the letter, in part perhaps because he had been a sea captain symbolically adopted by the wealthy Sloss and Gerstle families of the Alaska Commercial Company. He expected no less from the nephew and niece of his wife Susan, when they came to live with them after the death of their parents.

Louis Shingleberger and his sister were raised by the Niebaums in luxury, sent to the finest private schools and often spent summers at Inglenook with horses to ride, bathing pools and servants. Gustave and Susan had high hopes for the marriage of the children into proper San Francisco families, undoubtedly Sloss or Gerstle. Instead, Louis ran off with a budding actress who took him to Hollywood and his sister married someone rumored to be the chauffeur, far down the social ladder. Both were cut out of the will, although just months before his death, peace was restored between the adopted niece and Niebaum.

Never published in the newspaper columns, however, was any mention of the translation by Niebaum of documents and accounts of explorations on the northeast coast of America by the Norsemen. Some of these were published by research societies. Scholars at major universities sought Niebaum's assistance. His lifelong collection of Alaska and Canadian Indian artifacts, particularly totem poles, formed the nucleus of the collection begun by the new Department of Anthropology at the University of California, Berkeley.

There was no obvious scandal associated with the death on February 11, 1910 of John Benson, founder of the Far Niente winery. He had been a bachelor all his 81 years and moved to the Napa Valley after his favorite haunt, the Pacific Union Club, was burned out in the '06 earthquake and fire. (His wine was served almost exclusively there.)

Benson dutifully left everything he possessed to two nieces, Virginia and Josephine Johnson. They spent summers in Italy or occasionally in Bermuda. They had not lived in the United States for some years when their uncle left the Far Niente estate in far off Napa Valley. They had a few friends in San Francisco, but life in rural Napa would be quite a change! Why they didn't sell Far Niente immediately, without journeying all that long distance, remains unanswered.

Virginia and Josephine may have spent weekends thereafter in the summer at Far Niente but they spent more time in San Francisco, closer to the literati of the bay city. Virginia had written many children's books and gained even more fame by serving as a young female model for magazine and book illustrations executed by her cousin, Winslow Homer.

If Homer was Virginia's cousin, then Benson was his uncle. Benson never breathed a word, it seems, to anyone that the two were related. When Benson died, his will contained long lists of barrels, fermenters and wine making equipment plus the contents of his home. Not one reference to a painting by Homer, though he had by 1910 become one of the best known illustrators and artists in the United States.

Virginia Johnson died in January 1916 and her sister Josephine two years later. Neither had married, although they in turn had plenty of nieces and nephews to inherit the proceeds of Far Niente which had been sold about a year before Josephine died. If any treasured correspondence existed between Homer and his cousins, or they held a collection of his artworks, all seems to have disappeared. Surely Homer's artworks hung at Far Niente and/or Benson's home, later that of his nieces. What family ghosts hung in the closet as well, sealing the lips of Benson and the Johnsons?*

There were other deaths of distinguished Napa wine makers in these same years, but most departed this earthly existence being fondly remembered only by close friends and relatives. Giacomo Migliavacca died in November 1911, 78 years after his birth in Pavis, Italy. His pioneering efforts in behalf of the sons of Italy should have merited a granite bust in some public square in Napa.

Jacob Beringer died in October 1915, ending a 45-year career in Napa wine making. He had received his California training, like so many other later luminaries (Ernest Wente, Charles Wetmore), at the Krug cellar. The German native was the trained in the art of the cooper as well, which set him apart from many of his contemporaries. He was always ready to debate California redwood, French or American oak, used in wine production. With Jacob's death the German immigrant influence in valley wine making declined significantly.

There was a new German native in the valley who might have stepped into Jacob Beringer's shoes except that he called Oakland home, operated a wine cellar there, had extensive vineyards in Livermore and only found time now and then to visit his new winery in the Napa Redwoods. He always showed up, of course, when Turn Verein, a German singing society paid a visit, which was often.

Theodore Gier was so active in state matters regarding the wine industry that he somewhat transcended any local identification. He

---

*A new biography of artist Winslow Homer is being written by Eric Rudd of Falmouth, Mass. Exhaustively researched, the Napa Valley connection via Benson, will be detailed for the first time.

had been in the forefront of the California Grape Growers Association. He was active with the Oakland and California Chamber of Commerce. He deserved much of the credit for pushing for the first highway tunnel through the Oakland hills so that Contra Costa County might be easily reached (later enlarged, the shortcut was called the "Caldicott Tunnel").

Gier liked the hillsides of the Napa Redwoods for grape growing, and in the spring of 1903 on what was commonly known as the "old Hudeman place" began construction of a large stone winery. It would be 80 feet long, 60 feet wide, three stories with a distillery 40 x 30 feet nearby.* Eight years later he added a 120 foot wooden addition with a total capacity now of more than a half million gallons. This did not match his Livermore cellar, however, which could hold three million gallons.

Gier's name or picture appeared so often in newspapers or the *Wine and Spirit Review* that he did not need any publicity, but in 1913 he topped every wine maker in the state. At the Ghent, Belgium Universal Exposition, his wines were awarded the Diploma de Honeur and a special Gold medal. In reporting the story, the *Star* claimed for Napa Valley much of the credit, although no individual entries were named. Twenty-seven of the thirty-five judges were French—this was the kind of recognition California and Napa wanted.

The wines from Napa Valley sent by Gier were undoubtedly in the style of French clarets or Burgundies, since Livermore wines were generally of the white varieties. To Kalon, incidentally, won a Silver medal, the only two honorees in the valley.

Between 1900 and 1915 as many new wineries opened in Napa Valley as during the peak boom years of the 1880s. Many that would survive for decades to come were built of stone but by far the majority were wooden, usually redwood.

These new wine cellars were being built by Italian immigrants or Swiss Italian. Unfortunately, most of these men did not seek public recognition for what they were doing. Because of language problems

---

*In 1930 the Christian Bros. moved from Martinez to this winery. Here Bro. Timothy spent more than fifty years overseeing wine production. In 1987 the Hess Collection wine facilities moved into the Gier winery, leasing from the Christian Bros.

or just the wish to remain quietly in the background, they did not seek out the editor of a local newspaper to describe these activities. The Italian population in California jumped from barely 15,000 in 1890, when they constituted about 2 percent of the labor force, to 63,601 twenty years later.

Luigi Domeniconi was typical of this influx of immigrants, coming from the Italian-speaking portion of Switzerland in 1894. He made chocolate at the Ghirardelli chocolate factory in San Francisco, then put in some apprentice time at Italian Swiss Colony in Sonoma County. In July 1902 Domeniconi purchased fifty acres in the Stag's Leap area and promptly began building a house with a full stone basement devoted to wine production.

Domeniconi never attempted to show his wine at various competitions and none of it was ever bottled. He simply wanted to earn enough to support his family and he did so, rather well it seems, by placing two puncheons in a horse drawn wagon and peddled the white or red wine door-to-door in Napa. There is no record of what year he had his first crush, but it likely was '02 for he began buying grapes of his neighbors immediately.*

For twenty years the Italian-speaking immigrant succeeded remarkably well, increasing his cooperage and expanding his small wine operation. Much of the crushing was done by stomping the grapes, with neighborhood youth helping out. Thompson Parker returned home from this task, purple head to toe and shocked his wealthy San Francisco parents who had just moved to Stag's Leap.[VI.7]

Prohibition forced Domeniconi to sell, but rumors were rife in the area for years thereafter that the winery continued operating as before and the quality was exceptionally high. The new owners had purchased tanks filled with finely aged wine.

Giuseppi Brovelli took over the Laurent winery north of St. Helena in 1909 and not only made fine wines which he shipped East to dealers, he sold just as much out the door every Saturday night at winery dances. Italians came from miles to attend. Brovelli paid for the orchestra and the entire family prepared huge midnight suppers. He won a top prize every year at the St. Helena Wine Festival for his elaborate displays of wine and grapes.

----

*Since 1978 when Gary Andrus reopened the cellar, the wines have been known as "Pine Ridge."

This kind of participation in the local wine industry won for Brovelli and the Italian immigrant high praise and acceptance among longtime residents. He made a point, too, of mastering quickly the English language. Brovelli let the local newspaper editor know every time he had been East on a successful wine selling trip. He gave the editor a photograph of his winning wine displays, if the newspaper had overlooked it in the previous week's edition.

There were many other Italians who followed in these same footsteps, the Bartoluccis at Oakville, the Fagianis who purchased the Mt. Eden winery in 1911 east of the same town, Giuseppi Navone and his partner V. Valente who purchased the Anton Rossi farm in Spring Valley, and Carl Conradi on Spring Mountain.

Actually Conradi was one of those deceptive names, it ended in an "i," so typical of Italian yet the family's immediate origins were in Germany. Like the Justis of Glen Ellen and others similarly named, their distant antecedents were from Italy but had migrated to Germany a generation or two before moving on to California.

Conradi was a cigar and newspaper vendor in Oakland who dutifully put away half of each dollar he earned and on January 27, 1904 high on Spring Mountain, began construction of a stone wine cellar. He had vineyards in production as early as 1892 for he was included in the Priber survey of phylloxera damage of Napa County in that year. The unavailability of Napa wines may have induced him to enter wine production so long after planting his first vines.

The stone for the two story 85 x 50 foot cellar was quarried nearby by two Italian stone masons who deftly cut each stone by hand and fitted it snugly into place. "Guigni" and "Bognotti" were their names. Italian stone masons built most of the stone wineries constructed in the three decades previous to Prohibition, including Greystone.

The decision by the Conradis to settle on Spring Mountain represents quite a departure for someone of German nationality. First it was popular to be near Charles Krug, then the Napa Redwoods where Gier built his winery. There was no German community on Spring Mountain.

Charles Wagner had no Teutonic neighbors either east of Rutherford where he settled after leaving his homeland.

Wagner cleared out "a large hay barn" for his first winery, according to the Star of October 8, 1915, and besides wine making equipment manufactured locally by Henry Hortop, he installed electric motors to bring modern efficiency to his entire operation. His old-world relatives might have disdained such laborsaving devices, why he could almost run his winery from a chair near the on and off switch.*

There is some suggestion that Napa Valley residents in this period came to think of themselves more and more as one community, spread out over thirty-five miles. It was possible to hear a neighbor's rooster crowing on opposite sides of the valley, in the narrowest places. This may explain the concept behind building a second railroad. It was to be run by electricity—a sort of electric streetcar with frequent stops. It would run so often children could take it to school.

Although fresh milk, eggs and butter could be shipped on the electric train, the primary emphasis was on the rapid and frequent movement of people. An electric railway had been built in Vallejo in '02 from a wharf on Virginia Street with plans ultimately to run the line to Napa City.

An entire decade was needed to find the financing and solve other problems before the electric road was completed to Calistoga. Local business boosters hoped it might renew the town's future as is evident in this quote in a local newspaper:

> The completion of the electric road into Calistoga means much for the little town, and one may expect to see great progress made there in the next few years.[IV.8]

A timetable for the "San Francisco, Napa and Calistoga Electric Railway" for 1914 indicates the trip from the upper end of the valley to a ferry wharf in Vallejo took just under an hour and a half. There were twenty-two stops and the engineer would halt the train almost anyplace if potential passengers were sufficiently demonstrative (frantic waving of a sweater helped).

There were seven departures a day from Calistoga to Napa City, and a half dozen more just from Napa to Vallejo.

Two steamers plied the waters between Napa City or Vallejo to San Francisco, the "Zinfandel" (there were several ships over the

---

*Charles Wagner, a son of the winery's founder, resumed family wine making under the Caymus Vineyards name in 1971, not far from the original winery. World War II closed down the first Wagner wine cellar.

years with this name) and the "St. Helena." This trip usually took less than an hour.

Traveling a dusty road by horse and carriage from an outlying farm just to shop in St. Helena was bad enough, but attempting to make this trip all the way to Napa was an unpleasant adventure (and recounted frequently in newspaper columns). Promoters of the electric line no doubt had this in mind. Horses kicked up dust especially as the summer months became warmer and the last rainfall faded into a memory. Women covered themselves head to toe with heavy veils to avoid the dust.

Napa County supervisors paid to have the county roads, the main thoroughfares at least, watered once a day. That did wet down the dust for the first travelers.

What a relief it must have been when local newspapers began carrying stories that a technique had been discovered to lay oil on roadways, controlling the dust. Within a few more years came the technology to "macadamize" roads—lay down a thick layer of gravel mixed with oil, which lasted for several years.

The firm of Lindow and Johnson sprayed oil on county roads in 1902 with the first experimentation having been carried out by L. B. DeCamp the previous year. Thirty-five miles of county road were contracted by county supervisors in April 1903 to be "oiled."

By 1910 the League of California Municipalities was sponsoring experimental work being done in Alameda to find the right combination of gravel and heavy oil which would harden into a semi-permanent road surface. J. L. Webber, a county supervisor, did a test strip in Napa Valley a year earlier which demonstrated the concept would work. Gravel was taken from a hill near Yountville, crushed and spread on a one mile test strip near the Sonoma County boundary. It stood up well over the following winter.

Despite the technology being placed, public pressure had to be applied to county supervisors to finance the new so-called oil roads. Webber had estimated it would cost $2,500 a mile, this probably came as a shock to county officials.

By 1913, the Napa Chamber of Commerce organized a "Good Roads" mass meeting in Napa. Hundreds of citizens attended and experts brought in from Sonoma County where oiled roads were already being laid. A bond issue of $263,000 to cover the cost of the new roads, was one of the topics argued for several hours. The Good

Roads Committee named included many wine makers and vineyardists: H. L. Johnston, Henry Brown, Jos. A. Migliavacca, J. E. Beard, E. Light, Homer Hewens, Frank Pellet, E. A. Burge, D. A. Dunlap, H. C. Melone, Morton Duhig and W. J. Stearns.

A new highway route was also discussed at the meetings. The state wanted to build a major new highway from Napa into Marin County via what was referred to as "Black Point." This would mean bridging the Petaluma River near where Sonoma and Marin counties met at the north end of San Francisco Bay.

This highway would be carried around a second point on the Sears ranch and up to Schellville just south of Sonoma. At many places, existing roads would be used. In Marin County, there were a half dozen ferry slips for the trip across the bay for Napa and Sonoma travelers.

With this kind of momentum, the improvement of Napa Valley's roads could not be stopped and dust-free oiled roadways quickly became a reality—at least the major thoroughfares.

All of this concern with roads provided the opportunity for valley residents on the eastern side to speak up about their being slighted one time too many over the years. When was the county going to do something about the "East Side Road?" What hurt more was their road often being called "The old Back Road."

A Committee to find a new name for the old Back Road, from the Soda Canyon Farm Center induced the *Napa Daily Journal* to carry a long article on this subject in the issue of April 21, 1921. "No doubt it will be of interest to many of us to know that none of the roads in our county have official names," began the story. It was not just enough to repair the old Back Road, locals wanted a formal name like "Silverado Trail." That was the most popular suggestion out of a half dozen names put forward.

An informal referendum was held on the name and duly adopted with the Board of Supervisors acquiescing. The resurgence of interest in Robert Louis Stevenson may have contributed to the name selection. A decade earlier the New Century Club of Napa had set out to have Stevenson's Mt. St. Helena cabin site marked with a granite tablet. Suddenly, his book "Silverado Squatters" became fashionable to read and discuss again. Many residents who had not heard of his summer spent in the valley thought it was time to name a school after this famous author, or a park or a street. Let bygones be bygones.

If a few hardy souls picked their way through the brush and avoided Stevenson's rattlesnakes on Mt. St. Helena, seeking inspiration at his shrine, this in no way compared to what was happening on nearby Howell Mountain. A flood of newcomers were inundating the old resort opened in 1874 by Edwin Angwin. They came to worship too, at a sanctuary for the Seventh Day Adventist religion.

Angwin had sold his hilltop retreat in the summer of '09 to the Adventists who wanted the site for a new college. Never mind that the institution of higher learning and inspiration would be located in the heart of wine country. The large Angwin hotel would be the center of the new college, there were cottages for staff and students, a swimming pool and barns for horses and stock raising. The only missing ingredient was a church. Classes began at the new Pacific Union College in September 1912.

Angwin's Resort had become an institution in its own right since opening thirty-five years previously. The first vineyards had followed shortly thereafter on Howell Mountain, and some of the finest Napa wines came from cellars with views which took in the Pacific Ocean and the great bay of San Francisco. Brun & Chaix was the largest, W. S. Keyes was the best known because of his Paris wine medals, the Hess winery and the G. H. Richard winery (on the opposite side, halfway up, or down, the steep Ink Grade).

This closing of Angwin's Resort was significant as it came in the same year as the destruction by fire of Walter's Springs Resort in nearby Pope Valley. Napa Soda Springs was declining rapidly, White Sulphur Springs operated erratically and somehow, Calistoga could never recapture the glamour and lure of the 1860s and 1870s. Thousands of vacationers still came to Napa Valley, staying more often in cabins or homes rented out for the summer by families. This major shift in the valley's economy was blamed on the automobile, or on all the new oiled roads being built. Anyone with the means, drove to the Sierras, to mountain lakes like Donner and Tahoe or Yosemite Park.

The automobile made possible a minor shift in the distribution of wine. Visitors to Napa wine cellars who arrived by car, began leaving with casks, small barrels of wine, or even cases. No one left a memoir when the first automobile drove down Main Street in St. Helena with a wine cask in the back seat, but the sight would have caused heads to turn and perhaps gales of laughter. The wine could be taken undisturbed all the way home and stored in the basement.

The first automobile with a flatbed projecting out the back end, a truck as it would shortly be nicknamed, could also have produced stares of amazement. Carefully loaded with puncheons of wine this too suggested dramatic changes ahead for the valley. The truck moved faster than horse and wagon and soon would replace it. All that was needed now were bridges across Carquinez Strait or somehow span the great San Francisco Bay. Wine could reach the masses without transferring or a stop in-between. No wine left soaking up the sun on wharves. This would surely improve the quality.

With the near total destruction of Napa Valley vineyards by the phylloxera, there came the realization that a golden opportunity existed to upgrade the varieties of vines to be planted henceforth. This catastrophe had a brighter side—if farmers would not plant the Mission or Zinfandel again in such large quantities. Napa had the opportunity to once more jump out ahead of other wine regions in California if the emphasis was put on the quality grapes and the finest wines.

Curiously, there was no single spokesman for this cause—perhaps there was no need since the refrain was being echoed from Charles Krug's grave and Henry W. Crabb and Judge Stanly. Georges de Latour did not push one variety over another—at least there is no record of such recommendations.

Maybe the credit belonged to George Husmann, Jr. who was in charge of Viticulture research for the Department of Agriculture in Washington, D.C. He had grown up in Napa Valley and listened nightly to his father expound on the problems of grape growing. The elder Husmann's ideas were often controversial and sometimes dead wrong, as was his championing of the Lenoir vine as the best resistant root for California.

George, Jr. came up with the brilliant idea of establishing viticulture experiment stations in California, at least three, to test under scientific controlled conditions, the vines and soils. His father had started this kind of work at the Simonton ranch, but the death of Simonton ended it after five years. Crabb had hundreds of grape varieties growing at his To Kalon farm at Oakville but his approach was that of a farmer, not the scientist. He did not keep copious records, too much was in his head.

George Husmann, Jr. found an ally in this cause in E. W. Churchill, the cashier of the Goodman Bank of Napa and the new owner of To Kalon. Churchill gave twenty acres of land fronting on Oakville Grade Road to the Department of Agriculture for an experimental station, with the option of expanding the size if required later. In March 1903, Husmann announced the establishment of the station at Oakville, plus one at Fresno and a third for an unchosen site in Southern California.

Churchill also offered the services, apparently at no charge, of his ranch foreman, Hans Hansen, to oversee the experimental plots. Hansen was among the most respected farm superintendents in the county by virtue of having worked for Crabb. Every variety of grape including those for raisins and table grapes, were available for the taking at To Kalon, they numbered in the hundreds!

(Barely two months after the agreement with Churchill was legalized, he died. The family, fortunately, did not make any changes in the agreement, even allowing Hansen time to oversee the experimental plots.)

A decade later Husmann told a Napa gathering of wine makers that over 12,000 tests had been conducted to determine sugar and acid makeup of grapes produced at the experimental station. For the first time vintners who relied on taste buds or on intuition had data to confirm or discard old practices. Science had arrived in Napa Valley wine making.

Unquestionably the greatest efforts put forth under Husmann's direction at Oakville were in the area of phylloxera resistant rootstock. Husmann and his colleagues certainly knew of the successes of Georges de Latour at Rutherford, but they may have suspected this was some sort of temporary aberration. Would his vines die out too, in a decade

Almost simultaneous with the Oakville Experiment Station came the funding by the California State Legislature of a new agricultural college and ranch. It would be operated under the direction of the University of California, Berkeley, but would be located in farming country—not in the East Bay. The site chosen eventually was Davis, California, barely qualifying in size as a village.

Between the Agricultural Experiment Station and the University of California, including its new college at Davis, pressure began to mount to shift from the Zinfandel and Mission grape in Napa Valley to the better varieties. There were Cabernet Sauvignon grapes, for example, already in the Parrott Vineyard on Spring Mountain at Salmina's Larkmead; and naturally, To Kalon at Inglenook. De Latour planted twenty acres in 1910, probably the largest planting of the variety then in California. Beringers grew the grape too, as early as 1900.

Theodore Gier had the same variety in the Napa Redwoods, in small amounts. Morris Estee had grown it and produced Cabernet wine at Hedgeside winery; and Fawver grew it at the winery at Yountville.

There had been only two prices for grapes in the previous century, one for red and one for white grapes. Now red grape prices were split, with the bottom figure for Zinfandel and other lesser varieties and the top price for grapes like Cabernet. The Repsold winery advertised in the *Napa Daily Journal* of September 1915 offering to pay top price, $25 a ton for "Cabernet Sauvignon and Cabernet Franc."

As early as 1909 the Brun & Chaix cellar of the California Wine Association advised it would pay $16 a ton for the "Choicest varieties such as Alicante Bouschet, Petite Sirah, Cabernet and one or two other fine varieties." The Alicante Bouschet was a shining star being touted then as the best grape to grow for adding deep red color to wine. It was a hybrid developed a few decades previously in France when red varieties in that country, as in California, were having problems with good color.

Unquestionably Napa Valley led every other wine region in the state in the production of Cabernet Sauvignon wine by 1915 when the giant Panama Pacific International Exposition opened in San Francisco. The Panama Canal, which it honored, was opened officially but mud slides effectively prevented any ships from passing through. The Exposition included the largest wine competition ever held in the country. Fairgoers tasted freely of the wine and ate tons of fresh grapes.

This was the first American wine competition in which Cabernet Sauvignon was a major competitor under its own name. Twelve medals were awarded in the category, only four of which went to Napa Valley producers. A. Finke's Widow won a Gold for its Cabernet, as did Salmina's and A. Repsold. Beringers and Krug picked up Silvers.

Napa Valley may actually have won five of the twelve medals given out to Cabernets, a Gold also going to the California Wine Association. The CWA entries were generally not identified by locale, their "Cabernet Claret" being one example. The CWA won the Grand Prize for four wines identified as "Greystone, Hock, Cerrito, Sauterne." Were all four produced at Greystone, and the Cabernet?

Over two hundred wine medals were awarded to California wineries, somewhat diminishing the value. A. Repsold was proud, however, to announce in the *Wine and Spirit Review* of June 30, 1915 that it had been awarded fourteen Gold medals and two diplomas. "All the wines exhibited by the Repsold Company were produced in Napa County. The awards attest to the excellence of the wines of Napa County."

Other Napa vintners honored by the wine judges included Inglenook (twenty awards), the French-American Wine Company and Theodore Gier (his "Cabernet-Pride of Livermore" won a Silver). It should be noted that Krug and Inglenook were two of fifteen honorees in the "Grand Prize" or highest award. Still, Napa Valley came out poorly considering its domination in past events.

Wine, grapes and Napa County were a prominent part of the huge Panama Pacific Exposition regardless of the number of wine medals. A three foot wide by eighty foot long bridge was built for the Napa exhibit with waterfalls, miniature roadways and baskets of every fruit grown in the county, grain, grapes and wine. October 8 was designated "Grape Day" with 700 crates of grapes given away—the grapes from nearly every grape growing county in the state. Wine by the bottle was also free, but not exactly to everyone who entered the Napa showcase.

This was the first World's Fair to make wholesale use of the electric light bulb and visitors stood in awe of the spectacular displays of lights at night. Few events could thereafter leave such a lasting impression, especially on children.

If there was some disappointment at To Kalon, Krugs, Beringers or the dozens of other wine cellars over the small number of wine awards in 1915, it did not compare to the concern over lagging wine sales. The market for California wine had stalled after the heavy growth years of the first decade of the century. In fact, in some years it declined sharply and '15 was one of them.

There was a bright spot for Napa Valley, however, in that dry table wines by the end of the second decade were up while sweet wines plummeted. This latter category dropped from 15 million gallons to 6 million by 1918 (higher federal taxes were a factor). Total production of table wines still stood ten million gallons less than the ten years earlier.

It was not difficult to pinpoint the major problem the wine and liquor industry was having—Prohibition. The Prohibitionists knew they had won the fight when grape grower associations split apart in confusion and especially when the wine and beer industry sought to separate itself from distilled beverages. "United we stand or divided we fall" could have been the rallying cry, but the famous words of John Paul Jones went unheeded.

Warning cries on Prohibition were being published almost monthly in the San Francisco based *Pacific Wine and Spirit Review*. In May 1902 the journal carried a story titled "Going Dry Too Fast" and listed five dry states (Kansas, Maine, New Hampshire, North Dakota and Vermont) and six more close to totally prohibiting the sale or manufacture of wine and other alcoholic beverages.

Every state in the nation was on this list because counties and cities by the hundreds were banning use of alcohol in any form. California had 175 cities or towns in this category. Six on the latter list had been amended to show 60 "incorporated" cities under Prohibition. These were not small rural villages.

The year of 1908 finally prompted a move to unite grape growers and wine makers in this battle for survival. The "Grape Growers Protective Association" was formed with Pietro Rossi and Andrea Sbarboro providing the real leadership. Both men had been pushing for a nationwide organization for some years. The Sonomans had no counterparts in Napa Valley, which had provided leadership on most issues in the past.

Some inspiration may have been provided by the astonishing election results that fall in Lake County—not normally considered a bastion of the Prohibitionists. Lake County voted in a local option ordinance, which allowed cities and towns to ban all alcoholic beverages. Some of the best known resort cities suddenly found they could serve no alcohol after November. In 1912 the complete county went dry.

At this same general election, Napa wine men spent some sleepless nights less the same thing happen in three local supervisorial districts. The Anti-Saloon League had succeeded, almost without being noticed, in putting a local-option initiative on the ballot. The Prohibitionist movement was stronger in the southern end of the county, and it was recognized that the same sentiment existed up at Angwin.

The *Star* carried a full page advertisement "A Warning to the Voters of Napa County" in its October 25 issue. Napa City newspapers carried long Letters to the Editors reflecting the anxiety of local wine producers, at last fully awake to what could happen. One letter quoted Joseph Migliavacca as pointing out that he paid annually $80,000 for grapes brought to his Napa winery. That money was largely spent in Napa City.

The "Drys" were defeated handily in all three districts. Every vintner with a car or grape grower with one raced from precinct to precinct looking for eligible voters who needed a ride to the polls. The Lodi precinct north of St. Helena voted 114 to go "dry" and 69 "wet," but the vote was overwhelmed in other areas.

In April 1913 the *Wine and Spirit Review* required two full pages to list every city and town that had gone dry in California!

In St. Helena in September 1914, Prohibitionist and their children marched up and down Main Street with banners advocating their cause. This was done regularly too, in Napa City but that evening when they sat down to listen to a speaker for their cause, carefully planted wine supporters broke up the meeting with jeers and shouts. The Anti-Saloon League should have guessed it was tempting fate by meeting in the heart of Napa Valley.

That year the state ballot carried an initiative which would have given state law protection to the so-called "Local Option Ordinance." Many had been declared illegal in local courts. This went down to defeat ultimately too, but only the heavy population centers in Northern California prevented the southern part of the state from carrying the Prohibitionist cause.

Napa County's vote proved again how many local residents were quite willing to destroy the county's economy and the tax base which provided most of the schools, roads, police protection, etc. Voters numbering 5,324 opposed the state vote in Napa County but 2,043 approved of it. Nearly 40 percent of the electorate in Napa

County would have pulled out every grapevine in 1914 and turned loose the spigots on wine tanks locally—or at least this would have been an end result of the Local Option law.

The Drys did not give up easily, and in 1916 California voters had another opportunity to drive alcohol forever from their midst. This was Amendment Number 1 on the ballot, outlawing completely the manufacture, sale or possession of any alcoholic beverage! It was all or nothing this time around.

Wine men had marshalled their forces more aggressively in this battle and won easily, even in Napa County where only 1,985 voted for the measure and over 5,000 opposed.

In 1917 the fight resumed all over again. This time the wine industry made a serious tactical error.

The passage of an Amendment to the U.S. Constitution on prohibiting the manufacture and sale of alcoholic beverages seemed a foregone conclusion. Congress had approved such an Amendment and sent it to the various states for adoption or rejection.

In California, a bill was introduced in the State Legislature which would have allowed wine and beer to be served as a part of meals, etc., in restaurants and consumed at home but would forbid the manufacture or sale of any other such beverages. Andrea Sbarboro immediately came out in favor of the attempt to save the wine industry but pull in the life preservers for any other portion of the liquor industry. Wine men had always wanted wine, and perhaps beer, to be considered foods.

The California Grape Protective Association immediately endorsed Sbarboro's position. Napa County's wing of the same group shortly voted to cancel its membership stating it would have no part of partial Prohibitionism, as it were.

The Prohibitionists had succeeded in destroying their opposition in essence for now the wine industry was not able to effectively fight the Eighteenth Amendment when it came before the Legislature. On January 11, 1919 the Amendment received the endorsement of the California Legislature. The Senate voted 24-15 in favor, the Assembly 48-28 in favor.

There was one last crushing defeat yet to be endured by the wine men.

In September 1917, Congress passed legislation banning the use of food products in making distilled beverages. This was to aid the war effort. The wine industry through some effective assistance from Congressional allies gained a delay on wine and beer until June 30, 1919. In November, of course, the Armistice was signed, and wine producers breathed a sigh of relief. As soon as President Woodrow Wilson signed a bill ending the mobilization, wartime restrictions would cease.

There was still the matter of the Eighteenth Amendment, but now it was one step at a time. The Supreme Court would hopefully declare the law enforcing Prohibition as unconstitutional.

President Wilson refused to act to prevent wine manufacturing coming under the wartime restrictions act. June 30, 1919 was to be the final day of legal wine making in California, perhaps forever.

In Santa Clara County 76 wineries would close. In Sonoma County 256 wine cellars ceased operations. In Napa County the total number of wineries closing was 120, a goodly number of smaller cellars already having gone out of business. Wine production in the county had risen to four million gallons or very close to that figure.[VI.9] No one knew how many acres of grapes had been pulled out already, that activity had proceeded at such a fast pace. There were anywhere from 13,000 acres to 15,000 acres.[VI.10] All of these vines would supposedly be pulled out.

If there were tears shed profusely between Napa City and Calistoga, or from the Napa Redwoods to Pope Valley over this dire situation, they could be dried quickly. Less than a week after Wartime Prohibition began, Fred Mercer arrived in St. Helena, stating he wanted to buy wine grapes to ship to an unnamed Eastern buyer. Mercer would pay $37.50 a ton.

Several weeks later L. Dellarro, representing a group called the "California Grape Association" of San Francisco, was in St. Helena offering to buy 2,000 to 3,000 tons of grapes. Forty dollars a ton was the suggested price.

By September 26, 1919 the *Star* could headline: "Grapes Being Shipped in Large Quantities." F. S. Cairns and F. J. Merriam advertised in the same newspaper for 4,000 tons of grapes but would only pay $25 per ton, "F.O.B. St. Helena Calistoga or Rutherford."

What was happening should have been foreseen by someone who spoke Italiano. Hundreds of thousands of immigrants from Italy, or France, or Yugoslavia, to name a few representative countries, and who worked in the inner cities for the steel industry or in similar occupations, began asking local produce distributors for wine grapes for home wine production. Their supply of vino or *vin ordinaire* was about to be cut off, they would make it themselves.

A price of $50 a ton had rarely been paid for any grapes in pre-Prohibition California. It became the standard rate for most Napa Valley grapes by October, at least those of the red variety. These home wine makers wanted red grapes, few of the white. Their favorite red was the Alicante Bouschet.

Most winery owners had their own vineyards so everyone shared in the totally unexpected profits.

There also came the slowly dawning realization that the provisions for the enforcement of Prohibition, whether wartime or the Eighteenth Amendment, were not in place. No sheriff or policeman in Napa County was likely to notice a truck of wine moving down the highway at night. It might be his brother or uncle, or certainly a cousin.

In Napa Valley as the decade ended and a new era began (which undeniably was to have its own frustrations), the future was not exactly as dark as had been prophesied. It just might be that Americans would drink more wine in the years ahead than in the past. No one would win a Gold medal, there would be no free samples or artistic displays at an exposition honoring an American explorer or construction of some earth moving project.

The real question suddenly before the country was, "What had been or was being prohibited?" The answer would come in about fourteen years, or less!

FOOTNOTES

Chapter One

I.1 Elizabeth Cyrus Wright, "Early Upper Napa Valley," Napa County Historical Society, Series No. 1, December 1978.

I.2 A. H. Grossman, letter to the *Napa Register*, August 2, 1889: "... Let us go back to '72. In that season I leased the Huicha Vineyard of W. H. Winters for a term of six years. It was then the largest vineyard in Napa county."

I.3 History of Howard and Cooper Counties, Missouri, 1883, pp. 152-156.

I.4 Robert Kirsch and William S. Murphy, *West of the West* (New York: E. P. Dutton & Co., 1967), p. 194.

I.5 Charles Brown manuscript, D53 (Berkeley: University of California, Bancroft Library), p. 8.

I.6 *St. Helena Star*, March 18, 1875: "Mr. John York—one of the respected citizens and pioneers who settled way back in 1845, and planted the first vineyard in the county ... informs us that his grapes have never failed to produce a crop during all that time."

I.7 *Official Report of the California State Agricultural Society's Third Annual Fair*, 1856, p. 11.

I.8 *Transactions of the California State Agricultural Society During the Year 1858*, 1859, p. 240.

I.9 See "The Chronicles of George Yount," p. 65.

I.10 "William A. Trubody and the Overland Pioneers of 1847," California Historical Society Quarterly, June 1937,

I.11 *History of Solano and Napa Counties*, vol. I, p. 341.

I.12 Page 203.

I.13 August 10, 1860, p. 1.

I.14 *Independent Calistogian*, Calistoga, Ca., Jan. 23, 1878.

I.15 *Farmer*, July 1, 1859.

I.16 *Star*, December 19, 1890.

I.17 "Sonoma and Napa Horticultural Association," *California Farmer*, May 20, 1859. Letter of William Boggs, *St. Helena Star*, June 8, 1885.

I.18 *Farmer*, November 4, 1859.

I.19 Ibid., September 18, 1859.

I.20 *Report of Special Committee on the Culture of the Grapevine in California* (Sacramento: State Printer, 1859), pp. 4-5.

Chapter Two

II.1 *California Farmer*, August 3, 1860, see "Napa and Napa Valley."

II.2 (New Haven, Conn.: Yale University Press, 1930).

II.3 August 10, 1860.

II.4 *Star*, December 19, 1890.

II.5 Ibid. There are two stories in the *Star* written by Crane for this quotation; see "Viticulture: Looking Back Some Thirty Years." The other story, "Pioneer Days," also includes some viticultural references.

II.6 July 29, 1864.

II.7 *Alta California*, March 11, 1866.

II.8   *Star*, December 19, 1890.

II.9   *Farmer*, May 15, 1866.

II.10 *Star*, December 19, 1890.

II.11 *Farmer*, June 22, 1860.

II.12 August 30, 1866.

II.13 As quoted in the *History of Napa and Lake Counties*, 1881, p. 328. Copies of the *Register* for this date do not exist.

II.14 *Alta*, May 7, 1866.

II.15 Ibid., December 6, 1858.

II.16 September 10, 1870.

Chapter Three

III.1   *History of Napa and Lake Counties*, 1881, p. 470.

III.2   Menefee, *Historical Sketch Book*, p. 207.

III.3   Report of the State Board of Equalization, For 1870-71 (published 1872), pp. 22-23.

III.4   *Alta California*, San Francisco, Ca., January 14, 1870.

III.5   *Pacific Bank Handbook* (San Francisco: Pacific Bank, 1888).

III.6   As reprinted in the *California Farmer*, October 25, 1866.

III.7   W. W. Lyman, "The Lyman Family," *Napa County Historical Society, Gleanings*, April, 1980.

III.8   *Napa Register*, August 2, 1889. Letter of A. H. Grossman, "The Reason Wines Are Cheap."

III.9. Menefee, *Sketch Book*, p. 213.

III.10 *Napa Reporter*, October 11, 1873, "Itinerant Field-Notes."

III.11 Ibid., April 19, 1873.

III.12 Ibid., September 27, 1873.

III.13 *History of Napa and Lake Counties*, 1881, p. 204.

III.14 December 16, 1875.

III.15 For construction of Pope Valley Road see the *Napa Reporter* of October 11, 1873. Lewelling's fire story is in the *Star*, July 29, 1875. See the *Star* also for Thompson story, January 5, 1877.

III.16 *Star*, November 15, 1878. 17 Ibid, May 27, 1877; Napa Register, August 25, 1885.

III.17 Ibid., May 27, 1877: *Napa Register*, Aug. 25, 1885.

III.18 William F. Heintz, "The Role of Chinese in Nineteenth Century Viticulture and Wine-Making in California" (Master's thesis, Sonoma State University, Rohnert Park, Ca., 1977).

III.19 *Star*, October 23, 1874.

III.20 Ibid., February 4, 1875.

III.21 *Napa Reporter*, February 22, 1873.

III.22 *Star*, July 25, 1879.

III.23 As quoted in the *Star*, October 27, 1876.

III.24 *Star*, October 20, 1876.

III.25 Ibid., October 16, 1874.

III.26 Ibid., October 14, 1875.

III.27 Bancroft Scraps, vol. 19, Part II, See letter signed "R. W. Montgomery."

III.28 *Star*, October 29, 1874.

III.29 Ibid., April 15, 1876.

III.30 Ibid., March 4, 1876.

III.31 Ibid. See issues of November 16, 23, 30 and December 7, 14, 1877.

III.32 As reprinted in the *Star*, March 1, 1873.

III.33 *Illustrations of Napa County*, 1878, p. 7.

III.34 *Star*, June 7, 1878.

III.35 Ibid., September 19, 1879.

III.36 Ibid., same date.

Chapter Four

IV.1 *For The Years 1882-3 and 1883-4*. (Sacramento: State Printer, 1884), p. 42.

IV.2 *Star*, August 25, 1882.

IV.3 February 26, 1876

IV.4 As reprinted in the *Star*, December 5, 1879.

IV.5 Ibid., as reprinted on January 31, 1879.

IV.6 Ibid., as reprinted on December 19, 1879.

IV.7 *Russian River Flag*, February 26, 1880.

IV.8 *Healdsburg Enterprise*, January 26, 1882.

IV.9 Ibid., same date.

IV.10 As reprinted in the *Star*, April 2, 1880.

IV.11 *Star*, July 2, 1880.

IV.12 *First Annual Report of the Board of State Viticultural Commissioners* (Sacramento: 1881), p. 9.

IV.13 *Star*, October 25, 1878.

IV.14 Ibid., August 21, 1884.

IV.15 Several writers on early Napa Valley history erroneously claim Watson ran a health resort. Early descriptive pieces on Inglenook were written in such a manner as to convey the concept that paying guests were accepted at the ranch.

IV.16 *Star*, July 1, 1881: ". . . The cellar rebuilt on its new site with the addition of a crushing room, covers a space of 55 x 120 ft."

IV.17 Ibid., August 12, 1881.

IV.18 Ibid., October 27, 1882.

IV.19 See issue of August 5 1881, for example, and many subsequent issues.

IV.20 *Report of the Sixth Annual State Viticultural Convention, San Francisco March 7, 8, 9, 10, 1888*. (Sacramento: State Office, 1888), p. 86.

IV.21 *Napa Register*, October 4, 1889.

IV.22 *The Life of Henry Wadsworth Longfellow*, Extracts from Journals and Correspondence, 3 vols. Edited by Samuel Longfellow, 1891. See vol. I, p. 187.

IV.23 *Napa Register*, August 25, 1885

IV.24 See issue of March 9, 1889.

IV.25 *San Francisco Merchant*, April 11, 1884.

IV.26 Reprinted in the *Star*, April 29, 1881.

IV.27 Ibid., May 6, 1881.

IV.28 *Annual Report, For the Year 1887*, p. 44.

IV.29 *Star*, June 8, 1885.

IV.30 The Laurent winery survives down to the present time, renamed the "Markham winery." Remodeled and enlarged by Bruce Markham, the facility has gone through a myriad of owners and troubled times. Laurent died in October 1890.

IV.31 September 22, 1876.

IV.32 Ibid., August 12, 1881.

IV.33 *Annual Report of the Board of State Viticultural Commissioners, For 1887* (Sacramento: 1888), p. 45.

IV.34 Reprinted in the *Resources of California*, San Francisco, April 1883.

IV.35 *Star*, March 9.

IV.36 Ibid., October 18, 1889.

IV.37 August 2, 1889.

IV.38 *Report of the Sixth Annual State Viticultural Convention* (Sacramento: Board of State Viticultural Commissioners, 1888), p. 11.

IV.39 *Second Annual Report of the Chief Executive Officer*, Board of State Viticultural Commissioners (Sacramento: 1884), p. 127.

IV.40 The March 14, 1884 *Napa County Reporter*, "Visit to Hudeman's" claimed "Twelve acres have already been put into vines and the ground is now being worked for more." Because it was difficult to transport grapes in those years from the redwoods to a sufficiently large commercial winery, it is certain Hudeman produced wine himself. Wine making at Mont LaSalle dates to the early 1880s, if not the late 1870s.

IV.41 *San Francisco Merchant*, August 14, 1885.

IV.42 *Napa County Reporter*, September 30, 1881.

IV.43 *First Annual Report of the Chief Executive Officer*, Board of State Viticultural Commissioners (Sacramento, 1882), p. xxxvii.

IV.44 *Pacific Wine and Spirit Review*, San Francisco, December 9, 1895.

Chapter Five

V.1 D. Leigh Colvin, *Prohibition in the United States*, 1926.

V.2 *Healdsburg Tribune*, February 28, 1891. Excerpted from *The Annual Report of the Board of State Viticultural Commissioners* with no date cited.

V.3 *Napa Register*, December 12, 1890.

V.4 As reprinted in the *Napa Register* of May 31 1890.

V.5 October 6, 1889.

V.6 May 31, 1891.

V.7 *Wine and Spirit Review*, March 15, 1891; *San Francisco Argonaut*, October 30, 1890; *Illustrated American*, as reprinted in *Wine & Spirit Review*, September 5, 1891.

V.8 *History of Fresno County*, pp. 831-832.

V.9 *Memoir of Jack Becker*, "Rennie Brothers Winery," sent to the author, February 20, 1985. Becker is a grandson of William Rennie.

V.10 Ira B. Cross, *Financing An Empire. History of Banking in California* (Chicago: S. J. Clarke Co., 1927), pp. 616-624.

V.11 See "Report of H. W. Crabb," *Report of the Board of State Viticultural Commissioners, 1893-94.* (Sacramento: 1894), p. 28.

V.12 *Star*, September 30, 1887 and September 6, 1889; *Independent Calistogian*, August 14, 1889

V.13 *Star*, January 24, 1894.

V.14 See "California Wines at the Columbian Exposition" N. A. in Charles Wetmore, *Treatise on Wine Production* (Sacramento: Board of State Viticultural Commissioners, 1894), p. 43.

V.15 *Report of the Board of State Viticultural Commissioners, For 1893-94* (Sacramento: 1894), p. 6.

V.16 As reproduced and translated to English in the *Wine & Spirit Review*, December 9, 1895.

V.17 April 21, 1893.

V.18 Ibid., April 8, 1892.

V.19 *Healdsburg Tribune*, April 23, 1896.

V.20 *Star*, May 19, 1882.

V.21 Arthur P. Hayne, Ph.D., *Resistant Vines* (Sacramento: University of California–College of Agriculture, 1897). For the Lenoir see especially pages 34-35.

V.22 *Report of the Board of State Viticultural Commissioners, For 1893-94* (Sacramento: 1894), p. 23.

V.23 February 16, 1900.

V.24 See issue of February 1, 1901; also February 16, 1900, January 26, 1900 and April 27, 1900.

V.25 *Napa Register*, April 10, 1896.

V.26 March 25, 1895 and probably later issues. For reprints of several of the articles in one issue see the *Register*, March 29, 1895.

V.27 Updated and unattributed newspaper clipping in the "Napa County" scrapbook, California History Room, State Library, Sacramento, Ca. The opening remark that "Napa County" lies 40 miles north and east of San Francisco and "70 miles southwest of Sacramento" leads one to believe it was a Sacramento newspaper. San Francisco publications generally would not mention the county's distance from so distant a point as the state capital.

Chapter Six

VI.1 From a taped interview with Ponti, by the author, at his Rutherford home on November 13, 1973. Ponti died in February 1975.

VI.2 Harrison should long ago have been honored for his early contribution to Napa Valley architecture and building. A small fraction of his buildings include all or part of: the Sunny St. Helena winery, the Jackse winery (across the street from the new St. Helena Public Library), Keller Market, buildings at Inglenook, the Martinelli Olive factory, and dozens of others scattered about the valley.

VI.3 Taped interview with Forni on February 13, 1975 in St. Helena by the author.

VI.4 For quoted material see issue of January 31, 1904. The Italian Swiss Colony story is told in the issue of August 31, 1905. Cecil Munsey's book, *The Illustrated Guide to Collecting Bottles*, published in 1970, gives the history of Owens and his bottle machine.

VI.5 *Wine and Spirit Review*, May 31, 1910.

VI.6 Ibid., May 31, 1903, "The Manufacture of Wine in California."

VI.7 Taped interviews at his home in St. Helena, Ca. December 16, 1980 and November 4, 1987.

VI.8 *Star*, September 6, 1912.

VI.9 Ibid., August 15, 1919.

VI.10 The State Board of Viticultural Commissioners in Bulletin #2, dated June 15, 1915 estimated Napa County grape acreage at 13,000 acres. A report by D. Butler, Agricultural Commissioner for Napa County, issued in 1921 gave the county 15,000 acres in vines and 400 newly planted acres. The latter source is under *Annual Crop Reports for Napa County, California*, in the Napa City/County Library.

ACKNOWLEDGMENTS

It would have been almost impossible to research this book without the aid of many public libraries and the men and women who work in the various departments! The St. Helena Public Library in particular, with Librarian Clayla Davis and her staff have come to my aid so many times that I cannot count them all. Librarians across the country have long deserved to be honored in some special way for their huge contribution to literature in America.

The Napa City and County Library, headed by Nan Vaaler and Assistant Librarian Tom Trice, have greeted me almost daily as well, always with a smile and the upmost patience. This library maintains and continues to expand an historical index of all Napa City newspapers and this has been a major resource. The staff at the Audio-Visual desk here, as in St. Helena, have unlocked the microfilm cabinets of these newspapers so many, many times or located a misplaced roll of film. (I should replace some of their chairs I have sat in them so often.)

At the San Francisco Public Library, Gladys Hansen and her assistants in the "San Francisco Archives" have dutifully brought out the large, dusty, bound volumes of the *San Francisco Merchant and Viticulturist*, each time I arrived. Often they have just asked "What Year?" and depart for the inner sanctum repository without further direction.

Bancroft Library, at the University of California, Berkeley, has opened dozens of secret wine treasures for me, like the *Land Cases of the Northern District Court of California*. Here I first came across evidence of precisely where George Yount planted his first vines in Napa Valley, circa 1838. Bancroft Is The Library of Western American history.

John Skarstad of the Special Collections Department, University of California, Davis (Shields Library), along with new wine librarian Axel Borg, are two of the finest librarians an author could meet. They have the patience and true love of their profession which makes working with them so pleasurable. A separate new wine library, headed by Borg and within the Shields Library, will soon give California its most important wine library for historical research.

The Napa County Historical Society museum and library is small by comparison to all of the above institutions but President Jess Doud and all of the staff make up for this shortcoming by their energy and enthusiasm. Besides there is a mystical quality to research in the historic Goodman library building—built of fine valley stone and whose walls could tell so many tales.

Every page of this manuscript was written the old-fashioned way on an electric typewriter. Lynne Ingraham has patiently retyped each page as well, after editing and corrections were made—sometimes many times over. My long-hand corrections have not been easy to decipher, nor those long pencilled tags which show just where to insert an additional comment.

Ruth Teiser of San Francisco digs into wine history on a daily basis, as I do, and is always willing to share or point me in some totally unexpected direction for research. It was she who first told me about the 1920-1950 Bureau of Alcohol, Tobacco and Firearms records concerning wineries at the University of California, Davis.

Vera Lewelling of St. Helena was once a school teacher and next to librarians, that profession stands highest with me in personal esteem. Taping her recollections of family history in the historic Lewelling house was most memorable. She generously made available the photographs in the Hanson-Lewelling Album.

Robert Mondavi initially set this book into motion by proposing it after my ninety long minutes of history testimony in 1980 at the Napa Valley appellation hearings. His enthusiasm for the subject of wine history would inspire any historian.

There are many other individuals who deserve some passing acknowledgment of a special contribution: Hanns Kornell, Brother Timothy of the Christian Brothers, Charles Carpy, the entire Raymond family, Carl Doumoni, Gil Nickel, Peter Mondavi and sons, Louis P. Martini, Warren Winiarski, Alden Yates, Irene Simpson Neasham, Rene di Rosa, John Wright, Lila and Bill Jeager and Roberg Craig and John Hess.

I also should include Francis Mahoney (who majored in History in college), Arthur Schmidt, Justin Meyer, Norman deLeuze, Mario Perelli-Minetti, John and Janet Trefethen, Ivan Schock, William Westgate, Tom May, William Collins, Barney and Belle Rhodes, James and Anne McWilliams, Dr. William J. Casey, Thomas E. Burgess, APM Cork Company, Pauline K. Solari, Jerry Luper and hundreds of others who allowed me to tape their oral history.

Mary Edwards of Sonoma has never owned even a potted grape vine but she graciously loaned me funds at a most crucial time to continue the writing. A former landlord, Myron Freiberg once let my office rent slide for six months without calling it to my attention. There have been many other similarly generous individuals.

Finally, two other friends with far differing talents must be noted because they made such key contributions to this book.

Jess Doud of Napa absolutely delights in every new historical discovery made about Napa Valley and he and I have shared many such euphoric moments over the past years. He also read the manuscript for historical errors and though should a few slip into print, the blame is mine, not his.

To Robert E. Berner who understands better than any other person the frustrations of the creative process and the personal rewards, there is no way to extend my appreciation adequately. With him, it need not be stated, it has always been understood.

If there has been one overriding concern while writing this book it has been that so much pioneering ground had to be turned over, where no historian had gone before. That makes for a lonely journey at times, and one with hazards as to accuracy.

WILLIAM F. HEINTZ
OCTOBER 1989